On Extended Wings

D0783187

> . . . *Casual flocks of pigeons make*
> *Ambiguous undulations as they sink,*
> *Downward to darkness, on extended wings.*

On Extended Wings

Wallace Stevens' Longer Poems

by Helen Hennessy Vendler

Harvard University Press
Cambridge, Massachusetts
and London, England

Library of Congress Catalog Card Number 70–82299
ISBN 0–674–63436–5

Printed in the United States of America

To I. A. RICHARDS

Acknowledgments

I am grateful to the libraries of Harvard University where, in records, books, and manuscripts, I first came to know Stevens' poetry. The libraries of Swarthmore College, Smith College, and Boston University have continued that service.

My reading of Stevens has benefited from conversations with Harold Bloom, Alvin Feinman, Allen Grossman, John Hollander, Samuel Hynes, Robert Levine, Francis Murphy, Margaret Shook, and Marguerite Stewart. Marie Borroff and Reuben Brower read the manuscript and gave indispensable commentaries. Grants-in-aid from the American Council of Learned Societies and the Graduate School of Boston University gave me free time in which to write, and the Department of English at Boston University provided a grant for secretarial work. Encouragement in obtaining support came generously from Reuben Brower and Morton Berman, to whom I am deeply indebted, and from the late Rosemond Tuve, who was to me, as to so many others, an unstinting giver of interest and help. To all previous critics of Stevens, both those quoted and those not mentioned, I am of course grateful; even when their writings were not of direct relevance to my own, they contributed to that general understanding needed by all readers of poetry.

I must thank the following for permission to reprint, with some changes, chapters of this book which have already been published: The Johns Hopkins Press ("The Qualified Assertions of Wallace Stevens," in *The Act of the Mind*, ed. Roy Harvey Pearce and J. Hillis Miller, Baltimore, 1966), and the *Massachusetts Review* ("Stevens' 'Like Decorations in a Nigger Cemetery,'" 7:136–146, Spring 1966).

Acknowledgments

Contents

Contents

On Extended Wings

Introduction: The Two Poetries

Every poem is a poem within a poem: the poem of the idea within the poem of the words.

Stevens, like Keats, believed in writing long poems, and defended the practice to Harriet Monroe in 1922: "The desire to write a long poem or two is not obsequiousness to the judgment of people. On the contrary, I find that prolonged attention to a single subject has the same result that prolonged attention to a senora has, according to the authorities. All manner of favors drop from it. Only it requires a skill in the varying of the serenade that occasionally makes me feel like a Guatemalan when one particularly wants to feel like an Italian" (*L*, 230).[1] He continued in his next letter, "I wish that I could put everything else aside and amuse myself on a large scale for a while. One never gets anywhere in writing or thinking or observing unless one can do long stretches at a time. Often I have to let go, in the most insignificant poem, which scarcely serves to remind me of it, the most skyey of skyey sheets. And often when I have a real fury for indulgence I must stint myself" (*L*, 231). For the rest of Stevens' life, long poems alternated with short ones, and while it may be that Stevens will be forever anthologized as the poet of "The Snow Man," his own sense of balance required verse on a large scale. He thought of calling *Harmonium* "The Grand Poem: Preliminary Minutiae," and at one time he wanted his collected poems called

The Whole of Harmonium: both titles were perhaps evoked by Shelley's assertion in the *Defense of Poetry* that all poems are "episodes to that great poem, which all poets, like the co-operating thoughts of one great mind, have built up since the beginning of the world."

The long poem was a discipline to the poet, but we may suspect that it was a liberation as well: when Stevens speaks of the effect of reading a long poem, he is probably drawing on the experience of writing one. A long poem, he says, "comes to possess the reader and . . . naturalizes him in its own imagination and liberates him there" (*NA*, 50): "In a long poem, so many emotions, so many sensations, are stirred up into activity that, after a time, the reader finds himself in a state of such sensibility that it cannot be said that the scale and deliberateness of allegory fail to produce an emotional effect. A prolonged reading of Spenser's Faerie Queene, for instance, creates just such a state of sensibility. In general, long poems have this attribute, derived from their very length, assuming that they have been charged throughout with the emotions of the poet" (*NA*, 111–112). Though Stevens never wrote anything approaching the length of *The Faerie Queene*, he implies that his own long poems can have the same naturalizing power, and in fact they do. We become most acclimated to Stevens in reading them, and they form the illumined large to which the lyrics, volume by volume, attach themselves. In each period of Stevens' life as a poet, they are characteristic, and to read them in sequence is one way, if not the only way, of tracing both his states of feeling and his enterprises and inventions. It is also true that his greatest poems, by almost any judgment, are the longer ones, whether one agrees with Yvor Winters' preference for "Sunday Morning," Harold Bloom's for *Notes toward a Supreme Fiction*, Daniel Fuchs' for *Esthetique du Mal*, or yet choose, as I am sometimes inclined to do, *The Auroras of Autumn*.[2]

Through the long poems Stevens discovered his own strengths.

It was, for instance, not until 1942, in *Notes*, that he settled on his final metrical form. Even then, he deserted that form to write *Esthetique du Mal* in 1944, and returned to it only in 1948, with *The Auroras of Autumn*. Those triads, as everyone has recognized, somehow organize his mind in its long stretches better than any other alternative, and yet to reach them he had to experiment with blank verse, couplets, ballads, terza rima, sonnetlike forms, and so on. This is the most obvious instance of Stevens' patient experimentation toward his own voice, but others come to light in reading the long poems. They are all directed toward a proper mode for his austere temperament, which is as different as can be from the temperament of Whitman or Wordsworth or Keats or Tennyson, those poets from whom he learned and to whom he is often compared. Neither is his sense of the world that of the French poets, however much he learned from them in his Harvard years. His manner was slow in evolving, and it evolved through his sense of himself and through a search for his own style: "A man's sense of the world is born with him and persists, and penetrates the ameliorations of education and experience of life. His species is as fixed as his genus. For each man, then, certain subjects are congenital. Now, the poet manifests his personality, first of all, by his choice of subject. Temperament is a more explicit word than personality and would no doubt be the exact word to use, since it emphasizes the manner of thinking and feeling" (*NA*, 120).

Most criticism of Stevens has been concerned, understandably, with his "choice of subject" — variously defined. Some readers have seen his subject as an epistemological one, and have written about his views on the imagination and its uneasy rapport with reality. Others have seen his subject as a moral one, a justification of an aesthetic hedonism. Still others have seen his subject as a native humanist one, the quest of the American Adam for a Paradise in the wilderness. Stevens of course offers justification for all these views, and it is perhaps partial, in view of his many letters and essays on reality and the imagination, to prefer one of his more wayward statements, as usual objectively put, of what his own subject was, and how it developed through his life. Nevertheless, this brief summation seems closest in spirit to the Stevens one finds in the greatest poems: "One's cry of O Jerusalem becomes little by little a cry to something a little nearer and nearer until at last one cries out to a living name, a living place, a living thing, and in crying out confesses openly all the bitter secretions of experience" (*OP*, 260). This confession needs to be completed by the third stage of that repeated cry: after O Jerusalem, after the cry to something near, comes that final unseeking cry of the very late poems, notably "The Course of a Particular." A year or so earlier, Stevens had written that the poem was the "cry of its occasion, / Part of the res itself and not about it," but he could not rest in this partial identification of cry and creation. At last the cry is entirely simple:

> Today the leaves cry, hanging on branches swept by wind,
> Yet the nothingness of winter becomes a little less.
> It is still full of icy shades and shapen snow.
>
> The leaves cry . . . One holds off and merely hears the
>   cry.
> It is a busy cry, concerning someone else.
> And though one says that one is part of everything,
>
> There is a conflict, there is a resistance involved;
> And being part is an exertion that declines:
> One feels the life of that which gives life as it is.
>
> The leaves cry. It is not a cry of divine attention,
> Nor the smoke drift of puffed-out heroes, nor human cry.
> It is the cry of leaves that do not transcend themselves.

In the absence of fantasia, without meaning more
Than they are in the final finding of the ear, in the thing
Itself, until, at last, the cry concerns no one at all.

(*OP* 96–97)[3]

This is, of Stevens, "the text he should be born that he might write," to paraphrase his own line in *Description without Place*. One can hardly doubt that the leaves, as well as being leaves, are Stevens too, and that he has gone beyond crying out to Jerusalem, beyond crying out even to a living name or place or thing, beyond all directed cries at all. Utterance is utterance, and the exertion to make it something more has disappeared. Stevens recapitulates in this poem all his previous efforts — his efforts to be part of the universe, his efforts to create divinities, heroes, and human beings, all his fantasia — and dismisses those attempts at self-transcendence in the presence of this pure sound. This is "the authentic and fluent speech" he told Harriet Monroe (*L*, 231) he hoped eventually to perfect for himself, a syllable intoning "its single emptiness":

It is here, in this bad, that we reach
The last purity of the knowledge of good.   (294)

But before the authentic came many trials of the less and the more authentic, and before the fluent came episodes of the halting and the borrowed, times when Stevens wanted to feel like an Italian and felt instead like a Guatemalan, as he wryly said. All these "trials of device" are recorded in his major poems, and underneath them all is the fatal stratum he will at last discover in *The Auroras of Autumn*, that blank which Harold Bloom rightly traces back to Emerson's *Nature*: "The ruin or the blank that we see when we look at nature, is in our own eye,"[4] or as Stevens writes,

A blank underlies the trials of device,
The dominant blank, the unapproachable.   (477)

If we find, in reading Stevens, that he tries and discards mode after mode, genre after genre, form after form, voice after voice, model after model, topic after topic, we also find a marvelous sureness mysteriously shaping his experiments. The story does not have an entirely happy ending: *An Ordinary Evening in New Haven* represents a decline from *Notes toward a Supreme Fiction* and *The Auroras of Autumn*, as even Stevens himself seems to have recognized when he called it "this endlessly elaborating poem" and wished that it could have been written by "a more severe, more harassing master" who could propose "subtler, more urgent proof" than he could himself (486). On the other hand, there are short pieces written in Stevens' last years which are the equal of anything he ever wrote, and, some would say, the best poems he ever wrote. Each poem is of course autonomous: "We never arrive intellectually," as Stevens said, "but emotionally we arrive constantly (as in poetry, happiness, high mountains, vistas)" (*OP*, 173). But each is also a stage in a sequence of development.

We keep, in reading Stevens, a double attitude, seeing the major poems both as things in themselves and as steps in a long progress toward his most complete incarnations of his sense of the world: "What is the poet's subject? It is his sense of the world. For him, it is inevitable and inexhaustible. If he departs from it he becomes artificial and laborious and while his artifice may be skillful and his labor perceptive no one knows better than he that what he is doing, under such circumstances, is not essential to him" (*NA*, 121). This is Stevens speaking, no doubt, of his own writing, and if we call him at times artificial and laborious we may be forgiven since he was there before us. There was no way for him to leap over those artifices; he had to go on by way of them: "The truth is that a man's sense of the

6

world dictates his subjects to him and that this sense is derived from his personality, his temperament, over which he has little control and possibly none, except superficially. It is not a literary problem. It is the problem of his mind and nerves. These sayings are another form of the saying that poets are born not made" (*NA*, 122). That is Stevens' bluntest statement of what he clearly thought about his own poetry, and he gives instances: "A poet writes of twilight because he shrinks from noon-day. He writes about the country because he dislikes the city . . . There are stresses that he invites; there are stresses that he avoids . . . In music he likes the strings. But the horn shocks him. A flat land-scape extending in all directions to immense distances placates him. But he shrugs his shoulders at mountains" (*NA*, 122). The long poems give us very clearly Stevens' world, and naturalize us in it, so that we may be forgiven also if we say he invites this, he avoids that, he shrinks from this, he is shocked by this, he is indifferent to something else, he is consoled by these things. This is not censure, it is classification in the human world.

In the same essay, "Effects of Analogy," Stevens adds that the second way by which a poet manifests his personality is by his style: "What has just been said with respect to choice of subject applies equally to style. The individual dialect of a poet who happens to have one, analogous to the speech common to his time and place and yet not that common speech, is in the same position as the language of poetry generally when the language of poetry generally is not the common speech" (*NA*, 123). Describing the individual dialect proper to any poet is difficult, the more so in the case of Stevens since there are such marked changes in his style. As Marianne Moore once said, his poems "suggest a linguist creating several languages within a single language." [5] There are some general traits which survive from *Harmonium* to *The Rock*, and which are in combination dis-tinctive to Stevens; these habits of language are briefly set forth below, in the chapter prefacing the individual commentaries on the long poems. A style is not easily describable as a whole, and summaries tend to be general or misleading,[6] since the same attitude can take different forms, or the same form embody different attitudes. In specific instances where only a single poem is in question, more justice can be done both to Stevens and to the poem at hand.

Stevens' "progress" has sometimes been put in terms of the "abandonment of rhetoric" after *Owl's Clover*.[7] Stevens himself gave currency to this legendary account of his progress by Crispin's rejection of the exotic, and by some of his disparaging remarks on rhetoric in *The Necessary Angel*: "What then, is it to live in the mind with the imagination, yet not too near to the fountains of its rhetoric, so that one does not have a consciousness only of grandeurs, of incessant departures from the idiom and of inherent altitudes?" (*NA*, 141). But *The Man with the Blue Guitar* is by no means unrhetorical, and to define Stevens' new spareness we need to see its own rhetoric, as in winter he reminded himself that the branches were not "bare" but that the junipers were shagged with ice and the spruces were rough in the distant glitter of the January sun.

To make Stevens' poetic arrangements clear to the eye I have not hesitated to realign certain poems according to their rhetorical rather than their metrical shape, to reprint others to show their true rhythmic form rather than their putative one, and in general to violate, for a purpose, Stevens' own lineation, assuming always a *Collected Poems* near at hand for the reader where the true poem can be found.

Stevens has suffered, as Shakespeare, Pope, Wordsworth, and others have, from the dreadful repetitive effect of moral paraphrase by his critics. Shaw notoriously believed, or said he did, that Shakespeare was no more than platitudes combined with superb "word music." A. Alvarez has, however unwillingly, put the same objection in regard to Stevens: "It is this that, for me, makes many of his long poems almost unreadable: they are difficult, very difficult, but below the trouble is a certain steady repetition; you work down to what he is saying on *this* topic only to find that it is much the same as he has always said about everything else . . . Often his abstractions can rouse him to no more than stylistic device; and then the repetition is not solely in the theme . . . Often there is a disparity between his elaborate furnishings and the rather stringent bareness of the ideas . . . Often the gestures claim all of your attention . . . and then the poems hardly exist below the level of style." [8]

If I seem to neglect the poet as philosopher, it is because I believe he has often been badly served in being considered one, as Alvarez's disappointment betrays when he asks for more in the way of "ideas" than Stevens apparently offers him. I should like to redress that balance, and also to distinguish Stevens from other poets or thinkers who may share his interest in the source and value of the creative imagination in this world. In my chosen emphasis I am concerned neither with the aesthetics of doctrine nor, at the other extreme, with the realm of metrics and sound. The first — the aesthetics of doctrine — is the most massive area of "style," what Stevens called "the poem of the idea." In Stevens' case, to study "the poem of the idea" would require seeing, in each of his volumes, which aspects of his "doctrine" are ignored, which emphasized, how these are juxtaposed, from what distance they are viewed, by which persons they are expressed, and in what images they are incarnated.[9] Just now, the criticism of Stevens needs a less sweeping survey. For the same reason, I do not scan the development of Stevens' imagery, though the subject naturally appears from time to time. Stevens' imagery is not particularly obscure once one knows the *Collected Poems*: it is a system of self-reference, and is its own explanation. I assume here a familiarity with its special meanings. Also, since criticism has yet to find a way of making notes on cadence, rhythms, and sounds both reliable and readable, I resort to only occasional remarks on these subjects. Stevens' lines, as critics have shown, are variously indebted; R. P. Blackmur found echoes of Marlowe and Lyly, Samuel French Morse and Daniel Fuchs added echoes of Jonson, J. V. Cunningham found Wordsworth, Robert Buttel found the Milton of *Comus*, Harold Bloom found Emerson, and others have added Keats, Tennyson, Browning, and Shakespeare. But the minute details of Stevens' inheritance, in spite of the contribution they make to his distinctive voice, must wait for a more general book than this.

I should like to follow, by means of the long poems, some of the experiments in style Stevens undertook — experiments in diction, in rhetoric, in syntax, in genre, in imagery, in voice, and in meter. The touchstone has been the best Stevens could do — those poems in which he seems most himself, most original. In this I am not in accord with some anthologists and critics: I choose, if I am pressed, "The Snow Man" over "Peter Quince at the Clavier" and "The Auroras of Autumn" over "Sunday Morning," and in general the later Stevens over the Stevens of *Harmonium* (but of course one sees the pathos of the later Stevens only by knowing the earlier one). These preferences, like others, have probably a moral basis, a sense of the poet's self to which one wants him to be true.

Of all the generalizations about Stevens, there are two I feel most central. One, concerning "the poem of the idea," comes from John Malcolm Brinnin: "Stevens is the banished poet storming the Republic . . . involved by nature or by the Platonic equivalent of original sin in sensuous reality and sensuous imagination, yet burning to come to whiteness and ascetic innocence." [10] The other, concerning "the poem of the words," comes from Blackmur: "I would think that he has all his life wanted to make supreme statements discreetly, so that their beauty would show before their force." [11] An ascetic by nature and temperament, thinking less of doctrine than of feeling: this

Stevens is of course the obverse of that other Stevens shown us by critics, the doctrinal poet of ideas, advocate of hedonism. Both views will be corrected by history:

> The laughing sky will see the two of us
> Washed into rinds by rotting winter rains.

And in the end, all the views will combine to redescribe the "total grandeur of a total edifice,/ Chosen by an inquisitor of structures/ For himself." Of that total edifice, the long poems are a considerable and imposing part, and since "a change of style is a change of subject" (*OP*, 171), it is to Stevens' style, and to his changes in styles, that we must look in order to understand those residual satisfactions, beyond the intellectual, offered by his poems.

I. The Pensive Man: The Pensive Style

The pensive man . . . He sees that eagle float
For which the intricate Alps are a single nest

Though Wallace Stevens' idiosyncratic vocabulary and imagery have been blamed and praised ever since his first poems appeared in print, his equally odd syntax has been less noticed. It shares nevertheless in his act of the mind, and differentiates him noticeably from other poets, whether the Romantic poets whose dependent heir he is, or his contemporaries in England and America. Abstractly considered, Stevens' "themes" are familiar, not to say banal, ones, but his poetry reproduces them in a new form, chiefly in an elaborately mannered movement of thought, which changes very little in the course of the *Collected Poems*. It is, needless to say, expressive of several moods, but three large manners can be distinguished, all of them present in Stevens' long poems. The first, in an ecstatic idiom, proclaims, sometimes defiantly, the pure good of being, the worth of vigorous life, the earthy marriages, the secular joys of ploughing on Sunday. The second, despairingly and in tones of apathy, anatomizes a stale and withered life. The third and most characteristic form is a tentative, diffident, and reluctant search for a middle route between ecstasy and apathy, a sensible ecstasy of pauvred color, to use Stevens' own phrase. Because commentary must ask how poems differ from each other, something beyond philosophical explication is needed: Stevens is notoriously "narrow" in subject, as he realized in having frequent recourse to a form that approximates the musical theme with variations. In these long poems, manner is, if not everything, at least of superlative importance. Words and images can best be seen in their place within the poems, but some general description of Stevens' characteristic rhetoric and syntax can be made before we come individually to the long poems themselves.

When Stevens is most himself, he is a severe and harassing master, allowing himself no delusory hopes, no forced feelings. And so he puts out faint feelers: maybe, say that, perhaps, suppose, tokens of fastidious truth:

> Suppose these couriers brought amid their train
> A damsel heightened by eternal bloom.   (15)

> Say that the hero is his nation,
> In him made one.   (279)

> Perhaps these forms are seeking to escape
> Cadaverous undulations.   (354)

With such suppositions Stevens is committed to nothing except a wish, and interpretations of the world become so many hypotheses, necessarily entertained but of questionable solidity:

> It is not in the premise that reality
> Is a solid. It may be a shade that traverses
> A dust, a force that traverses a shade.   (489)

By this skeptical music Stevens can be chiefly distinguished from the other poets who share his theme, not only by words of uncertainty as in the first quotations above, but by syntactic uncertainty, as in the triad last quoted. Stevens resorts repeatedly to may, might, must, could, should, and would to resolve his poems, and examples can be found on almost any page of the *Collected Poems*:

> If we propose
> A large-sculptured, platonic person, free from time,
> And imagine for him the speech he cannot speak,
>
> A form, then, protected from the battering may
> Mature: A capable being may replace
> Dark horse and walker walking rapidly.   (330)

The probability of the ending depends on the preceding hypothesis, and the whole construct is a nebulous one. Stevens never puts his hypotheses into the present tense ("When we propose a platonic person, a form matures"): such a construction would imply that the action has been successfully performed in the past with certified results, and can successfully be performed again. Stevens' action has not yet been tried, is entirely tentative. If "may" is congenial to Stevens, "might" is even more so. In fact, his constant sense of disparity between the thing and his description of the thing is bridged only by his notion of possibility, that perhaps some day one name might be accurate:

> How close
>
> To the unstated theme each variation comes . . .
> In that one ear it might strike perfectly:
>
> State the disclosure. In that one eye the dove
> Might spring to sight and yet remain a dove.
>
> The fisherman might be the single man
> In whose breast the dove, alighting, would grow still.
>
> (356–357)

This passage, where Stevens suggests rather than asserts, is typical in its imperceptible drift from one mood to another. Usually in Stevens the direction is from the less certain to the more certain; here Stevens substitutes for the expected "might" in the final line the far more conclusive "would," as the poem rises from the possible to the probable.

In other ways, too, Stevens induces us to forget his conditional propositions, often by making a great deal depend on them in a syntactic sequence, as he does in "Landscape with Boats." Though he is engaged in rejecting the search for an absolute truth, "the" truth, in favor of an amassing whole, he will not say so directly, but rather chooses to present his preference as a possible supposition. However, by the repeated apposition of the word "part" with the elements of the world he causes the original tentative "might" to fade away and to leave only the convincing force of the appositions:

> He never supposed that he might be
>   truth, himself,   or   part of it,
> that the things that he rejected might
>   be   part
> and the irregular turquoise,   part,
> the perceptible blue grown denser,   part,
> the eye so touched, so played upon
>   by clouds,
> the ear so magnified by thunder,   parts,
> and all these things together,   parts,
> and more things,   parts.   (242)

Then the poem returns to "might" again, but even so, Stevens' regular antiphony of "part" and a series of nouns affirms a real identity more than a conditional one, and his credence has been conveyed, even if indirectly and equivocally, that these things are all genuinely parts of the truth.

Often, where one of Stevens' Romantic predecessors might have made a straightforward claim, Stevens temporizes, either by "might" or by "may," and these forms compose some of his most characteristic aphorisms:

> It may be that the ignorant man, alone,
> Has any chance to mate his life with life
> That is the sensual, pearly spouse. (222)

> Crow is realist. But, then,
> Oriole, also, may be realist. (154)

Though "might" and "may" recur often in Stevens, they are common poetic property, and his most distinctive form of assertion seems his appropriation of "must" and its related forms "had to" and "cannot" or "could not," usually found in conjunction with some other mood. Sometimes the joining can seem dogmatic, a willed wrenching of reality:

> She must come now. The grass is in seed and high.
> Come now. (119)

> The utmost must be good and is. (374)

> But see him for yourself,
> The fictive man. He may be seated in
> A cafe. There may be a dish of country cheese
> And a pineapple on the table. It must be so. (335)

From "must come" to "come"; from "must" to "is"; from "may be" to "must be"; this fluidity of mood, although not peculiar to Stevens' constructions of obligation, is frequent in them. It accounts for the alternately strained and persuasive tone of many of his "didactic" statements, and poses an obstacle for any critic who would rephrase Stevens' ideas in the more dogmatic indicative mood. The constraint, the sadness, the attempts at self-conviction, the wishful longing — all of these are missing from a portrait of Stevens in the indicative mood. "A necessary function of the imagination," we might represent Stevens as saying, "is to imagine its own absence." But that condensation is untrue to his lines:

> Yet the absence of the imagination had
> Itself to be imagined . . .
>
> The great pond and its waste of the lilies, all this
> Had to be imagined as an inevitable knowledge,
> Required, as a necessity requires.   (503)

The pathos of this passage arises not only from the desolate imagery and the reluctant repetition but also from the hard necessity in the strange phrase "had to be imagined." We rarely use "must" or its variants except in cases of exterior obligation; Stevens here implies obligations or destinies of a more interior and evolutionary sort.

Fluctuations of mood are one way of intimating a shifting sense of the subject; questions are another, and certain questions in Stevens' poetry serve as a qualified way to put a premise. There are poems, like "The Man on the Dump," which are resolved mainly by a series of interrogations functioning more as hints than as easily answerable rhetorical questions. In proposing the attitudes to be taken by the modern imagination, Stevens rejects, by his image of the dump, all transcendence, ornament, and falsification of scene. There are three possible attitudes: to sit on the dump and say "I am sitting on a dump"; to sit and say "This is not a dump but a garden"; to sit, see that the scene is a dump, and nevertheless say "This dump is a flower garden."

Stevens is unwilling, as a poet, to give in to the depressing natural-
ism of the first; the second seems to him a romantic falsification;
but he does not quite know whether the third is possible, and
therefore resorts to questions, followed by two enigmatic words:

> One sits and beats an old tin can, lard pail.
> One beats and beats for that which one believes.
> That's what one wants to get near. Could it after all
> Be merely oneself, as superior as the ear
> To a crow's voice? Did the nightingale torture the ear,
> Pack the heart and scratch the mind? And does the ear
> Solace itself in peevish birds? Is it peace,
> Is it a philosopher's honeymoon, one finds
> On the dump? Is it to sit among mattresses of the dead,
> Bottles, pots, shoes and grass and murmur *aptest eve*:
> Is it to hear the blatter of grackles and say
> *Invisible priest*; is it to eject, to pull
> The day to pieces and cry *stanza my stone*?
> Where was it one first heard of the truth? The the.
>   (202–203)

"That which one believes" is "the truth," and Stevens suspects
that truth is not a transcendence, but merely oneself. Oneself
is the dump out of which must be constructed apt eves, invisible
priests, and stanzas. Oneself, as Stevens has said elsewhere, is the
the:

> There was that difference between the and an,
> The difference between himself and no man.   (255) [1]

All the questions preceding the final phrase converge toward the
notion that no absolute, but rather his own self, is a poet's true
object, but they tend toward it as suggestions, not as statements.
   If Stevens is a didactic poet, as he is so often said to be, it

is with a diffident didacticism. Over and over in the *Collected Poems* he closes poems with a question:

> Is this picture . . . a picture of ourselves?
> Do I sit, deformed?
> Have I been destroyed?
> Am I a man that is dead?
> Is my thought a memory, not alive?
> Is the spot on the floor, there, wine or blood
> And whichever it may be, is it mine?   (173)

These questions compose the total structure of one of the poems in *The Man with the Blue Guitar*. Though a totally interrogative poem is a rarity in Stevens, still there are enough questions at crucial points to make us see the question as one of the natural forms into which his mind casts its observations. The evasion of direct statement, which he regarded as central to poetry,[2] continues, and even the past, whether of personal history or of myth, is not safe from questions. Stevens is full of forms half-glimpsed whose meaning he debates:

> Who was it passed her there on a horse all will,
> What figure of capable imagination? . . .
>   Was it a rider intent on the sun,
> A youth, a lover with phosphorescent hair,
> Dressed poorly, arrogant of his streaming forces,
> Lost in an integration of the martyrs' bones,
> Rushing from what was real; and capable?   (249)

We can, theoretically (though not practically), take our choice of answers to Stevens' question: perhaps it was a rider of just this sort, perhaps not. The figure remains deliberately undefined, since the description is interrogative.

The mood of uncertainty in Stevens, whether marked by

direct questions or by implicit qualification, sometimes yields to
a mood of desperate assertion, where a passionate insistence is
based on fear, a fear of a dreadful disintegration if the assertions
prove false:

> To discover winter and know it well, to find
> Not to impose, not to have reasoned at all,
> Out of nothing to have come on major weather,
>
> It is possible, possible, possible. It must
> Be possible. It must be that in time
> The real will from its crude compoundings come,
>
> Seeming, at first, a beast disgorged, unlike,
> Warmed by a desperate milk.   (404)

This is anything but serene formulation; it is not even a passionate creed, since creeds and beliefs do not take on such hectic
phrasings. "Must" is not a word of faith but a word of doubt,
implying as it does an unbearable alternative. "The utmost must
be good and is," says Stevens in *Credences of Summer*, because
if the utmost were evil his credences would be hollow, as they
sometimes can seem to him. "Poetry / Exceeding music must
take the place / Of empty heaven and its hymns" because if not,
man is lost in the terrible spaces of inhuman auroras. In spite
of his announced intent to remain the poet of reality, to "hasp
on the surviving form / Of shall or ought to be in is," to assert
that "For realist, what is is what should be," Stevens always
knew that reality was composed of more than the present indicative. Again and again, he found himself seduced away to
what ought to be, forsaking all description and reporting of
present and past in favor of the normative and the optative, the
willed and the desired.

Often a poem will end with one of these clauses of will or

desire: "he wanted," "he sought," "he needed," or a variant on these, and these verbs lead him to the inevitable syntactic form of the infinitive as complement:

> He wanted to feel the same way over and over.

> He wanted the river to go on flowing the same way,
> To keep on flowing. He wanted to walk beside it . . .

> He wanted his heart to stop beating.   (425)

And just as he leads us in some poems from the conditional to the present tense to give the illusion that his speculations are facts, so he leads us from desire to timeless states by his use of the perpetually tenseless infinitive. As the poem just quoted goes on, first to a cluster of more infinitives and then to a present participle, it almost succeeds in obliterating that far-forgotten governing unaccomplished phrase, "he wanted":

> He wanted his heart to stop beating and his mind to rest

> In a permanent realization, without any wild ducks
> Or mountains that were not mountains, just to know how
> it would be,

> Just to know how it would feel, released from destruction,
> To be a bronze man breathing under archaic lapis,

> Without the oscillations of planetary pass-pass,
> Breathing his bronzen breath at the azury centre of time.
> (425)

By the end of the poem Stevens has done his best to give the bronze man a fictional existence, to make him something more solid than a mere object of desire. The peculiar, timeless, unqualified nature of infinitives suits his purpose exactly, and explains why so many of his poems include infinitive phrases. They imply a future, usually, but without reminding us that it is in fact a future and not yet accomplished:

> Bastard chateaux and smoky demoiselles,
> No more. I can build towers of my own,
> There to behold, there to proclaim, the grace
>
> And free requiting of responsive fact,
> To project the naked man.   (263)

In such a sequence of infinitives, potentiality is almost forgotten. When Stevens wishes to be even more independent of his own limitations, he uses the infinitive alone, syntactically independent:

> To change nature, not merely to change ideas,
> To escape from the body, so to feel
> Those feelings that the body balks.   (234)
>
> To think of a dove with an eye of grenadine
> And pines that are cornets, so it occurs,
> And a little island full of geese and stars.   (222)

The reader must supply his own main verb — "it is necessary," or "it is exhilarating," or anything that seems to fit. In Stevens' quasi-French constructions with infinitives, the reader must supply a noun — "our duty" or "our fate" for the expletive "it":

> So it is to sit and to balance things
> To and to and to the point of still,
>
> To say of one mask it is like,
> To say of another it is like,

> To know that the balance does not quite rest,
> That the mask is strange, however like.   (181)

> It is of him, ephebe, to make, to confect
> The final elegance, not to console
> Nor sanctify, but plainly to propound.   (389)

These are programs for action, not descriptions of action; manifestos, not reports; potentialities, not completions.

Just as Stevens tries to veil possibility by following conditional verbs with the present tense, and veils unsatisfied desire with independent infinitives, so he tries to veil infinitives with something more positive. In one canto (vii) of *Credences of Summer*, the veiling device is the past participle. The poem begins with desire, and then with no warning except a pause, slips into the present tense as the self grips the object; from there, it goes into a procession of infinitives of purpose, and then ends deceptively with two past participles, as if to imply that desire had found its object:

> They sang desiring an object that was near,
> In face of which desire no longer moved,
> Nor made of itself that which it could not find . . .
> Three times the concentred self takes hold, three times
> The thrice concentred self, having possessed

> The object, grips it in savage scrutiny,
> Once to make captive, once to subjugate
> Or yield to subjugation, once to proclaim
> The meaning of the capture, this hard prize,
> Fully made, fully apparent, fully found.   (376)

Such resolutions of infinitive phrases are not common in Stevens. More often the infinitive closes the poem, looking forward to "the hopeful waste of the future," to a place "where we have yet to live."

When Stevens seems to be asserting unconditionally, not using the mitigating auxiliaries, nor infinitives, nor questions, he nevertheless can escape being final. Sometimes he escapes semantically, as he does in his constant use of the word "seem" and his meditations on it:

> It is possible that to seem — it is to be,
> As the sun is something seeming and it is.   (339)

Where we might expect "is," especially at the end of a poem, we find the more delicate "seems":

> In that cry they hear
> Themselves transposed, muted and comforted . . .

> So that this cold, a children's tale of ice,
> Seems like a sheen of heat romanticized.   (467–468)

"Seems" introduces the uncertainty of knowledge, the likelihood of deception, the possible quicksand of nature.

Stevens is also likely to end a poem with a verb which implies a future, though cast in the present tense; of these, "become" is his favorite, though he uses, too, such verbs as "promise" and "foretell":

> The blue guitar
> Becomes the place of things as they are.   (168)

> The yellow grassman's mind is still immense,
> Still promises perfections cast away.   (318)

> The clouds foretell a swampy rain.   (161)

Poets have often used the future to resolve a poem, and very satisfactorily, since the future is always a fiction. But Stevens, though he will use the simple future tense, prefers a more devious future, the sort expressed in English by "when" or "until" followed by the present tense — a future in disguise, so to speak. "Until" can imply either finished action in the future or hopeless effort which may never bear fruit, and Stevens relies on that equivocal implication. He adjures the muses, for instance, to repeat *To Be Itself* until —

> Until the sharply-colored glass transforms
> Itself into the speech of the spirit, until
> The porcelain bell-borrowings become
> Implicit clarities in the way you cry
> And are your feelings changed to sound, without
> A change, until the waterish ditherings turn
> To the tense, the maudlin, true meridian
> That is yourselves, when, at last, you are yourselves,
> Speaking and strutting broadly, fair and bloomed,
> No longer of air but of the breathing earth,
> Impassioned seducers and seduced, the pale
> Pitched into swelling bodies, upward, drift
> In a storm blown into glittering shapes, and flames
> Wind-beaten into freshest, brightest fire.   (*OP*, 52)

This passage, the conclusion to one of the cantos in *Owl's Clover*, is clearly and consciously the enacting of a wish-fulfillment, not the statement of a fact: it is an apotheosis, but exists very far from a direct future of apotheosis like Milton's celestial time when

> Attired with stars, we shall forever sit
> Triumphing over Death and Chance and Thee, O Time.

Stevens' passage is a whirl of willed confusion, as "until" modulates into "when" (l. 8), and the present-tense "are" replaces the more obviously future-in-intent "transforms," "become," and "turn." The passage ends with one of Stevens' barrages of apposition, which serve as smoke screens over the terms they juxtapose. Even here, the implicit futurity is remarkable: the pale Muses are to be "pitched into swelling bodies," they are to be "drift . . . blown into glittering shapes," and "flames/ Wind-beaten into . . . fire." It is a second-order futurity: they will be X which will then itself be transformed into Y. And the final superlatives, representing the ecstasy of that moment, obscure too the possible delineation of this projected time; they simply ask us to imagine the Anselmian unimaginable, the brightness and freshness beyond which there is no better brightness and freshness. The trouble with this ineffability is that it is ungrounded, not extrapolated from any present out of which it naturally grows, and so the future rings false.

When Stevens is reluctant to assert even an equivocal present or future, he resorts to hypothesis and supposition, chiefly by using his indispensable hypothetical "if," which takes away with one hand what the poet has already given with the other:

> Or, if the music sticks, if the anecdote
> Is false, if Crispin is a profitless
> Philosopher, beginning with green brag,
> Concluding fadedly, if as a man
> Prone to distemper he abates in taste . . .
> And so distorting, proving what he proves
> Is nothing, what can all this matter since
> The relation comes, benignly, to its end? (45–46)

This is one of the most satisfying of Stevens' shrugs of disavowal, coming as it does in what is, superficially at least, a witty and ironic poem. Other instances can seem merely evidence of a repetitive manner: "the summer came,/ If ever, whisked and wet" (35); "Moonlight was an evasion, or, if not,/ A minor meeting" (35); "You are the will, if there is a will" (233); "There's no such thing as life; or if there is,/ It is faster than the weather" (192). These "ifs" are like marks of punctuation, like small question marks inserted in the sentence. More powerful instances arise in Stevens' ample hypotheses of desire:

> Perhaps, if winter once could penetrate
> Through all its purples to the final slate . . .
>
> One might in turn become less diffident . . .
> One might. One might. But time will not relent.   (96)
>
> If they could gather their theses into one,
> Collect their thoughts together into one,
> Into a single thought, thus: into a queen,
> An intercessor by innate rapport . . .
> If they could!   (254)

These remain hypotheses, not truths, and they are denied, in the first case by the obstructive and final "But time will not relent," and in the second case by the violence of the closing optative. Sometimes, though, there is no such denial present, and the hypothesis becomes a softened way of assertion:

> This day writhes with what? . . .
> If the day writhes, it is not with revelations.   (429)

These "ifs" of uncommitted assertion serve as points from which Stevens can suspend long deductions, making us disregard the shaky status of the antecedent in the accretion of apparent logic that follows, as we tend to do for instance in the eighth canto of "It Must Give Pleasure" from *Notes toward a Supreme Fiction*:

What am I to believe? If the angel in his cloud . . .
Leaps downward through evening's revelations and . . .
Forgets the gold centre . . .
Am I that imagine this angel less satisfied? . . .
Is it he or is it I that experience this?
It is I then that keep saying there is an hour
Filled with expressible bliss . . .
And if there is an hour there is a day,
There is a month, a year, there is a time
In which majesty is a mirror of the self.   (404–405)

The combination in this poem of hypothesis and question finally collapses as the critical mind strikes the midnight end to these filaments of speculation:

These external regions, what do we fill them with
Except reflections, the escapades of death,
Cinderella fulfilling herself beneath the roof?   (405)

Finally, Stevens uses "if" as he had used "when" and until": as a conjunction introducing a solid-seeming tense which is in fact not solid at all. Just as "when" and "until" make the present tense do duty for the future, so "if" makes the past tense, with all its impression of solid historical fact, do duty for the subjunctive. "If one went to the moon," Stevens begins, meaning "If one were to have gone to the moon":

So that if one went to the moon,
Or anywhere beyond, to a different element,
One would be drowned in the air of difference . . .
And then returning from the moon, if one breathed
The cold evening . . .
                    If then
One breathed the cold evening, the deepest inhalation
Would come from that return to the subtle centre.   (258)

This passage serves, supposedly, as a long simile, a description of a lunar experiment to confirm the poet's belief in the absolute uniqueness of the earth, even at its barest moments. But the experiment, like some epic similes, becomes lost in the experience recounted, which takes on an actuality of its own. This is true of another passage from the same poem, using again the same quasi-historical past following "if":

> But would it be amen, in choirs, if once
> In total war we died and after death
> Returned, unable to die again, fated
> To endure thereafter every mortal wound,
> Beyond a second death, as evil's end?   (258)

And this hypothesis is continued, and vivified, and taken seriously as a vehicle for reflection.

Another manner of indeterminacy is permitted by the imperative, and Stevens takes full advantage of it, often to resolve poems. Since all poems of prayer, command, and exhortation choose this means, it is only remarkable in Stevens in conjunction with his other reticences of mood, and in view of its imitation of a religious tradition. Stevens' divinities have a shadowy *ad hoc* existence, materializing momentarily as an interior paramour, a rabbi, a green queen, or even an unnamed presence:

> Oh! Rabbi, rabbi, fend my soul for me
> And true savant of this dark nature be.   (134)

> Unreal, give back to us what once you gave:
> The imagination that we spurned and crave.   (88)

Nothing in an imperative implies that it will be complied with, and the poem retains the same unsettled sort of ending that Stevens arranges elsewhere with other means. As he addresses the musician at the piano, "Be seated, thou" (132), or tells his imaginary rustics, "Clog, therefore, purple Jack and crimson Jill" (154), the action summoned, whether playing or dancing, remains still unperformed.

In all the cases mentioned above, Stevens at least concludes, finishes his sentence, even if the end is tentative at best, destructive at worst. When the statement he is theoretically pursuing escapes formulation altogether, he breaks off suddenly, as the mind retreats from something, whether blissful or disastrous, that it cannot compass:

> It was an old rebellious song,
> An edge of song that never clears:
> But if it did . . . If the cloud that hangs
> Upon the heart and round the mind
> Cleared from the north and in that height
> The sun appeared and reddened great
> Belshazzar's brow, O ruler, rude
> With rubies then, attend me now.   (207)

Here the syntactic connections break in the wistful third line and again in the seventh line as the interjection interrupts the hypothesis. The unsayable is, in these cases, hovering just beyond the sentence:

> If the stars that move together as one, disband,
> Flying like insects of fire in a cavern of night,
> Pipperoo, pippera, pipperum . . . The rest is rot.   (230)

Whenever the sentence expands and threatens to dodge conception to the bourne of heaven, it bursts like a bubble, sometimes in hope, as it does in the first quotation above, sometimes into cynical irony, as in the second.

When the ending is not quite unsayable, Stevens modulates

into conjecture, with his characteristic "as if." Usually currents of feeling have become so entangled by the end of any poem ending with "as if" that the logical sense of the ending is dissolved in the affective result of the comparison. So it is in the eighth canto of *The Auroras of Autumn*, where Stevens, faced with the terrifying aurora, must decide whether it is malign or innocent. In accents of desperation he insists on the reality of innocence, "But it exists,/ It exists, it is visible, it is, it is." The spent and childlike conclusion follows:

> So, then, these lights are not a spell of light,
> A saying out of a cloud, but innocence.
> An innocence of the earth and no false sign
>
> Or symbol of malice. That we partake thereof,
> Lie down like children in this holiness,
> As if, awake, we lay in the quiet of sleep,
>
> As if the innocent mother sang in the dark
> Of the room and on an accordion, half-heard,
> Created the time and place in which we breathed . . .
>
> (418–419)

The last four lines are an attempt to soothe by conjuring up a nursery peace, a solace in the comforts of childhood. Stevens does not say, "Let us lie down as if we *were lying* in the quiet of sleep," but uses the past tense to invoke recollection of a real past experience of such quiet. There is no innocent mother singing in the present, but Stevens' lulling lines hope for her presence as a counterforce to his apprehensions, even though she exists only in his shadowy "as if."

Such an "as if" is pure invention, and recognized as such. In other poems, a quasi existence is given to the presences invoked in the "as if," especially when Stevens in some cases uses "was" as his verb instead of the more usual "were":

> And we feel, in a way apart, for a moment, as if
> There was a bright *scienza* outside of ourselves,
>
> A gaiety that is being, not merely knowing,
> The will to be and to be total in belief,
> Provoking a laughter, an agreement, by surprise.   (248)

Without committing himself to the existence of the bright *scienza* Stevens nevertheless neutralizes the effect of the tentative "feel . . . for a moment, as if" by the ripple of description that closes the poem. The same technique of a neutralized "as if" resolves *Esthétique du Mal*:

> And out of what one sees and hears and out
> Of what one feels, who could have thought to make
> So many selves, so many sensuous worlds
> As if the air, the mid-day air, was swarming
> With the metaphysical changes that occur,
> Merely in living as and where we live.   (326)

The use of "was" here is deliberate, as it is in several other poems,[3] all of which underscore the affirmation beneath the hypothesis.

"As if" forms a bridge between perception and reflection; we stop the film to analyze it. This analysis often goes unremarked unless we sense a departure from the expected tense and mood, as we frequently do in Stevens, but even so, the use of the past tense after "as if" is only intermittently surprising, since it occurs in ordinary speech.

A stranger case of the unexpected comes in the conclusion of Stevens' elegy on Santayana, "To an Old Philosopher in

Rome." Santayana is "on the threshold of heaven," in the last tenuous earthly room, and after describing him there, Stevens concludes:

> It is a kind of total grandeur at the end . . .
>
> Total grandeur of a total edifice,
> Chosen by an inquisitor of structures
> For himself. He stops upon this threshold,
> As if the design of all his words takes form
> And frame from thinking and is realized.   (510–511)

The "as if" is followed here, quite oddly, by the present tense and the indicative mood, deliberately forcing the poem to end on a note of present happening, of actual event, almost giving the lie to the "as if." Santayana has been addressed before the last stanza as "you": suddenly he becomes at the end a sublime "inquisitor of structures," a Platonic person moving among the possible shapes of life to choose one suitably noble, a "total edifice." Having chosen it, "he stops upon this threshold," and we are no longer sure whether this is the threshold of heaven mentioned earlier in the poem or whether it is the threshold of the "total edifice," the construct of Santayana's life and work, now combined into a perfect whole, as one exemplifies the other. Santayana, in his exemplary function, has created his own heavenly mansion. In default of picturing to us a mansion in "that more merciful Rome beyond," Stevens has established a new threshold on which, in a moment of arrested motion, we last see the old philosopher. Like a legendary castle that springs up overnight, Santayana's total meaning, "the design of all his words," "takes form and frame from thinking," takes on architectural substance from something insubstantial, and "is realized," made real in the edifice which he in himself is, by what he has chosen, by what he represents, by what he has written. This is the modern elegiac consolation, as the poet becomes his poems, the philosopher becomes his system. The final "as if" gives Santayana a place to go, so to speak, at the end. The poet cannot leave him in Rome, cannot take him to a fictive heaven, and cannot, in one sense, leave him on the threshold, not if it is a threshold to emptiness. The "total edifice," at first clearly metaphorical, becomes strangely real as the present tense follows "as if," and, as it is realized, resolves the poem.

Stevens' language is such that it modulates from "reality" to the realm of "as if" very easily, making the two almost interchangeable at times; one poem begins,

> All night I sat reading a book,
> Sat reading as if in a book
> Of sombre pages.   (146)

In the second line we are told by the "as if" of the metaphorical nature of this "book" (which turns out to be the heavens filled with falling stars) but after this momentary withdrawal from the fiction, we once again re-enter the metaphor and the sombre pages remain pages. The effect is of something half-glimpsed, half-seen, and that is, finally, what Stevens achieves over and over: if he has a dogma, it is the dogma of the shadowy, the ephemeral, the barely perceived, the iridescent:

> It is not in the premise that reality
> Is a solid. It may be a shade that traverses
> A dust, a force that traverses a shade.   (489)

In his witty moments, Stevens practices legerdemain with the world's "reality" and produces a fantasia of shifting possibles, the brilliant changes of "Sea Surface Full of Clouds." In the more reflective poems, he juggles with logic as he juggles with colors and shapes, often less successfully, but sometimes with the confident disposition of alternatives he displays in "The Idea of Order at Key West":

> She sang beyond the genius of the sea . . .
>
> The sea was not a mask. No more was she.
> The song and water were not medleyed sound
> Even if what she sang was what she heard,
> Since what she sang was uttered word by word.
> It may be that in all her phrases stirred
> The grinding water and the gasping wind;
> But it was she and not the sea we heard . . .
>
> If it was only the dark voice of the sea
> That rose, or even colored by many waves;
> If it was only the outer voice of sky
> And cloud, of the sunken coral water-walled,
> However clear, it would have been deep air,
> The heaving speech of air, a summer sound
> Repeated in a summer without end
> And sound alone. But it was more than that,
> More even than her voice, and ours, among
> The meaningless plungings of water and the wind,
> Theatrical distances, bronze shadows heaped
> On high horizons, mountainous atmospheres
> Of sky and sea.   (128–129)

The apparent structure of the poem is one of logical discrimination, but actually the complicated "even if . . . since . . . it may be . . . if . . . or . . ." and so on simply serve to implicate the various alternatives ever more deeply with each other so that the sea, the girl, the water, the song, the wind, the air, the sky and cloud, the voices of the spectators, all become indistinguishable from each other, as Stevens wants them to be.

To separate out his inferences and insist on the demarcations of his logic would be to run counter to the intent of the poem. This is true in general of Stevens' use of logical form: he uses it not as a logician, but as a sleight-of-hand man. He is attached to paradoxical logic, especially in the realm of existence — "He is and may be but oh! he is, he is" (388), he says in many ways, denying and affirming at the same time. The irresolution of his lines sometimes defies all logic:

> In the little of his voice, or the like,
> Or less, he found a man, or more, against
> Calamity, proclaimed himself, was proclaimed.   (230)

Such passages can be parsed into sense, but not very rewardingly, since Stevens' use of "or" in this way is one more device for hovering over the statement rather than making it. The atmosphere of false precision sometimes conferred by this language of logical discrimination is deceptive: Stevens is not at pains to distinguish between the little, the like, and the less in the passage above, but to identify them with each other.

Stevens' nuances of feeling, determined though they are in particular poems by each special context, are nevertheless better sensed if we see the general patterns into which his voice falls. Even in the simplest and shortest poems the characteristic sentence forms, the characteristic logic, the characteristic resolutions appear. It is against the background of these idiosyncratic but persistent armatures of thought that we can see the individual departures or emphases in each poem. To follow the development of his life in poetry we must turn first to the bravura of *The Comedian as the Letter C* and of *Sunday Morning*, and go on from there to the thirty years of publishing following that first éclat.

II. Fugal Requiems

> Was he to bray this in profoundest brass
> Arointing his dreams with fugal requiems?

Commentaries on *The Comedian as the Letter C* (1923) [1] have in general ended with its ending, seeing what happens in the poem as the equivalent of what happens in its fable. But this poem speaks one language in its narrative plot, another in the success or failure of its rhetoric. As Lawrence said about earlier American writers, we must not trust the artist, but the tale. Nevertheless, behind the poet stands the man, who may be engaged in an effort to believe what the poet in him cannot enact. A separation of these strands of saying can lessen certain kinds of unease that anyone reading this first of Stevens' long poems must feel.

The plot of the *Comedian* is an epic one — the grand voyage and the return home. The ironic treatment of the voyager, critics have been quick to say, makes this poem a mock epic,[2] and the genre, asserted in the title, is comedy. But Stevens' more accurate readers, notably R. P. Blackmur,[3] have seen that no matter how slyly and briskly the poem moves, its subject is serious and skirts the tragic, and that in spite of its mock-heroic mode the poem conveys some sort of heroism, at least in its first cantos. All paraphrases unite in rendering the poem, in spite of its self-minimizing shrugs, as a testament, a reflection of the odyssey of one modern poet. Such summaries do not match the tone of the poem as we have it, and conclude in paying homage to the "seriousness" of its intent while honoring the surface of the poem, if at all, as the sparkling but almost irrelevant iridescence over the serious "topic."

The Comedian as the Letter C is fantastic in its language, and belongs, in the spectrum of poetic effort, at the end where we find anagrams, schemes, acrostics, figure poems, double sestinas, and so on — the poetry of ingenuity, the poetry with overt verbal designs on its readers. At least, that is our first impression. Then we notice a strange ebb and flow to that fantasy of language so that together with the obvious simplicity of the plot we have occasional corresponding simplicities of speech, lulls in the erratic gothic harmonies of the words. These simplicities are of several kinds, just as the coruscations are; together they bound the stylistic extremes of the poem and frame its rhetorical architecture.

Since all language in a poem is deliberate language, even simplicities, especially in strategic locations, have their wit. One form of simplicity that the *Comedian* and later poems depend on is the epigram, where the concepts may not be simple, but the rhetoric is:

> Man is the intelligence of his soil . . .
> His soil is man's intelligence.

These are punctuations in the poem, where it finds momentary pause. So are the titles of the cantos, deliberately laconic or banal — "The Idea of a Colony," "A Nice Shady Home" — which seem all the plainer when we reflect on the vagaries of entitling that Stevens allows himself in the *Collected Poems*. Equally plain is the final optative of the *Comedian*, which stands as Crispin's epitaph: "So may the relation of each man be clipped." Nothing of this prosaic sort occurs in Stevens' serious Romantic models, those voyages of nineteenth-century heroes in narrative verse. Around these dryly-put themes Stevens clusters his variations.

Stevens' range, beyond this primary level, makes simple definition awkward. He joins "high" syntax — an imposing parade of appositions, for instance — with mixed high and low diction in his first description of Crispin: "Socrates of snails, lutanist of fleas, imperative haw of hum." [4] The high syntax and some of the diction of royal address persist, but are diminished in their sphere of operation by Crispin's Lilliputian domestic range. If incongruity between high and low is the basis for the self-irony in such passages, there is no such incongruity in some other equally ironic appositions:

> An eye most apt in   gelatines
>   and jupes,
>   [and] berries of villages,
>
>   a barber's eye,
>   an eye   of land,
>   of simple salad beds,
>   of honest quilts,
>
>   the eye of Crispin.

The earlier appositive epithets had pointed to Crispin's exaltation of himself as "principium and lex." But these later ones point to his simultaneous defensive diminution of self into the *honnête homme, l'homme moyen sensuel*. The protesting rusticity in "simple" and "honest" comes from Crispin's intimidation by the sea; what results is a scared claim for the decent reliable God-fearing land inhabitant. These simplicities are Crispin's two forms of romanticizing the self, and whether he sees himself as an exalted personage ruling a minute kingdom or, plaintively, as just an ordinary man like everyone else, these delusions have their appropriate forms of speech. The exalted personage talks in theological and philosophical terms, the *hon-nête homme* in ostentatiously *villageois* language.

Although the *Comedian* is written in the third person, there is no consistent speaking voice. Some readers have seen the speaker as an older Crispin ironically retelling his past voyage, but the narrator can be placed equally well at a further remove, as a third voice which modulates into both of the voices of Crispin, high and low. Crispin in fact is dead, and the third voice claims no temporal continuity with him at all, however much it may be true that all three are Stevens. The third voice speaks the "neutral" lines: "Crispin was washed away by magnitude." And this grave third voice, expressing itself often without irony, gives the poem its claim to high seriousness on life and fate. When it becomes fussily scholastic, a didactic voice retelling an exemplary voyage, we are given the mock hagiographer or anatomist. The "Nota" and "Sed quaeritur" of the opening are *its* mode of irony,[5] as it goes on with scholarly detachment to preach or to expound, via the life of its safely entombed exemplum, the anecdote of Crispin, of which the *sentence* is *De te fabula*. Pseudo-scholarly interest in a historical precedent is the governing ironic mode of the whole: we are given Crispin as zoological sample ideally preserved, as an exemplary allegorical model to be followed, as anything but a taxing living creature. And the inclusive irony is that even the scientific examination of an instructive case is vitiated:

> What can all this matter since
> The relation comes, benignly, to its end?   (vi)

The only resolution is a temporal ending, not the moral resolution that the scholar-voice had intended, and the whole elaborate house of cards topples to the ground.

The sea and sky that wash Crispin away have, too, a double

stylistic self, just as he has: a self of immense simplicity and a self of decorative variety. The poem attempts to appreciate both the strict austerity of "one vast subjugating final tone" and the "gaudy gusty panoply . . . caparison of wind and cloud." As always, Stevens wants reality both as monad and as plenitude, as the impenetrable rock-face and as Madame La Fleurie. What he desires is not necessarily what he perceives, and the double vision of reality shared by the narrator and by Crispin is the source of some confusion.

For a voyager, Crispin, like his prototype in *Alastor*, is remarkably passive. Things happen to him — first the sea, then a thunderstorm, then a family. These passages are the most explicit in the poem as the narrator speaks of undeniable physical happenings:

> Crispin was washed away by magnitude.
> The whole of life that still remained in him
> Dwindled to one sound strumming in his ear,
> Ubiquitous concussion, slap and sigh,
> Polyphony beyond his baton's thrust. (i)

> The white cabildo darkened, the façade,
> As sullen as the sky, was swallowed up
> In swift, successive shadows, dolefully.
> The rumbling broadened as it fell. (ii)

> And so it came, his cabin shuffled up,
> His trees were planted, his duenna brought
> Her prismy blonde and clapped her in his hands . . .
> The chits came for his jigging, bluet-eyed. (v)

We may take this as swift and unequivocal narration, where the flickers of comedy are overcome by the general march of ceremonious narrative. But where the sea and sky are elemental fate, the daughters are human fate, and are not consequently either purely simple or purely decorative, as the sky and sea, in this poem, are free to be. The idiom of the last canto of the *Comedian*, in describing the daughters, becomes the most forced in the poem: except for the opening definitions of Crispin, there are no excesses of elaboration to equal the density of the picture of Crispin's cabin as he returns to social nature:

> The return to social nature, once begun,
> Anabasis or slump, ascent or chute,
> Involved him in midwifery so dense
> His cabin counted as phylactery,
> Then place of vexing palankeens, then haunt
> Of children nibbling at the sugared void,
> Infants yet eminently old, then dome
> And halidom for the unbraided femes,
> Green crammers of the green fruits of the world.   (vi)

The cabin, in a word, is not a place where anyone would want to live, or could live without being buried alive. The revulsion from the proliferation of life, subliminally ever present throughout Stevens, is nowhere clearer than in this account of Crispin's daughters, especially in what they have done to Crispin's cabin — deprived it of style, finally, with all those palankeens and fruit-crammings.

In the enumeration of the daughters, Stevens becomes more schematic than ever before or since, first announcing them in language that is a parody of an invocation to the Muse (vi, 1–8) [6] and then counting them, over and over: they are counted in their coming, counted in their growing, and counted, finally, in their being — an equivocal abacus, since the daughters, though insistently four, are scarcely differentiable [7] except for the one who becomes a queerly inane lady poet, "gaping at the orioles . . . a pearly poetess, peaked for rhapsody." The first two marry successively the same husband, who is presumably Cupid, "the full-pinioned one." The second sister has a chance because the first was inept:

> The second sister dallying was shy
> To fetch the one full-pinioned one himself
> Out of her botches, hot embosomer.   (vi)

The sexual flinching underlying the ostentatious lustiness of the last epithet resembles the revulsion from the flesh which dictates the gobbet-like description of the fourth baby, compounded of

> Mere blusteriness that gewgaws jollified
> All din and gobble, blasphemously pink.   (vi)

That daughter becomes tolerable only when she is the residual inhabitant, single, of the cabin, "pent now, a digit curious." Crispin, as we know him, is allegorized in his environment, and the moral explicitly drawn from marriage and the engendering of these overwhelming daughters is that this fertility and multiplication is a benign end, inundating the stage with new dramatis personae:

> Four daughters in a world too intricate
> In the beginning, four blithe instruments
> Of differing struts, four voices several
> In couch, four more personae, intimate
> As buffo, yet divers, four mirrors blue
> That should be silver, four accustomed seeds
> Hinting incredible hues, four selfsame lights
> That spread chromatics in hilarious dark,
> Four questioners and four sure answerers.   (vi)

This insistent summary of the daughters' effect, altogether milder than the din and gobble and nibbling children, excludes the more embarrassing of its own antecedents, especially the extinction of Crispin's self which necessarily precedes his marriage and family. That extinction of self offered him two choices in the way of song, and he considers the first at length: it is to sing fugal requiems, chant dirges, and wear mourning. He rejects that option in the *Comedian*, but the falling-off in poetry which comes when he decides for a posthumous family life makes us doubt the wisdom of the fatalist choice. As Stevens was to say in his last extended poem, he had an instinct for earth as well as an instinct for heaven, but in his earlier years he seems to have been mistaken about what parts of the earth he had an instinct for. He felt obliged to pretend an instinct for the fertility of earth, when his true instinct was for its austerities and its dilapidations. Pursuing the *ignis fatuus* of luxuriance, he came to grief, not only in the poetry of the daughters but in other parts of the *Comedian* as well, where in convulsions of diction violence is done to language by archaism, slang, and affectation all jumbled together.

Stevens' active repugnance in the presence of the sensual and social daughters is matched only by his response to the tropics in the poem. His exposure begins with the melodic and archaic vocabulary of celestial vision:

> The fabulous and its intrinsic verse
> Came like two spirits parleying, adorned
> In radiance from the Atlantic coign.

And then, revulsion:

> But they came parleying of such an earth,
> So thick with sides and jagged lops of green . . .
> So streaked with yellow, blue and green and red

In beak and bud and fruity gobbet-skins,
That earth was like a jostling festival
Of seeds grown fat, too juicily opulent,
Expanding in the gold's maternal warmth.   (ii)

This travesty of Porphyro's table offers a pulpy vocabulary of overripeness that we find elsewhere in Stevens:

Our bloom is gone. We are the fruit thereof.
Two golden gourds distended on our vines,
Into the autumn weather, splashed with frost,
Distorted by hale fatness, turned grotesque.
We hang like warty squashes, streaked and rayed,
The laughing sky will see the two of us
Washed into rinds by rotting winter rains.   (16)

When he acknowledges his own choking on the lush and opulent fruit of life, Stevens criticizes his incapacity — "Man proved a gobbet in my mincing world" (17) — but he cannot deny his reaction. He spits out gobbets, he draws back from the fat and fruity, in language as in experience. His verse describing "hale fatness" (a condition which he perceives as distention, distortion, grotesquerie) issues from the fastidious shudder of the involuntary ascetic.[8]

Stevens repudiates fertility in favor of discreet fineness; his gift above all others was to see, both comically and tragically, that "fluttering things have so distinct a shade." This capacity for the fluctuating engages us by virtuoso turns in "Sea Surface Full of Clouds" and by equivocal thresholds of expression in "To an Old Philosopher in Rome," where the physical and the spiritual are not placed in a mutually annihilatory relation, as they are in the *Comedian*. Stevens' best verse trembles always at halfway points, at the point of metamorphosis, when day is becoming darkness, when winter is becoming spring, when the rock is becoming the ivy, when a shadowy myth takes form before dissolving, when the revolving *mundo* hesitates in a pause. It is a poetry of the transitional moment, of the not-quite-here and the not-yet-gone, and is expressed, as Randall Jarrell finely said, in a dialectical movement: "In Stevens the unlikely tenderness of this movement — the one, the not-quite-that, the other, the not-exactly-the-other, the real one, the real other — is like the tenderness of the sculptor or draftsman, whose hand makes but looks as if it caressed." [9] Neither the unbodied nor the embodied engages Stevens for long; he is engrossed in "a voyaging up and down, between two elements," and the emphasis should be on the "between." Stevens is not a poet of antinomies, but a poet of the midworld between them, a world not of infinite Miltonic dimensions but of limited space. Stevens cannot go "on spredden wings" through "deep space" (404) like his angels and Canons for more than a moment, any more than he can range with natural flexibility through the earth, at least not without abnormal strains on his language.

Stevens' predicament, though it has been sometimes voiced, and by Stevens too, as a predicament of the modern agnostic, seems rather the result of a wintry temperament, as Stevens' saw when he wrote, "Life is an affair of people not of places. But for me life is an affair of places and that is the trouble" (*OP*, 158). The lively things of this world — human, animal, vegetable — do not touch him as they did Keats or Wordsworth; he cannot become a sparrow or a stoat; he is not transfixed by a girl, a gibbet, and a beacon; the minutiae of the scene pass by unobserved; the natural cast of his eyes is upward, and the only phenomenon to which he is passionately attached is the weather. Natural forms, even when they are drawn from particular Pennsylvania or Connecticut landscapes, are generalized, abstracted, made almost anonymous in his poetry.

The entire absence of immersed attention to the details of the natural scene is nowhere more striking than in Stevens' di-

47

vergence from his Romantic forebears, even when he is echoing them. The famous and beautiful ending of *Sunday Morning* derives, as everyone has noticed, from Keats's more famous and more beautiful final description of autumn:

> While barred clouds bloom the soft-dying day,
>   And touch the stubble-plains with rosy hue;
> Then in a wailful choir the small gnats mourn
>   Among the river swallows, borne aloft
>   Or sinking as the light wind lives or dies;
> And full-grown lambs loud bleat from hilly bourn;
>   Hedge-crickets sing; and now with treble soft
>   The red-breast whistles from a garden-croft;
>   And gathering swallows twitter in the skies.

In Stevens, this becomes:

> Deer walk upon our mountains, and the quail
> Whistle about us their spontaneous cries;
> Sweet berries ripen in the wilderness;
> And, in the isolation of the sky,
> At evening, casual flocks of pigeons make
> Ambiguous undulations as they sink
> Downward to darkness, on extended wings.   (viii)

Both passages seem to be generalized scenes, but in Keats the implication of a present event (this is happening *now*, not this is what happens on autumn days), perceptible in the use of "while" in lieu of the more usual "when," is made unequivocal as the poem focuses, with full pathos, in the mind of a single observer with a vantage point in space to which the sounds are referred: the red-breast whistles not in, but from, the garden croft; the lambs bleat from the hilly bourn. Keats's observer is also located at a single and particular moment in time — "And *now* with treble soft / The red-breast whistles." Although Autumn has been gently deified in the previous stanzas, the mythology is equally gently discarded, and Ceres is reabsorbed in the minimal natural sounds, "the concretions which must, in the end, speak for themselves." [10]

Though Stevens, like Keats, mentions natural objects, they are allegorical instances of the abstract formulation earlier in the poem:

> We live in an old chaos of the sun,
> Or old dependency of day and night,
> Or island solitude, unsponsored, free,
> Of that wide water, inescapable.   (viii)

Stevens' deer represent solitude, the spontaneous quail are unsponsored, the berries mature in the "free" wilderness, and the casual (also unsponsored) isolated (or islanded) pigeons make ambiguous undulations (close to chaos) as they sink (in dependency) downward to darkness (from day to night) on wings extended wide, hovering over that wide water. The scene, in short, is being used largely as an instance of a thesis, not surrendered to in and for itself.

Like Stevens, Crispin has only two choices in respect to the natural world: to be repelled by it, or to abstract it and make it scan. When Crispin "humbles himself" to the turnip, it has to be by a deliberate quelling of his natural fastidiousness, and with a *nostalgie de la boue* he hunts down all the "arrant stinks" that might help him "round his rude aesthetic out." There seems no middle ground in the *Comedian* — we have either the memorial gesturings of Triton or else resinous rankness, with the daughters, a simple perpetuation of self, no real poetic solution. The veritable small, the everyday, the sparrow at the window or the quarrel in the street — these, for all Crispin's pretensions to family life, are absent, and so is the visionary. Crispin's dilemma is not a universal one, as some readers of Stevens assume: it is only a dilemma for Stevens' very special vantage point in the person of Crispin, the vantage point of the man for whom the senses do not provide transcendent moments, who is repelled as the provocations of the senses reach excess, who is almost indifferent by temperament to any world except an arranged or speculative one — and who nevertheless "knows" that this world is all there is, that this is the unique item of ecstasy.

To embrace the quotidian is Stevens' "answer" in the *Comedian*, but it is not his only, nor his most characteristic answer, since in other poems he chooses to emphasize the world as a construction of the imagination, to reject or at least to surpass the mediations and satisfactions of the senses. Stevens' self seems to have presented him with a world excessively interior, in which the senses, with the exception of the eye, are atrophied or impoverished, and he writes about the world he has, putting in active terms, as a voyage, what is in fact involuntary. When the attempt at a transformation of reality fails, as it does with Crispin, when he is faced with the same insoluble lump only disastrously multiplied, he is embittered. Stevens certainly cannot write lovingly about a collection of raw turnips, though he conveys their appalling rawness by din and gobble; nor can he truly transform them, though he tries to cast the mantle of the transformed over what he feels as the deformed by calling the multiplied turnips "four questioners and four sure answerers."

Though Stevens writes superbly about the frail tentatives of reality — the single croak, the scrawny cry, the pre-history of February — when he is faced with the gross heterogeneity of the world he recoils. His preferred view of totality is not the heterogeneous but a great One — the Celestial Sun — which is, needless to say, still far away. When, on the other hand, Stevens exposes his dislike for that multiple reality which makes a dump of the world, the voice becomes unhampered, though self-critical; as soon as he tries to see the dump as fertile and prolific, the revulsion shows. He can ask finely of the present uncoiffed image,

> Why, without pity for these studious ghosts,
> Do you come dripping in your hair from sleep?   (14)

But when he tries to describe natural curls, as he does with the four daughters, he is balked, since he does not naturally perceive the world as an inrush of curls and riches — that inrush is the springlike song of the nightingale that he can never hear, bound as he is to an autumn refrain in this long "autumn compendium."

What can Stevens mean, then, when he talks of the "affluence" (532) of this planet? Certainly not the heterogeneity of the physical. The end of *Esthétique du Mal* suggests one answer, the one that Stevens will finally adopt after forsaking the false direction of the *Comedian*:

> And out of what one sees and hears and out
> Of what one feels, who could have thought to make
> So many selves, so many sensuous worlds,
> As if the air, the mid-day air, was swarming
> With the metaphysical changes that occur,
> Merely in living as and where we live.   (326)

Stevens' affluence is in that glass which catches the mannerism of nature and makes it into the mannerism of a spirit, "a glass aswarm with things going as far as they can" (510), "the swarming activities of the formulae of statement" (488), rather than in the false familial swarm of the daughters. The physical world will become, for Stevens, a minor *point d'appui* on which the immense structures of the imagination are erected, and his style, at the end, will be mercifully freed from those reproductive gestures toward jaunty fertility which so clog the texture of the *Comedian.*

The Comedian as the Letter C, like many of the poems in *Harmonium,* is an exercise in stressed physicality and stressed tropicality. Brilliant as it is, *Harmonium* gives sometimes the impression of a strained Dionysian *tripudium,* the classic instances being "Life Is Motion" and "Ploughing on Sunday." We recall that even *Sunday Morning,* in its original printing of stanzas chosen by Harriet Monroe but arranged by Stevens, ended with a prophetic vision of men chanting in orgy their boisterous devotion to the sun.[11] Stevens' resolute attempts to make himself into a ribald poet of boisterous devotion to the gaudy, the gusty, and the burly are a direct consequence of a depressing irony in respect to the self he was born with and an equally depressing delusion about the extent to which that self could be changed. These ribaldries take two stylistic forms in *Harmonium* — the willed and artificial primitivism of poems like "Earthy Anecdote," "Ploughing on Sunday," and so on, and the verbal mimetic reproduction, persistent only in the *Comedian,* of the actual density of the physical world. Neither is destined to become Stevens' persistent mode. Stevens as ironist never fades entirely (even in *The Rock,* Mr. Homburg is one of his *personae*), but the corrosive deflations of the *Comedian* are nowhere else so relentless.

The lines in the *Comedian* that are most continuous with *The Auroras of Autumn* or *The Rock* are the description of the divested Triton and the equally divested Crispin, as we see them unforcedly present:

> Triton incomplicate with that
> Which made him Triton, nothing left of him,
> Except in faint, memorial gesturings,
> That were like arms and shoulders in the waves,

Here, something in the rise and fall of wind
That seemed hallucinating horn, and here,
A sunken voice, both of remembering
And of forgetfulness, in alternate strain.   (i)

The salt hung on his spirit like a frost,
The dead brine melted in him like a dew
Of winter, until nothing of himself
Remained, except some starker, barer self
In a starker, barer, world.   (i)

The glimpse of Triton, the invisible voice, the hallucination in
surfaces, the voice of suggestion ("nothing except . . . like
. . . seemed . . . both, and") are all ways leading to the language of the older Stevens affirming that reality may be "a shade
that traverses/ A dust, a force that traverses a shade" (480).
And the bareness of the surviving Crispin will lead to a later
question:

Shall we be found hanging in the trees next spring?
Of what disaster is this the imminence;
Bare limbs, bare trees and a wind as sharp as salt?   (419)

Or we might choose, out of the *Comedian*, as central to the "continuous" Stevens, the picture not of the myth divested but of
the world endowed, the plum hazily and beautifully bloomed
by its poems:

The plum survives its poems. It may hang
In the sunshine placidly, colored by ground
Obliquities of those who pass beneath,
Harlequined and mazily dewed and mauved
In bloom.   (v)

This is Stevens at his adorning best, happy in the reflections cast by the mind on the world. But as soon as he attempts the gross *Ding an sich*, the old shudder returns:

> . . . Mazily dewed and mauved
> In bloom. Yet it survives in its own form,
> Beyond these changes, good, fat, guzzly fruit.   (v)

Stevens' Guzzla Gracile, his appetite for both the dewed and the guzzly, chokes on its own avidity. We learn to trust the Stevens of obliquities and appearances, the Stevens of "like," "as," and "seem," the Stevens of phenomena in all their shimmers of investiture and raggedness. But the Stevens of guzzling, rankness, and bluster disappoints and is false, except when he is engaged in such charming self-parodies as "Bantams in Pine-Woods."

The true tale of Crispin, then, is a tale of false attempts and real regrets, which presumes intellectually on its felt satisfactions, asserting an ironic benignity it cannot render without revulsion, refusing to acknowledge an asceticism it cannot hide. The veiled autobiography, the semi-ironic confessional, is the form Stevens elected for his first long poem, but never took up again, no doubt because the narrative progress was deeply uncongenial to his mind, which moved always in eddies, never in dramatic sequence. Stevens' tendency, as he says in *An Ordinary Evening in New Haven*, is to branch, to proliferate, to multiply, not to come to an end. Crispin's voyages and plans are, after all, rhetorical variations on a single theme, the mutual accommodation of the self and the world, and in the nature of things any "end" to such a theme must be falsely concocted, as Stevens came to realize in his ever more tentative resolutions.

It is odd, and can probably be explained only in terms of such Romantic models as *Alastor*, that Stevens should have attempted a quasi-narrative at all, especially since he had already found an apt form in the "magnificent measure" of *Sunday Morning*

(1915) and *Le Monocle de Mon Oncle* (1917).¹² Together with the *Comedian*, these poems show us what Stevens was capable of, and show his somewhat intractable extremes. The relative proportions of elegy, gusto, and irony are still uncertain in *Harmonium*. No later long poem will ever be so purely archaic and nostalgic at once as *Sunday Morning*, and no single one will ever muster the heavy irony of the *Comedian*, an irony which can only be understood as a flight from the mournfulness of his "noble accents and lucid inescapable rhythms" as they appear in his poem of the *Götterdämmerung, Sunday Morning*. "To see the gods dispelled in mid-air and dissolve like clouds is one of the great human experiences. It is not as if they had gone over the horizon to disappear for a time; nor as if they had been overcome by other gods of greater power and profounder knowledge. It is simply that they came to nothing. Since we have always shared all things with them and have always had a part of their strength and, certainly, all of their knowledge, we shared likewise this experience of annihilation. It was their annihilation, not ours, and yet it left us feeling that in a measure, we, too, had been annihilated" (*OP*, 206–207). So it is his own annihilation as well as that of the gods that Stevens mourns in this "poem of long celestial death." Stevens has no Nietzschean brio, and his prophecies of a new divinity are wistfully and even disbelievingly made. At their least exalted, they spring from self-pity:

> The sky will be much friendlier then than now . . .
> Not this dividing and indifferent blue.   (iii)

At their most delusory, the prophecies spring from an anachronistic primitivism masked as prediction:

> Supple and turbulent, a ring of men
> Shall chant in orgy on a summer morn
> Their boisterous devotion to the sun.   (vii)

At their best, the stanzas of *Sunday Morning* are always elegiac, even in passion:

> The maidens taste
> And stray impassioned in the littering leaves. (v)

The apparently non-elegiac phrases of the poem are inevitably embedded in an autumnal text, as the bough of summer is reduced to the winter branch, and as elations are surrounded by sadder motions of the soul:

> Divinity must live within herself:
> Passions of rain, or moods in falling snow;
> Grievings in loneliness, or unsubdued
> Elations when the forest blooms; gusty
> Emotions on wet roads on autumn nights;
> All pleasures and all pains, remembering
> The bough of summer and the winter branch.
> These are the measures destined for her soul. (ii)

These gravities of resignation belong to the preceptor who speaks the poem, and whose grieving measured tones correct the woman's protestations:

> "But in contentment I still feel
> The need of some imperishable bliss."

She cries this need, and is answered by a voice of disembodied and ghostly wisdom:

> Death is the mother of beauty, hence from her
> Alone, shall come fulfillment to our dreams. (v)

For this older voice, all sorrow, triumph, and love are infinitely distanced in some remote and remembered pathos of the past, re-enacted now in equal pathos by the young, unaware of death:

> Although she strews the leaves
> Of sure obliteration on our paths,
> The path sick sorrow took, the many paths
> Where triumph rang its brassy phrase, or love
> Whispered a little out of tenderness,
> She makes the willow shiver in the sun
> For maidens who were wont to sit and gaze
> Upon the grass, relinquished to their feet.
> She causes boys to pile new plums and pears
> On disregarded plate. The maidens taste
> And stray impassioned in the littering leaves.   (v)

It is a voice from the sepulcher that speaks these lines, one who has himself long since relinquished the taste of that early autumnal fruit.

The exquisite cadences of *Sunday Morning* are in fact corpse-like, existing around the woman's desires in a waxy perfection of resignation. Some remnant of the last claims made on life exist in the person of the woman, the pre-sepulchral self of the poet, but he has given up all active engagement and deals in bleak and funereal finalities. In the most oracular of them, he becomes a voice out of the air:

> The tomb in Palestine
> Is not the porch of spirits lingering,
> It is the grave of Jesus, where he lay.

Nevertheless, there is no suicidal thrust to the poem. The poet decides to prolong his posthumous life, to bide his time in the twilight of the gods, to live, perhaps, in a suspended animation.

The close of the poem reflects his suspension as it broadens to as reluctant a construction as a sentence can have, pause by pause:

And,
> in the isolation of the sky,
>> at evening,
>>> casual flocks of pigeons make ambiguous undulations
>>> as they sink,
>>>> downward to darkness,
>>>> on extended wings.

The final clause floats in its own equilibrium, knowing its inevitable direction, but not hastening the drift, just as the noting eye sees the undulations but deliberately, phrase by phrase, waits to locate them in time and space before giving them a name.[13]

The brisk ironic resignation of Crispin and the elegiac resignation of *Sunday Morning* both testify to throes which must have preceded their final stances. The memorial to these throes is a poem more radically imperfect, perhaps, than the *Comedian*, and more stylistically impure than the serener *Sunday Morning*, but indispensable as the clue to them both, the poem in which Stevens represses nothing, neither his sadness as he does in the *Comedian* nor his irony as he does in *Sunday Morning*. Grotesque as it sometimes becomes, *Le Monocle de Mon Oncle* comes nearer to encompassing, however awkwardly, the whole of Stevens. Here the skeleton is still alive, still pursuing the origin and course of love, not yet resigned, not yet posthumous, not yet wise.[14] The poem sees a dreadful paralysis on the horizon, but has not yet succumbed to it.

We witness in the poem the death-in-life — summed up in the death of love — of a young man turning old. The lover turns into a monocled avuncular sage:

When amorists grow bald, then amours shrink
Into the compass and curriculum
Of introspective exiles, lecturing.   (vi)

We are to follow this shrinking of the soul as Stevens begins
to turn into the final dwarf of himself, but not without watching
the anguished and unwilling struggle of the last vanquished
adolescent energies of love and faith, now exhausted in a de-
pleted marriage. A sardonic pity and antagonism separate the
conscious poet from his self-deceiving wife: [15]

And so I mocked her in magnificent measure.
Or was it that I mocked myself alone?
I wish that I might be a thinking stone.
The sea of spuming thought foists up again
The radiant bubble that she was. And then
A deep up-pouring from some saltier well
Within me, burst its watery syllable.   (i)

On the poignant, Stevens superimposes the mordant, taking the
model readiest to hand for grim wit, Hamlet in the graveyard,
and in that borrowed voice scrutinizing his own elegiac forms.
The Ananke of the last poems appears here as the Newtonian
apple of disillusion, falling inevitably and necessarily "of its
own weight":

The luscious and impeccable fruit of life
Falls, it appears, of its own weight to earth.
When you were Eve, its acrid juice was sweet,
Untasted, in its heavenly, orchard air.
An apple serves as well as any skull
To be the book in which to read a round,
And is as excellent, in that it is composed
Of what, like skulls, comes rotting back to ground.   (iv)

But this heavy grotesquerie, though Stevens is clearly driven to it as an antidote to his fugal requiems, goes too far into the anatomy of decay, and forms too pat and "metaphysical" a parallel between apple and skull.

The other and more physical antidote is a grossly cynical counterpoint to the harmonies of love, as a frog booms "from his very belly/ Odious chords" of sex, insisting on the ruthless necessity of sex even while the poet recognizes its insufficiency. The dubiousness of blaming the entire melancholy of forty on an absence of desire is antithetical to Stevens' taste for finding all the contexts of a given whole, but simple rage prevails against elegiac feeling for one stanza:

> If sex were all, then every trembling hand
> Could make us squeak, like dolls, the wished-for words.
> But note the unconscionable treachery of fate,
> That makes us weep, laugh, grunt and groan, and shout
> Doleful heroics, pinching gestures forth
> From madness or delight, without regard
> To that first, foremost law. Anguishing hour!
> Last night, we sat beside a pool of pink,
> Clippered with lilies scudding the bright chromes,
> Keen to the point of starlight, while a frog
> Boomed from his very belly odious chords.   (xi)

Though the violence here is not typical of Stevens, the argument is conducted in his manner as he puts two untenable hypotheses: if sex were all, if love were enough. The tyranny of the body is unsparingly voiced: sex is not all, but it is the first, foremost law, and everything else must follow on it. The early theatrical gestures of romantic love, made when Eve's apple was as yet untasted, disappear forever when the essential sexual instinct is found to be absent. Eve, like the pool, is still pink, bright, chromatic, lilied, starry like her *connaissance*, but she and her Adam lack what even the odious frogs possess by nature.

It is not often that Stevens will try the ultimate in determinism — that men's gestures, determined by fate, are absurd and puppetlike, and deserve a puppet language; more usually, he will prefer the stoic defense, but that too requires an assent to a virtual death. He seems to escape that death in one mysterious stanza of *Le Monocle*, where a parable adopts a stoic stance but saves itself by a myth of uncertain reference. Stevens begins by disavowing rapturous memories of inspiration and the effeminate poetry they produce:

> The fops of fancy in their poems leave
> Memorabilia of the mystic spouts,
> Spontaneously watering their gritty soils.
> I am a yeoman, as such fellows go.
> I know no magic trees, no balmy boughs,
> No silver-ruddy, gold-vermilion fruits.   (x)

This is the stance that will be taken up in the *Comedian*, a dismissal of rhapsodies in favor of yeoman plainness, in itself a stoic choice. But Stevens cannot rest in pure self-sufficiency; he may dismiss mystic inspiration, but he retains a source of unending nourishment:

> But, after all, I know a tree that bears
> A semblance to the thing I have in mind.
> It stands gigantic, with a certain tip
> To which all birds come sometime in their time.
> But when they go that tip still tips the tree.   (x)

This is yeoman language to suit a yeoman mystique, but the magic tree in the second half of the poem seems only another version of the dismissed magic trees in the first half. The parable is more intelligible rewritten in *Esthétique du Mal*, vi (318), in the serious but charming image of the mutual sustenance of sun and bird. This kind of plain parable offers a middle ground between the personal and the abstract, always with a slight overlay of fairy-tale pleasure, subduing private tone to public manner but without the blankness of public generalization. Nevertheless, Stevens is no staunch peasant, and the stoicism of yeomanry is no true solution to his melancholy.

There are other possible defenses against requiems, and *Le Monocle* tries two with great success. One is wry history, as the poet realizes the recurrent cycles of success and failure, which Stevens represents by the ceaseless decorative efforts of coiffeurs. Against their strategies he sets the obdurate return of hair to its uncoiffed state:

> Is it for nothing, then, that old Chinese
> Sat tittivating by their mountain pools
> Or in the Yangtse studied out their beards?
> I shall not play the flat historic scale.
> You know how Utamaro's beauties sought
> The end of love in their all-speaking braids.
> You know the mountainous coiffures of Bath.
> Alas! Have all the barbers lived in vain
> That not one curl in nature has survived?
> Why, without pity on these studious ghosts,
> Do you come dripping in your hair from sleep?   (iii)

This stanza forecasts the relation of subject and style in the *Comedian* — exaggeration and comedy in the surface of language, with tittivating Chinese, barbers, and Bath coiffures like mountains, but not a shred of comedy in the emotion undergone. This manner, found in shorter poems too, succeeds as one tone among many, but the veil in the *Comedian* will become tedious in its discrepancy with matter or, as Joseph Riddel has put it, in the conflict between language and meaning.[16] Stevens' truer defense against elegy is to see the decline into the nonchromatic as offering a new and haunting color to be explored:

> If men at forty will be painting lakes
> The ephemeral blues must merge for them in one,
> The basic slate, the universal hue.

Riddel has very truly called this "the most prophetic stanza in early Stevens," just as he rightly praised *Le Monocle* for "an emotional variety which is rare throughout [Stevens'] canon." [17] Stevens chooses to abandon both the star of Venus and the odious frogs for a new intermediate area of life, the "little kin" of fireflies and crickets, descended, no doubt, from Keats's gnats:

> In the high west there burns a furious star.
> It is for fiery boys that star was set
> And for sweet-smelling virgins close to them.
> The measure of the intensity of love
> Is measure, also, of the verve of earth.
> For me, the firefly's quick, electric stroke
> Ticks tediously the time of one more year.
> And you? Remember how the crickets came
> Out of their mother grass, like little kin,
> In the pale nights, when your first imagery
> Found inklings of your bond to all that dust.   (v)

These are the "fluttering things," Venus' doves turned to pigeons, the light of Venus diminished to fireflies, that have nevertheless "so distinct a shade."

In spite of these felicities, *Le Monocle de Mon Oncle* remains both uncertain and derivative, uncertain in its wild variations of mood and self-regard, derivative in its blank verse. These choiring verses are to give way to the sparer art of the wasted figure propounding blank final music; and the ravishing but inherited harmonies of *Sunday Morning*, so composed to console and sanctify, will yield to a wish for a sparer rhetoric, meant "plainly to propound." As for *The Comedian as the Letter C*, its torrential expansions will be mercilessly contracted, and its central personage totally expunged, as Stevens undertakes his next long poem, *Like Decorations in a Nigger Cemetery*.

III. The Sausage Maker

God of the sausage-makers, sacred guild.

"My poems are like decorations in a nigger cemetery." This is Stevens' flagrant borrowed simile for a chain of poems, fifty of them, an experiment in poetry as epigram, or poetry as fossil bones: "Piece the world together, boys, but not with your hands" (192).[1] The poem, a token of things to come, is, like many foretastes, perversely experimental. Though the poetry of disconnection is Stevens' most adequate form, and though the gaps from canto to canto in the long poems will always challenge the best efforts of critical articulation, still the discontinuity will never again be so arrogant as in this example. There are no bridges here for the magnifico; he must migrate from one "floral tribute" to another, some visionary, some cynical, some bitter, some prophetic, some comic. Each is a "nigger fragment, a *mystique*/ For the spirit left helpless by the intelligence" (265). They are fragments of vision seen in the mirror of the mind refusing to reconstruct itself, refusing the attempt to make a whole from the ruses that were shattered by the large. *Harmonium* was by no means a harmony: all of Stevens is in it, and not in embryo either; but although its tonal spectrum is as diverse as the one we find in *Decorations*, it is less shocking because the tones are presented in separate units, not heaped together ruthlessly in one poem. In *Decorations*, the work seems to be left to the reader, since he must do the ordering of impressions; these are haiku potentially articulable, like the *Adagia*. Whether *Decorations* is any more than fifty short pieces pretending to be one poem is debatable, but if we believe in Stevens' good faith we must assume he thought it a viable whole.[2] His wholes were always melting into each other, of course; his work was all one poem to him, clearly, but yet he did divide it into parts.

The sense of death and fatal chill is the "subject" of *Decorations*,[3] as it will be the subject of *The Auroras of Autumn*, but to read only physical death into Stevens' lines is to limit his range. To be dead is also not to live in a physical world, to "live a skeleton's life, / As a disbeliever in reality, / A countryman of all the bones in the world" (*OP*, 117), and Stevens is afraid, in his fifty-sixth year, that he is already shriveling into that dwarf form. His depletion is his specter, and his wrestlings with it make up *Decorations*. The resources of man facing death compose the metaphorical range of the poem; from legacies left to heirs to the desire for heaven, from stoicism to cynicism, from hedonism to nostalgia, from self-delusion to a willed belief that life is as real as death. Stevens chooses to express no preference among these responses, except by the implicit preference accorded by convention to the beginning and end.

The mythologizing of Whitman-as-sun into a prophetic figure begins the poem boldly, in a partially tempered version of Stevens' boisterous tone. Instead of the ring of men chanting in orgy on a summer morn, we have the Whitman-sun chanting on the ruddy shore of an autumn day. He is a Jovian figure, moving with large-mannered motions, "A giant, on the horizon, glistening" (442), "rugged and luminous" (479), one of Stevens' many chanting figures:

> Nothing is final, he chants. No man shall see the end.
> His beard is of fire and his staff is a leaping flame.

Like the "new resemblance of the sun" in *An Ordinary Evening in New Haven*, this sun is "a mythological form, a festival sphere

/ A great bosom, beard and being, alive with age" (466), with all the equivocal sentimentality still attached to our images of Jehovah.

From this rather self-indulgent flame, the poem proceeds to its ending in snow, and the immortality of the chanting sun gives way, finally, to the stoic's revenge — lopping off his feet, as Blake said, so as not to want shoes. Human solidarity (advocated in the penultimate stanza) is no defense against decay, since there is no strength that can withstand process; only wisdom, by its slyness, anticipates destruction, slipping from the grip of winter by anticipating its clasp. What can winter do to one who has already forsaken casinos for igloos?

> . . . Can all men, together, avenge
> One of the leaves that have fallen in autumn?
> But the wise man avenges by building his city in snow.   (1)

Neither sand nor rock, as in the Bible, but snow; and not a house but a city; and not "on," but "in," with its diffuseness of reference. This preventive avenging is stated as a proverb, and the suggested vengeance is reaffirmed by the telling dactyls of the last line. It is a remark, however, not an accomplishment; what it means to build a city in snow is to use this rhetoric of cunning, to put to bold use intimations of despair, to counter the erosions of process by one's own ice palace, not to regret autumn; to be the snow man, in short, and to decorate the cemetery.

To write of nothing that is not there is almost impossible to Stevens with his gift for nostalgic reminiscence, for the poetry of the vanished, but to write of the nothing that *is* there is more possible, and accounts for some of his most brilliant poems ("The Snow Man," "No Possum, No Sop, No Taters," "The Plain Sense of Things," "The Course of a Particular"). The full rhetoric of nostalgia and the taut rhetoric of the minimal are at war in him, profitably; sadness and stoicism contend, and forth the particulars of poetry come. There is a curiosity in Stevens' stoicism that redeems it from indifference or listlessness. As the joyless becomes the norm, the inveterate aesthetician's eye remarks the change:

> It was when the trees were leafless first in November
> And their blackness became apparent, that one first
> Knew the eccentric to be the base of design.   (iii)

We scarcely have a name for a tone of this sort, verging, as it does, as close to irony as extreme dryness can bring it, grafting schoolmaster's language and impersonal detachment onto a sinister paradox of disorder, all to express a tragic intimation. It is the tone of the doctor investigating his own mortal disease and writing his report, embodying an intrinsic pathos as the clinician records his own decline.

Stevens is remarkable in his evasions of the first person singular, and the options of avoidance are many — "one" and "he" and "we" are Stevens' favorites, as well as the "I" of dramatic monologue. "We" is perhaps tarnished for us by its long use in "high sentence": it belongs to the rhetoric of sermons, of political oratory, of moral verse. Though Stevens is fond of its oracular potentialities ("We live in an old chaos of the sun") he uses it chiefly as a signal of an experience not peculiar to the poet, reserving for that special case the particularized "he." In the long poems, Stevens is uncomfortable with any pronoun after a while, and prefers (abandoning his practice in the *Comedian*) to change from first person to third person to second person at will. In this respect again, *Decorations* is the most eccentric of the long poems, as the speaker metamorphoses from detached aesthetician and scholar ("one") to one of us ("we") to a man alone ("Shall I grapple with my destroyers?") to a man having a dialogue with a servant (xxvi) to a commentator on someone else ("It needed the heavy nights of drenching

weather / To make him return to people"). The extreme variation of speakers makes us, in defense, assume a single sensibility
"behind" the scene, a puppet master of whom we can say only
that he is a man revolving thoughts on middle age, death, and
the compensations of creation. This temptation to impose order
by a thematic statement explains the natural tendency to reduce
Stevens to his subject matter, to look for consistency of some
kind in such a welter of styles, even at the cost of making the
manner disappear entirely.

The speaker of *Decorations* has a horror of dying "a parish
death" (in which the cost of burial of a pauper is borne by the
parish), because the irony is too great: Death the priest in his
opulent purple and white vestments set against the pine coffin
and maimed rites of the pauper.[4] How to cheat death of that
triumph, how to redeem our own ignominy, is the question of
the poem, and the answer of course is both pitiful (we decorate
the cemetery with grotesque poem-bouquets) and stern (we
build our city in snow). The third "answer" — that the sun is
eternal and so our death is fictitious — begins the poem, but
never assumes any real importance in it, except in stanza xlvii,
where the sun's indifference to the world, its self-sustenance
("It must create its colors out of itself"), is insisted upon. The
stanzas explicitly about poetry [5] both attempt to exalt it by
Stevens' religious intonations (vii, xv, xxxvi, xlviii) and yet reduce it by revealing its carnality and its ineffectual "comedy of
hollow sounds" (xiii, xxii). In the most ironic passage of all,
Stevens visualizes his fifty stanzas as so many sausage links, pre-
sided over by the "god of the sausages" or possibly an even
more insignificant Muse, a mere patron saint sanctifying himself
by a complacent self-regard (xlii).[6]

The oddest characteristic of *Decorations* is its abjuring of
verbs. In at least a fifth of the poem the stanzas are syntactically
incomplete, and verbs have been dispensed with. Partly, this
yields a quality of epigram ("Out of sight, out of mind") which

helps to give the poem its extraordinary aridity, and partly it strengthens the sense that these are jottings, *adagia*, epitaphs, the daily *pensées* of the inspector of gravestones. Usually, the verbs can be easily supplied, since Stevens is not interested in mystification for its own sake, but the absence of an opening clause impersonalizes the topic further:

[What we confront in death is]
[What I want to write about is]
[What we truly experience is]

Not the ocean of the virtuosi
But the ugly alien, the mask that speaks
Things unintelligible, yet understood.   (xxxix)

The stanza could imply any of the previous beginnings, but its strength lies in not needing them. The formula used in this stanza (not X but Y) is one of Stevens' commonest, and is frequently preceded elsewhere by "he wanted" or "he saw." The absence here of such a verb creates the phrase as an immediate object of perception to the reader, with no intervening subject, as Stevens achieves the poetry of no perceiver, the landscape poetry of the mind, so to speak.[7] The personal voice, with its clamor of selfhood, is too desperately intrusive, and yet invented personae carry the immediate flavor of irony. One solution, adopted here, is to drop the subject voice entirely.

Another is to reproduce the interior musing of the mind, as the mind has no subject-relation to itself, needs no explanations to itself of its own hurdles, and can speak in ellipses:

The album of Corot is premature.
A little later when the sky is black.
Mist that is golden is not wholly mist.   (xxxviii)

If we supply the missing links, the verse might read: "[Do not offer me] the album [of reproductions of paintings of summer] of Corot. [That] is premature [— to solace myself with art in the absence of the reality it reproduces, since something of summer is still left. Give me the album] a little later when the sky is black. [It is true that the mists of autumn are around me, but they are tinged with the gold of summer still, and] mist that is golden is not wholly mist." Or, as Stevens put it briefly to Hi Simons, "Do not show me Corot while it is still summer; do not show me pictures of summer while it is still summer; even the mist is golden; wait until a little later" (L, 349). My amplification of the original lines, and Stevens' paraphrase of them, both lose the dryness of the poem, where Stevens' truncated dismissal of art is flavored with epigram in the punning near-chiasmus of sound — mist, golden, wholly, mist — and where something like malice supervenes on the foreboding of the second line.

One of Stevens' continuing triumphs is his rapidity of change as he is flicked by various feelings. Despair overlaid by wry cynicism — "There is no such thing as innocence in autumn" — is succeeded immediately by a pallor of hope — "Yet, it may be, innocence is never lost" (xliv). The autonomy of the stanzas of *Decorations* suggests that all its exertions exist simultaneously rather than successively.[8] Though Stevens can order his poems temporally, as his nostalgias, farewells, and prophecies attest, here, as in other long poems, the unity is radial, not linear. Stevens' true subject in *Decorations* becomes the complexity of mental response as he gives intimations, in these fifty stanzas, of almost all possible reactions to the decay that is the topic of the poem. If this is a poetry of meditation, it does not have the sustained progressive development that we know in other meditative poets; it is rather the staccato meditation of intimation and dismissal, of fits and starts, revulsions and shrugs, lightenings and sloughs, the play of the mind and sensibility over a topic.

Except for two sections (i and iv), the stanzas are of three or four lines, and depend almost entirely on very simple rhetorical figures for their form. Often the figure is antithesis, for instance, as in the dominating contrasts of summer and winter, rich and poor, the mechanical and the human, the social and the private:

> A bridge above the bright and blue of water
> And the same bridge when the river is frozen.
> Rich Tweedle-dum, poor Tweedle-dee.   (xxiv)

Such antitheses stress the indistinguishability of the basic forms underlying the qualitative apparel. The decorations are a mediation between the living and the dead, and the speaker, not yet dead but no longer quite alive, stands between the systems of antitheses,

> Between farewell and the absence of farewell,
> The final mercy and the final loss,
> The wind and the sudden falling of the wind.   (x)

Sometimes the rhetorical figure will come from logic, as in the deliberately trivial arithmetic by which one ascertains the density of life by dividing the number of legs one sees by two (xliii), or in the more enigmatic series of instances leading to an induction of stanza xxiii:

> The fish are in the fishman's window,
> The grain is in the baker's shop,
> The hunter shouts as the pheasant falls.
> Consider the odd morphology of regret.

Decorations is a poem of regret; placing decorations on graves is a gesture of regret; and yet these actions are reserved by the human world for its own members alone. No regret is expended on the deaths of the fish, the wheat, the pheasant. Rather, we buy, sell, and deal in death of all sorts without regret every day. But the compression of the verse forces us to leap from the three instances to the antithesis of the final ironic line without the explicit connectives of conventional logic.

The internal echoes in *Decorations* are casual, with certain spheres of metaphorical reference in the ascendant (sun and frost, wealth and poverty, vanished religion set against the new hymns sung by the various birds) but again, there is no particular consistency. There are, for instance, six poems about birds [9] (I omit the pheasant, who does not sing, but only falls) and they vary in symbolic meaning. The birds "singing in the yellow patios, / Pecking at more lascivious rinds than ours, / From sheer Gemütlichkeit" (xiii) are both satirized and envied in their sensual and sentimental ease. To equate lasciviousness with bourgeois Gemütlichkeit is to dismiss it aesthetically rather than morally. The absence of possible lasciviousness is the deprivation of the next bird, the unmated leaden pigeon who, Stevens conjectures, must miss the symmetry of a female leaden mate. Imagining her, he makes her better than she would have been in reality, makes her not a leaden mortal pigeon but a silver ideal dove, and creates a transcendent ethereal bird who, like other Stevensian ideal figures, lives in a place of perpetual undulation:

> The leaden pigeon on the entrance gate
> Must miss the symmetry of a leaden mate,
> Must see her fans of silver undulate.   (xiv)

Oriole and crow, the extremes of music in the natural world, form a simple opposition (xxv), and comment on the tendency of this declining decorator of cemeteries to distrust the beautiful and opulent. The sterile androgynous fowls of stanza xxx, one a day creature and one a night creature, are perhaps allied to the sun and moon, those two elements between which Crispin voyages. Singly, they are impotent, because creation requires the separation of genders.

> The hen-cock crows at midnight and lays no egg,
> The cock-hen crows all day. But cockerel shrieks,
> Hen shudders: the copious egg is made and laid.

The final fertility, Stevens might say in a less outrageous way, is in the journey back and forth between the antithetical states, not in any imagined confluence of opposites. Only with the inter-penetration, but no identification, of the antithetical elements can the shrill vocalism of crowing become the copious egg, an exhibit scrutinized here at arm's length.

As for the rare and royal purple bird (xxxiii), he finds his rarity not exalting but boring; like the poet of abnormal sensibility, he has no company, and must sing to himself, if only to provide some fictitious company. Though purple is the color of royalty, it is also, in Stevens, the color of middle age, of the malady of the quotidian, leading "through all its purples to the final slate" (96) of some unimaginable bleakness. Finally, Stevens leaves us with an image of the impotence of poetry — though it may live radiantly beyond much lustier blurs, it lives uncertainly and not for long (xxxii). Time, not the song of the cuckoo (even though cuckoos, if any bird, might appeal to the mad clockmaker of this universe), is the regulative principle of this clanking mechanism, the world:

> Everything ticks like a clock. The cabinet
> Of a man gone mad, after all, for time, in spite
> Of the cuckoos, a man with a mania for clocks.   (xlvi)

All that Stevens expects of his reader, then, is a hazy notion, certainly traditional enough, that birds are a figure for poetry.

It is understood that as the context differs, so will the bird. In a context of clock time, he will be a cuckoo; in a context of lonely regal rarity, he will be a purple bird; in a context of fertility and shrillness, cock and hen; in a context of the real and ideal, a pigeon-dove; in the context of beauty of song, oriole versus crow; and in the context of reality, in the yellow patios, an anonymous figure, a "meaningless natural effigy" (xx), trite and uninteresting until given a "revealing aberration" by the observant eye. This flexibility of reference is necessary in invoking other image clusters in the poem — the theater, the weather, and so on. Stevens' metaphors are extremely provisional in their species, but quite permanent in their genus, and the vegetation still abounds in forms, as the *Collected Poems* declare.

The alternative to varying the species of bird is of course to vary the environment of the bird, as Stevens had done in *Thirteen Ways of Looking at a Blackbird*,[10] an early poem that in its epigrammatic and elliptic form anticipates *Decorations* (just as its variational scheme resembles "Sea Surface Full of Clouds" or "Variations on a Summer Day," and as its theme is allied to "Domination of Black"). The Ananke or Necessity of *Decorations* appears in the *Blackbird* as the black principle, the eccentric which is the base of design, the strict, the final, the intrinsic, the limiting, the temporal. The blackbird is the only element in nature which is aesthetically compatible with bleak light and bare limbs: he is, we may say, a certain kind of language, opposed to euphony, to those "noble accents and lucid inescapable rhythms" which Stevens used so memorably elsewhere in *Harmonium*. To choose the blackbird over the pigeon is a possible aesthetic for Stevens, and it is different from the aesthetic of Crispin who chose arrant stinks, the anti-aesthetic. There are thirteen ways of looking at a blackbird because thirteen is the eccentric number; Stevens is almost medieval in his relish for external form. This poetry will be one of inflection and innuendo; the inflections are the heard melodies [11] (the whistling of the blackbird) and the innuendos are what is left out (the silence just after the whistling):

> I do not know which to prefer,
> The beauty of inflections
> Or the beauty of innuendoes,
> The blackbird whistling
> Or just after.   (v)

As a description of both *Blackbird* and *Decorations* this could hardly be bettered. Stevens himself called *Blackbird* a collection of sensations, rather than of epigrams or of ideas (*L*, 251), but the later remarks on it to Henry Church are intellectual ones: that the last section was intended to convey despair, that section xii existed to convey the "compulsion frequently back of the things that we do" (*L*, 240). We are not falsifying the poem entirely, then, if we ask how, by varying the blackbird's surroundings, Stevens conveys to us both the sensations and the ideas which exist with them.

The blackbird has perhaps something in common with Eliot's "shadow" that falls between potency and act, desire and consummation. But Stevens would deny that it is a remediable or accidental intrusion between two things that without it would be better off. It is, rather, of one substance with the things it relates:

> A man and a woman
> Are one.
> A man and a woman and a blackbird
> Are one.   (iv)

Between the man and the woman is the blackbird, one with them; between the man's mood and his environment is the blackbird, the indecipherable cause of the mood which is man's response to nature (vi); between the men of Haddam and their imagined golden birds is the blackbird, the real on which they construct their "artifice of eternity" (vii); between the haunted man and his protective glass coach is the terror of the blackbird (xi); it lies at the base even of our powerful verbal defenses, those beautiful glass coaches of euphony and lucidity. It is, finally, the principle of our final relation to the universe, our compulsions, first of all,

> The river is moving.
> The blackbird must be flying.   (xii)

and lastly, our despair at death:

> It was evening all afternoon.
> It was snowing
> And it was going to snow.
> The blackbird sat
> In the cedar-limbs.   (xiii)

But neurosis and death are only instances of a pervasive relational eccentricity. Our extent in space (as well as in time) goes only as far as the blackbird goes — the blackbird *is* our "line of vision" (ix), as it is our line of thought: when we are of two minds (or, as Stevens presses it, "of three minds"), it is not as if we had a blackbird, an oriole, and a pigeon in view, but only "a tree / In which there are three blackbirds" (ii). The blackbird is by no means all — it is surrounded by the vastness of twenty mountains, the autumn winds, the snow — but though only a small part, it is the determining focus of relation.

Blackbird is undoubtedly a more finished poem than *Decorations*, its fineness of structure making for remarkable strength, as Stevens pursues his single image for a single theme through several aspects. Its subject, the "new aesthetic" of the spare and the eccentric as it arises from flaw and mortality, prohibits the use of the oratorical mode of *Sunday Morning*, a mode which becomes a blemish in certain stanzas (notably viii and xlviii) of the usually tight-reined *Decorations*. *Blackbird* depends wholly on contraction, on the simple declarative sentence reduced almost to the infantile. Just as the declarative sentence is the simplest grammatical figure, so tautology is the simplest rhetorical form, and Stevens deliberately approaches it:

> A man and a woman
> Are one.
> A man and a woman and a blackbird
> Are one.   (iv)

> It was snowing
> And it was going to snow.   (xiii)

> I know . . . accents . . .
> But I know
> That the blackbird is involved
> In what I know.   (viii)

Like Stevens' *exotisme voulu*, this is simplicity *voulu*, calling flamboyant attention to itself in a way that the unobtrusive simplicity of colloquial language does not. As an instrument, it is brilliant but limited, and clearly will not do for much more than thirteen stanzas. The increased expanse of *Decorations* comes at the cost of high finish, but promises perfections still far away, in the greater long poems to come. Meanwhile, these two poems together represent Stevens' most remarkable compression of his naturally voluminous self, a new asperity of language over a long span, a daringly varied meditative form, and a willingness, in the case of the later poem, to sacrifice finish for experiment's sake.

IV. The Volcano Apostrophe, the Sea Behold

A sphere
Created, like a bubble, of bright sheens,
With a tendency to bulge as it floats away.

It is its myths which distinguish *Owl's Clover* (1936) [1] from
the long poems which preceded it. A great part of the poem is
mythical, not the "once upon a time there was" of folk tale but
rather the "my soul, there is a country" of myth still extant.
Once the poet's mythical images are established, he generally
intensifies their location: "*there* this happens, and *there* this is
true" — the "là-bas, là-bas" of *Notes toward a Supreme Fiction*
(393) or Goethe's "*Dahin, dahin.*" In this way, Stevens constructs a mythical half of *Owl's Clover*, while in the other half
he creates, in a mimicry of real reference, a country with which
he presumes us to be familiar — the land of the Bulgar or of
Basilewsky — as a stage, a *mise-en-scène* to play earth in respect to his mythological regions above and below. This mixture of genres is unsettling and new. The *Comedian*, based as
it is on the satiric reality of its narration, has no heaven and
no Hades, no visionary language invoked to express a reality
"beyond" Crispin. The sea, intimidating as it is, is nonetheless
the medium in which he voyages. But the Muses, Africa, the
Subman, and the Portent which appear in *Owl's Clover* are
mythical entities hovering around the park, the mob, the Old

Woman, and the Statue (though the status of the Statue, both mythical and real, remains equivocal).[2] The basic style of the "real" in the poem is low, satiric, even sardonic, while the style of the mythical is reverential, awed, or intimidated. But both are florid, and both the disparaging and the invocational come as enormous vocalisms after the laconic compressions of *Decorations*. They represent a ballooning music, a variant of the euphuism of the *Comedian*, soon to be checked by the relatively small-stringed guitar.

Stevens' massive cutting of the original poem is the work of a man embarrassed by his own rhetorical excesses. Since Stevens' way of writing is expansive rather than progressive, some of his second thoughts represent simple excision of expanded-upon words.[3] But such amputations — shortening a series of appositions, for instance — are less interesting than the substantial annihilations that take place. The first mythical personages of the poem, the Celestial Paramours or Muses, are most sharply diminished in these revisions, as cantos iv and vii of "Mr. Burnshaw and the Statue" are dropped entirely, and while the Muses remain in cantos ii and vi, their function is drastically reduced. In canto ii, they are summoned to chant a requiem for the Statue, but they are invoked as if they were the simpering Byzantines of "Peter Quince." Stevens' language is never more equivocal than in imagining these forms, tentative, awkward, infantine, dancing sallowly in their elegiac movements:

> Come, all celestial paramours,
> Whether in-dwelling haughty clouds, frigid
> And crisply musical, or holy caverns temple-toned,
> Entwine your arms and moving to and fro,
> Now like a ballet infantine in awkward steps,
> Chant sibilant requiems for this effigy. (47)

These elegiac Muses have some beauty, but they are debilitated, fragile, even frigid, and the squeamishness of concept embodied in a ballet infantine and a sibilant requiem invalidates these paramours as figures of power. Stevens' own explanation does not quite explain his tone: he wrote to Hi Simons that the paramours were "all the things in our nature that are celestial. In their very movements they are of the future (ballet infantine) (*L*, 367).

But to speak of celestial heralds of the future in terms that remove their celestial nature, as Stevens here does, betrays uncertainty of their capacity to do what they are asked to do — regenerate the Statue:

> Suddenly with lights
> Astral and Shelleyan, diffuse new day;
> And on this ring of marble horses shed
> The rainbow in its glistening serpentines
> Made by the sun ascending seventy seas.   (47)

This is mere fancy, and a surface transformation at that. Shelley is twice mentioned in *Owl's Clover*, and his rhapsodic claim that poets are the unacknowledged legislators of the world broods behind the poem as Stevens, while knowing the difficulties of the claim, nevertheless tries his voice against a social orchestra.[4] The insufficiency of a real Utopia to a poetic mind finally ensures the dismissal of the Shelleyan ideal: in Utopia the poet, with no occasion for comment and no scope for prophecy, would fall silent. The Shelleyan starry vision, once it has been realized, becomes

> An eternal vista, manqué and gold
> And brown, an Italy of the mind, a place
> Of fear before the disorder of the strange . . .
> A world impossible for poets.   (48)

Though the Muses can irradiate the "gawky plaster" of the Statue by bathing it in rainbow light, their real impotence leaves other things unaffected. Stevens' ambivalence is in his comment: "The astral and Shelleyan lights are not going to alter the structure of nature. Apples will always be apples, and whoever is a ploughman hereafter will be what the ploughman has always been. For all that, the astral and the Shelleyan will have transformed the world (*L*, 367). The poem puts it even more tentatively:

> Agree: the apple in the orchard, round
> And red, will not be redder, rounder then
> Than now. No: nor the ploughman in his bed
> Be free to sleep there sounder, for the plough
> And the dew and the ploughman still will best be one.
> But this gawky plaster will not be here.   (47–48)

The minimal and superficial power of "the things in our nature that are celestial" causes them to dance an unregarded elegy:

> And if you weep for peacocks that are gone
> Or dance the death of doves, most sallowly,
> Who knows?   (48)

Earlier, in "Botanist on Alp (No. 2)," Stevens had conceived of two poems worth singing:

> Chant, O ye faithful, in your paths
> The poem of long celestial death;
>
> For who could tolerate the earth
> Without that poem, or without
>
> An earthier one, tum, tum-ti-tum.   (*CP*, 136)

The elegy and the earthy celebration seem to him in some moments to be the only two possible modes for poetry. In *Owl's Clover* he appears to be rejecting, with both distaste and aplomb, the elegiac posture, even admonishing his Muses to give up their solemn mourning steps, their stylized awkward ballet (50). As choreographer of change, he drafts, in a passage later canceled, the new steps in which the Paramours are to leave their ineffectual grief, expressed in the poem of long celestial death, and are to begin to chant the earthier poem. If Stevens' language was uneasy in describing the original ballet, it is hallucinatory in prescribing the new one. In this "hallucinative" style, the object is to confuse the frame of reference by so confusing the syntax that a rational parsing of the sentence is no longer possible. It is the style of the sleight-of-hand man, making deceptive motions this way and that, in and out through the air, so that the provenance of his scarves and birds is no longer traceable.

The Muses dance barefoot in a ring, like the men in orgy on a summer morn; they are to be "damsels daubed" in hints of color which will deepen:

> Let your golden hands wave fastly and be gay
> And your braids bear brightening of crimson bands.   (51)

It is presumed that these dancers will create a new, self-sculpted Statue, and even more, that they will acquire new voices, not the glassy porcelain cries of their earlier fragility, nor the alto clank of the poem of death, but new implicit clarities. Finally, their watery ditherings will be turned to fire, their infantine ballet turned to broad strutting. Here, in all its interweavings, is the later canceled dance:

> In the glassy sound of your voices, the porcelain cries,
> The alto clank of the long recitation, in these
> Speak, and in these repeat: *To Be Itself,*

Until the sharply-colored glass transforms
Itself into the speech of the spirit, until
The porcelain bell-borrowings become
Implicit clarities in the way you cry
And are your feelings changed to sound, without
A change, until the waterish ditherings turn
To the tense, the maudlin, true meridian
That is yourselves, when, at last, you are yourselves,
Speaking and strutting broadly, fair and bloomed,
No longer of air but of the breathing earth,
Impassioned seducers and seduced, the pale
Pitched into swelling bodies, upward, drift
In a storm blown into glittering shapes, and flames
Wind-beaten into freshest, brightest fire.   (52)

The basic happening here, as I have said in Chapter I, is some X
being turned into a Y (glass transforming itself into speech)
which is then elaborated upon to become Y transformed into Z
(flames beaten into fire). The varying verbs all serve as so many
copulas, whether the things are said to transform themselves, be
changed, turn into something, be pitched, blown, or beaten into
something, or simply become. They are all signs of equation, and
all depend on the implicit futurity of "until" — the Muses are
to repeat the magic phrase *To Be Itself* until X will become Y
and Y will become Z. But Stevens chooses not to put it so simply. He begins with the deceptive present tense ("transforms"),
goes on to the even more deceptive past participle ("changed")
which implies the miracle already performed, and ends with
a cluster of present participles ("speaking," "strutting"), the
miracle now happening, and past participles ("pitched," "blown,"
and "beaten") again implying the miracle accomplished. He
concludes with the superlative degree, his final verbal signal of
the earthly paradise, in his "freshest, brightest fire."

These are Stevens' grammatical and syntactic equivalents to

his vocabulary of the gaudy and gusty, here represented by "the maudlin, true meridian," where the Muses are "speaking and strutting broadly," and so on. This apotheosis of the sallow Muses turned blooming is a confection without true conviction, written with the forced breathlessness of Stevens' more desperate inventions, and consequently canceled as he reread the whole. Stevens' recurrent poem is finally neither the elegy for the death of the gods nor the earthy tum-ti-tum, but in fact the elegy for the death of tum-ti-tum, the atrophy in life of the earthy poem. In compelling his Muses here to sing the maudlin meridian in such an exalted way, he exceeds their vocal range, and the strain shows, as he knew, in the overpitch of his rhetoric.

The Muses are replaced in the poem by the Subman, who is the Muse as Male, a mythic figure whom Stevens never re-employs as myth, though he will use again the notion he springs from. The Subman, roughly speaking, is "the imagination . . . as an activity of the sub-conscious" (*L*, 373); he lives below the mind which itself lives below the body, and so he is the man below the man below the man (66). Unlike the sickly Muses, he needs no transformations to be able to sing. He belongs to instinct, to night, to that November in which the trees too speak at a sublevel:

> So much less than feeling, so much less than speech,
>
> Saying and saying, the way things say
> On the level of that which is not yet knowledge. (OP, 115)

The Subman can reconcile sun and moon, the two poles of Crispin's journeying, but only in nighttime, when daytime order is destroyed:

> Summer night,
> Night bold, and winter night, night silver, these

Were the fluid, the cat-eyed atmosphere, in which
The man and the man below were reconciled.   (68)

The Subman is a familial figure, and Stevens introduces with him the tone of tenderness which will reappear in *The Owl in the Sarcophagus* and *The Auroras of Autumn*, a tone almost of lullaby, with a simple and solacing rhythm. This simplicity is worlds away from the angularities of his imagist spareness:

He was born within us as a second self,
A self of parents who have never died,
Whose lives return, simply, upon our lips,
Their words and ours . . .
He dwells below, the man below, in less
Than body and in less than mind, ogre,
Inhabitant, in less than shape, of shapes
That are dissembled in vague memory
Yet still retain resemblances, remain
Remembrances, a place of a field of lights,
As a church is a bell and people are an eye,
A cry, the pallor of a dress, a touch.   (67)

The line division is deceptive here, and once the lines are re-arranged their true nature as regular and irregular tetrameters reveals itself:

He dwells below, the man below,
In less than body and in less than mind,
Ogre, inhabitant, in less than shape,
Of shapes that are dissembled in vague memory
Yet still retain resemblances, remain
Remembrances, a place of a field of lights,
As a church is a bell, and people are an eye,
A cry, the pallor of a dress, a touch.

Though the pentameter rhythm reasserts itself later, the *berceuse* is clearly the Subman's music, "in an interior ocean's rocking/ Of long, capricious fugues and chorals." [5]

The Muses as Family — appearing as parents and Subman here, as "sister and solace, brother and delight" or as the pure perfections of parental space in other poems — will never replace for Stevens the interior paramour whom he still addresses in *The Rock*. Nevertheless, the tone of lover to beloved or subject to queen (as in "To the One of Fictive Music") will not do for all addresses by the poet to his creative faculty. The oddity, of course, of the first politely ironic address — "Mesdames" — to the Muses in *Owl's Clover* is that those ladies are addressed as a corps de ballet, as sorceresses outside of any special relation to the poet: they emphatically do not dwell below his other selves, or exert sovereignty over him. And even the Subman, though affectionately described, is totally unable to resolve *Owl's Clover*; he is finally dismissed (70) as impotent to save the Statue for us, since the Statue cannot be scaled to interior space alone, the space "in camera," immeasurable though it is, of the Subman. His space is one of minor and surrealistic emotional sounds, "the locust's titter and the turtle's sob," whereas the statue requires a cosmic space, in which it would soar "in a clamor thudding up from central earth." But even that apotheosis is a delusion. The Statue stands at last in true perspective, in hum-drum space (71).

After the Muses and the Subman, the other anthropomorphic mythical creation in *Owl's Clover* (and the most original and beautiful) is the Portent, which is allied to one of the mythical places in the poem, called "The End of the World" (49). The Portent and the World's End may be thought of, respectively, as the anti-Parousia and the anti-paradise of Stevens' religious imagination, his Abomination of Desolation. The Portent is the Future as menace (the Future as promise never quite convinces in this social poem) and the Trash Can at the End of the World is the Valley of Jehoshaphat before the command that the dry bones should live, or, as Stevens called it, "a panorama of things come to their end" (*L*, 368). The solemnity of Stevens' tone in describing his graveyard is given special weight by his use of the usually celestial mythic "there" as the rhetorical frame for his description: [6]

At some gigantic, solitary urn,
A trash can at the end of the world, the dead
Give up dead things and the living turn away.
There buzzards pile their sticks among the bones
Of buzzards and eat the bellies of the rich,
Fat with a thousand butters, and the crows
Sip the wild honey of the poor man's life,
The blood of his bitter brain; and *there* the sun
Shines without fire on columns intercrossed,
White slapped on white, majestic, marble heads,
Severe and tumbled into seedless grass,
Motionless, knowing neither dew nor frost.
There lies the head of the sculptor in which the thought
Of lizards, in its eye, is *more* acute
Than the thought that once was native to the skull;
And *there* are the white-maned horses' heads, *beyond*
The help of any wind or any sky:
Parts of the immense detritus of a world
That is completely waste, that moves from waste
To waste, out of the hopeless waste of the past
Into a hopeful waste to come. *There* even
The colorless light in which this wreckage lies
Has faint, portentous lustres.   (49)

The language here is the variable, while the syntax is the constant — not a grammatically confusing constant, like Stevens' collection of unattached appositions, but a gravely repetitive constant of the historical present which effaces itself. Even the diction depends on simple irony: a Keatsian urn is a trash can, butter becomes buzzards, columns intercrossed collapse to "white slapped on white." Two familiar signs of Stevens' paradise (the comparative "more" and the adverbial "beyond") appear ironically as in reality a less and a beneath. In this ravaged nobility, the majesty, solitude, and immensity, even of detritus, is unquestioned; this is the Roman Forum of the imagination. While the better known poem "The Man on the Dump" is a serio-comic version of the same image, centered on the personal dilemma of the poet as central *fantoche*, here the Solitary Urn is seen archaeologically, greatly distanced, in another country, as a tragic spectacle.

After a halfhearted attempt to imagine a rosy transfiguration of the wreckage (resembling, in syntax, the strained apotheosis of the Muses mentioned earlier) Stevens rejects, in the final bleak luster of the scene, the more sentimental rose-points, rose-breasted birds, and rose-beliefs:

> Above that urn two lights
> Commingle, not like the commingling of sun and moon
> At dawn, nor of summer-light and winter-light
> In an autumn afternoon, but two immense
> Reflections, whirling apart and wide away.

Stevens formulaic "not X, nor Y, but Z" invites us to consider the rejected alternatives as well as the proposed final image. Though "commingle" can be a word of communion, we are advised not to take it as we generally know it, as an embrace which is the origin of change:

> Winter and spring, cold copulars, embrace,
> And forth the particulars of rapture come.   (392)

The commingling, Stevens tells us, is neither the progressive warmth of the moon meeting the sun at dawn, nor the chilly decline of summer meeting winter at autumn,[7] but it is a commingling in a double mirror image, as these planetary lights, the past and the future,[8] though reflecting each other yet rush outward, like the universe, forever diverging.

At last the sprawling Portent takes form, becoming the genius of one of those lights, the one creating the future. Stevens presents his conjectures about it as eternal mythical truths told in the present tense which we use for timeless myth; as counterpoint to this "false" present tense he uses the "true" present of the quotidian (in the phrases I have italicized) to comment on the Portent's invisibility to us:

> High up in heaven a sprawling portent moves . . .
> *But this we cannot see.* The shaggy top
> Broods in tense meditation, constantly . . .
> *This is invisible.* The supporting arms
> Reach from the horizons, rim to rim,
> While the shaggy top collects itself to do
> And the shoulders turn, breathing immense intent.
> *All this is hidden from sight.*   (68)

Though hidden from us, the Portent is not hidden from the sight of the mythic Subman, whose voice Stevens uses to affirm its existence:

> The man below beholds the portent poised,
> An image of his making, beyond the eye.   (69)

As the Solitary Urn of the past and the Portent of the future stand in opposition, Stevens attempts, with characteristic insistence ("must") and speculation ("may"), a prophecy and recapitulation:

The future must bear with it every past . . .
The portent may itself be memory;
And memory may itself be time to come
And must be, when the portent, changed, takes on
A mask up-gathered brilliantly from the dirt,
And memory's lord is the lord of prophecy
And steps forth, priestly in severity,
Yet lord, a mask of flame, the sprawling form
A wandering orb upon a path grown clear.   (70)

The final transition, as the portent becomes a planet and sprawl-ing cosmic form becomes orbital motion, is successful in its pure likelihood: nothing is more probable than the condensation of a nebulous celestial mass into a planet. But the temple-trappings of the rather theatrical priest-lord are gratuitous and suffer accordingly.[9]

Even this envisaged resolution of planet-priest collapses in the conclusion as we return to present mythic fact: "High up in heaven the sprawling portent moves" (70). The only way to vanquish the menace of the alien future would be to see the statue resurrected, not scaled to a particular era but scaled to the cosmos, bigger than history, as relevant to the future as to the past. In that case, Stevens would have us believe, the portent would change in proportion to humanity's changes, being a meager thing to a race of dwarfs, but celestial to a race bound for the stars:

The portent would become man-haggard to
A race of dwarfs, the meditative arms
And head a shadow trampled under hoofs,
Man-misty to a race star-humped, astride
In a clamor thudding up from central earth.   (70)

Here, once again, the language becomes notably strained in grotesque compound epithets (man-haggard, man-misty, star-humped) as Stevens attempts yet another solace before the Portent (abandoning the notion that the future might really be only the past transformed). And, like the Subman, the Portent ends inconspicuously, in a return to *berceuse*, to night:

> The statue stands in true perspective. Crows
> Give only their color to the leaves. The trees
> Are full of fanfares of farewell, as night
> And the portent end in night, composed, before
> Its wheel begins to turn . .
>   It is, it is, let be
> The way it came, let be what it may become.
> Even the man below, the subverter, stops
> The flight of emblemata through his mind,
> Thoughts by descent. (71)

In that momentary equipoise between nostalgia and hope, the poem sinks downward to darkness, on extended wings — Stevens' rare acquiescent drift in the temporal stream.

Finally, the most unworthy mythical creature in *Owl's Clover* is the "buckskin, crosser of snowy divides" (61), the American frontiersman. Like Stevens' figure of Walt Whitman in *Decorations*, the pioneer horseman is meant to signify life-giving freedom, his riding to suggest the opposite of the machined fate of urban workers. Nothing much, in the end, is made of either Whitman or the pioneer: in fact the "broad-brim" (as the primitive Westerner is called in the revised version) is oddly possessed of scholar's outlines, prints of London, papers of Paris, and so on, since Stevens wanted a primitive blessed with all the advantages of civilization, a type that the legendary Whitman is tailored to fit. As Stevens said in his romanticizing of the pioneers, "The pioneers pushed out from a known world, a world that had a scholar's outline. The emigrant from England might well have read the print of poets, Italian lives — not particularly Plutarch, or Vasari, or that sort of thing, but the lives of acute men, Italian as in fine, Italian hand. The pioneers took these things with them (preserved them in the destitution of life in a new world)" (*L*, 371). What might have been true of the New England divine, Stevens wants to make true of the Western freeman, but since the myth cannot be sustained, this noble rider disappears and is not heard from again.

The mythical "more than natural figures" of *Owl's Clover* will remain a poetic resource for Stevens, though he may change their sexes and their functions, as the Subman becomes the Glass Man, or the Portent becomes the Aurora, or the Muses become the Mother. The same is not true of the powerful geographical myth of Africa. Though it is an image naturally developed from the venereal Florida of the earlier books and the barbarities of Yucatan in the *Comedian*, the powerful identification of tropical fertility with menacing death is never so strongly pursued in Stevens' later poems as it is in *Owl's Clover*. (If fertility is expressive of death, then, it must be added, asceticism paradoxically becomes the principle of life, as it does in Stevens.) [10]

We are presented, in "The Greenest Continent," with three images of paradise, or heaven, of which the third is Africa. The first, canceled in Stevens' revisions, is the "social" heaven of civilized Europe, annihilated by pretension, religion, decadent art, wealth, and finally war. While it was available, before its corruption, it was (to use Stevens' amplest superlative, characteristic of his tendency to understatement), "enough":

> The heaven of Europe is empty, like a Schloss
> Abandoned because of taxes . . . It was enough:
> It made up for everything, it was all selves
> Become rude robes among white candle lights,
> Motions of air, robes moving in torrents of air.   (53)

The second heaven, described in the "there" phrases of paradisal reference, rises in words belonging to the imagination's "room": cloud, solitude, transparence, immaculate fire. It refers, judging by later sections of the poem, to the secular imagination's power to conceive of transcendence, the episcopate of the spirit which created the classical and Christian pantheons — gods, angels, and saints. "The only marvelous bishops of heaven have always been those that made it seem like heaven" (*OP*, 208), as Stevens said in an essay especially relevant to this second "heaven." The preludes over, Stevens dismisses his second heaven and arrives at the third, a savage and deathly place:

> That was never the heaven of Africa, which had
> No heaven, had death without a heaven, death
> In a heaven of death.   (54)

The equivalence of death and this dark heaven is insistent: the tropic is a country of prey. In Crispin's voyage the tropic was relatively harmless, and panthers and serpents, though mentioned, were not major. Other poems in *Harmonium* ("Floral Decorations for Bananas," "O Florida, Venereal Soil," and "Nomad Exquisite") betray Stevens' mixed feelings about the savage and sullen hurricane shapes which represent to him the inevitable extrapolation of sensual pleasure, of the venereal soil as man's intelligence, the sexuality implicit in tropical metaphors. By the time Stevens writes *Owl's Clover*, the compensatory, if intimidating, beauties of the tropics are submerged entirely in the pervasive primacy of death, erected by our fear into a serpent-god, the black sublime. Green become greenest equals black, and the sun, become antiquest sun, is no longer life-giving but death-dealing.

The fertility of Stevens' diction in respect to the tropics is embarrassed, as we saw in the *Comedian*, when it is pressed into the repelled service of luxuriance:

On what strange froth does the gross Indian dote,
What Eden sapling gum, what honeyed gore,
What pulpy dram distilled of innocence,
That streaking gold should speak in him
Or bask within his images and words?   (*CP*, 38)

When the same opulence, forsaking its uncomfortable language
of fertile surfeit, is expended on prey and death, a masculine
force unlike anything else in Stevens emerges in the verse, a
force of strong and unequivocal syntax and almost unequivocal
language:

No god rules over Africa, no throne,
Single, of burly ivory, inched of gold,
. . . Except a throne raised up beyond
Men's bones, beyond their breaths, the black sublime,
Toward which, in the nights, the glittering serpents
    climb . . .
Death, only, sits upon the serpent throne . . .
And Africa, basking in antiquest sun,
Contains for its children not a gill of sweet.   (55)

The emancipating steady constancy of this final somber vision
collapses in an epicene angel-fight against Jaguar-men. This
"trinket pasticcio, flaunting skyey sheets," aims at a mythical
satire of myth, a mythical mock-epic, but Stevens, for all his
"imagination flashed with irony" is troubled in this episode by
divided feelings. These "effulgent hordes . . . affecting roseate
aureoles" are of course impotent against "the drenching reds,
the dark and drenching crimsons" of Africa. Whether or not
they are meant to represent the Italian aviators in Ethiopia, as
Henry Wells suggests,[11] they are verbally intolerable, a mas-
querade of "concentric bosh" as Stevens calls them. But after
the encounter, they return to their tabernacles, and are redeemed

by language quite other than the grotesqueries describing their African sortie: back they return

> To contemplate time's golden paladin
> And purpose, to hear the wild bee drone, to feel
> The ecstasy of sense in a sensuous air.   (56)

This is too close to approving passages in Stevens (the end of *Esthétique du Mal* for example) to be dismissed as a continuing satire on the angels, who are after all enjoying themselves:

> And out of what one sees and hears and out
> Of what one feels, who could have thought to make
> So many selves, so many sensuous worlds.

But the angels are a bypath, one of the abortive offshoots of the poem: the real question is whether the statue, not the filleted angels, can survive the African jungle.

These, then, are the chief myths of *Owl's Clover* — the enfeebled or meretriciously appareled Muses, the tender Subman, the learned-virile pioneer, the effete aesthete-seraphim of Europe, the menacing Portent, the Solitary Urn, and the powerful green continent, each with its appropriate language. One last mythical personage enters briefly: Ananke, or Necessity, resurrected from *Decorations* as a figure of final disposition and possible extinction, the Minos or Rhadamanthus of this world.[12] Ananke, the final god common to Europe, Africa, and the Statue, is expressed in abstract theological terms, in Stevens' hymn to God the Father, as it were, with none of the humanizing religious terms which occur in Stevens' frequent invocations to more accessible deities — the One of Fictive Music or Chocorua, for instance. Ananke looks, sees, knows, hears, and thinks — he presides, in short, but in the paradoxes of theology;

He sees but not by sight,
He does not hear by sound. His spirit knows
Each look and each necessitous cry, as a god
Knows, knowing that he does not care, and knows,
Knowing and meaning that he cannot care.

For this presider over the greenest continent Stevens uses phrases
derived from the paradoxes and abstractions of theology, just as
his peroration on Ananke borrows the tone of the sterner Latin
doxologies:

Be glory to this unmerciful pontifex,
Lord without any deviation, lord
And origin and resplendent end of law,
Sultan of African sultans, starless crown.   (60)

As the Subman, part of ourselves, knows all from below, Ananke
knows all from above, and both we and our statues must mediate
between these myths.

The nonmythical portions of *Owl's Clover* are of two sorts:
social commentary and reflections on the Statue. The social
scene elicits two sorts of poetry from Stevens, the poetry of
satire and the poetry of pity, of which the more equivocal is
the poetry of pity. It resorts to language suspiciously like the
diction of the poetry of fertility, with the ambiguous vocabulary
which recurs in Stevens whenever he speaks of "the squalid
whole" (57), for which the Statue was supposed to make "a
visible clear cap, a visible wreath" (57). The description of the
squalid whole appears chiefly in "A Duck for Dinner," where
the spirit of "the million" writhes

To see, once more, this hacked-up world of tools,
The heart in slattern pinnacles, the clouds,

> Which were their thoughts, squeezed into shapes, the sun
> Streamed white and stoked and engined wrick-a-wrack.
> In your cadaverous Eden, they desire
> The same down-dropping fruit in yellow leaves. (61)

Clearly the workers belong to the bananas, to those for whom floral decorations will not do, and they represent the same unaccommodating and unaesthetic element, those sullen hurricane shapes that wrench Stevens' language into grotesquerie. The acrid Bulgar openly satirizes the workers in their affectations — the watch chains aus Wien and so on (62) — but in his attempt to imagine an apocalypse for them he lapses into the language of a Magus:

> Of what . . .
> . . . Are they being part, feeling the strength,
> Seeing the fulgent shadows upward heaped,
> Spelling out pandects and haggard institutes? (62)

Stevens' inflation makes it hard to say whether this unwieldy vision is ironic or not; at least, the Bulgar ends by giving up his hopes for a Five-Year-Plan apocalypse and for a potential true community beneath the heterogeneous. But Stevens takes up the problem again in "A Duck for Dinner" envisaging, as always, not the raising of the million in their million "squalid cells" (63) but a miraculous transformation of the million by means of poetry, as one of them becomes an orator "twanging instruments/ Within us hitherto unknown." The familiar rhetoric of magical transfiguration reappears but subsides almost immediately in favor of a mitigated assertion that even "to think of the future is a genius." Finally, Stevens gives up on speculation: to think of men in the abstract is to falsify (65).

The uninflected language of meaninglessness (introduced with

a reminiscence of Emily Dickinson's "dimity convictions")
arises briefly:

> The civil fiction, the calico idea,
> The Johnsonian composition, abstract man,
> All are evasions like a repeated phrase,
> Which, by its repetition, comes to bear
> A meaning without a meaning.   (65)

When words become "only words" (as they seem to do in
"Repetitions of a Young Captain," iv) or when music becomes
only noise (as it does in "Jouga") there is a tendency toward
repetition into imbecility, described in the passage above on
abstraction, reaching its audible perfection in "Jouga":

> The physical world is meaningless tonight
> And there is no other. There is Ha-ee-me, who sits
> And plays his guitar. Ha-ee-me is a beast.
>
> Or perhaps his guitar is a beast or perhaps they are
> Two beasts. But of the same kind — two conjugal beasts.
> Ha-ee-me is the male beast . . . an imbecile,
>
> Who knocks out a noise. The guitar is another beast
> Beneath his tip-tap-tap. It is she that responds.
> Two beasts but two of a kind and then not beasts. (*CP*, 337)

The poem is a pun on *jugar* (to play), *con-jugar* (to play together, to be conjugal, to conjugate), guitar, and jaguar (the
final beast in the poem, greatness manifesting himself in "a little
sound"). The name of the player (Jaime) is deliberately spelled
phonetically to deprive it of familiar meaning, to reduce the

guitarist to the anonymity of the bestial world. Stevens touches this extreme — words reduced to their physical sound alone — only in moments of revulsion and staleness, but it remains a strong polarity of his world, even though he always turns hurriedly away from the abysses it reveals.

The satiric actors of *Owl's Clover* — the ironic and hedonistic diplomats in the cafe, the hopeful Bulgar, Basilewsky as the modern musician manqué — are convenient means of dramatic dissociation for Stevens, but the caricature of conversation among the diplomats and by the Bulgar is hardly sustained by any fictional energy, and dissolves very quickly into Stevens' own voice. The characters in later long poems — *Notes toward a Supreme Fiction* and *The Auroras of Autumn* especially — do not speak but are only described or addressed, and that convention is better suited to Stevens' gifts, which were never dramatic ones. When he speaks in his own voice (61) about the proletariat, sentimentality wars with revulsion. His contact with the individual poor is tenuous, not to say nonexistent, and it is only when one of them rises above the million-in-the-mass and becomes the Old Woman that he can grasp her. Even then, what he grasps in her is himself; she exists purely as a medium for the lyric voice. One feels very strongly in *Owl's Clover* Stevens' extreme distance before social questions of an immediate sort. Solitude, not society, is his subject as poet, whatever he may have felt as man, and he remains always a poet of "the organic consolation, the complete/ Society of the spirit when it is/ Alone" (CP, 309).

Stevens never deceived himself about the apparent irrelevance of poetry to practical social problems: "Given the mobs of contemporary life, however, it is impossible to project a world that will not appear to some one to be a deformation. This is especially true when the projection is that of the volcano Apostrophe, the sea Behold: poetry. At a time of severely practical requirements, the world of the imagination looks like something distorted. A man who spouts apostrophes is a volcano and in particular the volcano Apostrophe. A man full of behold this and behold that is the sea Behold" (*I*, 372). A discouragement of this order explains the satiric portions of the poem, and explains as well why Stevens never chose again in a long poem to speak against the backdrop of the masses. It also explains why the myths of the poem, since they are conceived (with the exception of Africa) against the low, appear by contrast as bubbles of bright sheens, "with a tendency to bulge" and sometimes, like Basilewsky's concerto, turn to caramel and refuse to float.

The peripheral parts of *Owl's Clover* — the myths and the social satire — exist for the Statue, which is neither satiric reality in its quotidian and cynical form (the diplomats, the parks) nor an invented myth like Africa. The poem is composed of a series of perspectives on the Statue, with Stevens' own stance, an elegiac one, encompassing the rest.[13] The simple wry statement of *Notes* — "Phoebus is dead, ephebe" — is not yet possible in the elegies of *Owl's Clover*, where the Statue is too much with us as the art we are, the only art we have, its sculptor our better voice. But in the midst of summer Stevens stops to imagine winter, both in the person of the Old Woman and in the Trash Can at the End of the World; he returns to summer in the mind of the sculptor; and, in the difficult balance at the end of the poem, pauses between summer and winter, wanting "the cloak to be clipped, the night to be re-designed."

In his first view of the Statue, Stevens mixes nostalgia with brio, and summons the superb past:

> Another evening in another park,
> A group of marble horses rose on wings
> In the midst of a circle of trees, from which the leaves
> Raced with the horses in bright hurricanes. (43)

The brilliant fact is orchestrated into Stevens' energetic display of the creative mind in act, the whole description a cluster of past participles, representing the Statue as a thing devised and made, and of present participles, evoking it as a thing awake in its own life. The two acts, making and wakening, are syntactically indistinguishable, a rhetorical image of genesis from without and from within.

> So much the sculptor had *foreseen*: autumn,
> The sky above the plaza *widening*
> Before the horses, clouds of bronze *imposed*
> On clouds of gold, and green *engulfing* bronze,
> The marble *leaping* in the storms of light.
> So much he had *devised*: white forelegs taut
> To the muscles' very tip for the vivid plunge,
> The heads *held* high and *gathered* in a ring
> At the center of the mass, the haunches low,
> *Contorted*, *staggering* from the thrust against
> The earth as the bodies rose on feathery wings,
> Clumped carvings, circular, like blunted fans,
> *Arranged* for phantasy to form an edge
> Of crisping light along the statue's rim.

It is no accident that so many adjectives in the passage are participial (clumped, blunted, crisping), that so many of the nouns are nominalized verbs (thrust, plunge, carving), and that other nouns are usable as verbs (storm, tip, ring, mass, wing, fan, edge, light, rim). As far as possible, this passage is composed wholly of verbs or verblike words, with a bright strength of motion resulting in the spectacle.

When the autumn wind makes a shadow of rotten leaves fall over the leaping marble, Stevens cannot rejoice in the prospect of revolution. Nothing in him could echo Shelley's invocation to the West Wind:

Make me thy lyre, even as the forest is:
What if my leaves are falling like its own!
The tumult of thy mighty harmonies

Will take from both a deep autumnal tone,
Sweet though in sadness. Be thou, spirit fierce,
My spirit! Be thou me, impetuous one!

To "cry hail" at the prospect of "the cycle of the solid having turned" is not in Stevens' power. The "Ode to the West Wind," a revolutionary hail, and the ode "To Autumn," a farewell ever unsubmissive to its own pathos, underlie all of Stevens' autumnal poems as the two extremes impossible to him. His variation on Shelley here is somber, elegiac, and ironic:

> The rotten leaves
> Swirled round them in immense autumnal sounds. (43)

The second perspective on the Statue, following Stevens' own, is the Old Woman's. Although she belongs to the generation of the Statue, its tumultuous art is not relevant to her present condition of poverty and destitution, both real and metaphorical. She is the denial of meaning, the Domination of Black (not the Snow Man, who has surmounted his terror), and she is reduced to fear alone in one of the step-by-step "stripping-off" sentences to which Stevens is addicted. "Nothing except," "nothing but," "no more than," and "only," are his marks of poverty:

> She was that tortured one,
> So destitute that nothing but herself remained and
> Nothing of herself except
> A fear too naked for
> Her shadow's
> Shape. (44)

For a moment, Stevens suddenly drops the third person description of the Old Woman, and her destitution is made ours by the universal "one" of a plea:

> To search for clearness all an afternoon
> And without knowing, and then upon the wind
> To hear the stroke of one's certain solitude,
> What sound could comfort away the sudden sense?   (44)

Her black domination "kills" the horses; they collapse to marble hulk, marble skulls, matchless skeletons, debris for the Trash Can at the End of the World. Even the starlight cannot reinvigorate the Old Woman or the horses; it simply washes over them, a transparent surface. The unity of man and nature, which usually appears in the conventional rhetoric of ecstatic identity, is ironically imitated in Stevens' copulas of unitive meaninglessness, as black becomes

> A mood that had become so fixed it was
> A manner of the mind, a mind in a night
> That was whatever the mind might make of it,
> A night that was that mind so magnified
> It lost the common shape of night and came
> To be the sovereign shape in a world of shapes.   (45)

This is a still point, but in a still world of fear. The old Woman is in "A place in which each thing was motionless/ Except the thing she felt but did not know." In this hellish version of Shelley's desire to be one with Nature, the voice of the Old Woman and the voice of the wind are one, but in an expunging blankness, not in ecstasy.

Stevens follows this annihilation in blackness with an apotheosis, irrelevant in its way, of evening untroubled by suffering, phrased in a nostalgic crescendo with the familiar evasiveness of tenses following "would" and "until." Without the "harridan self and ever maladive fate," night would become

> A yew
> Grown great and grave beyond imagined trees,
> Branching through heavens heavy with the sheen
> And shadowy hanging of it, thick with stars
> Of a lunar light, dark-belted sorcerers
> Dazzling by simplest beams and soothly still,
> The space beneath it still, a smooth domain,
> Untroubled by suffering, which fate assigns
> To the moment. There the horses *would rise* again,
> Yet hardly to be seen and again the legs
> *Would flash* in air, and the muscular bodies *thrust*
> Hoofs grinding against the stubborn earth, until
> The light wings *lifted* through the crystal space
> Of night. How clearly that would be defined!   (45–46).

In spite of this fantasy, the Old Woman's unity with night remains a sterile one, and we are expected to remember her desolate syllables when we reach the end of the poem, where a truer vision of unity, "Night and the imagination being one," depends on a recollection of her nightmare.

The Statue is next seen by the revolutionary mind that would jettison the past, like the lawyers in *Notes* who disbelieve in the statue of General Du Puy. Though this passage is in part satiric, still Stevens is intellectually committed to the desirability of revolution, to the return to the primitive. He has two chief metaphors for that return, diametrically opposed to each other: one is redness, ruddiness, hotness, vividness, and so on; the other is sparseness, scrawniness, austerity, the rock beneath the leaves. The red primitivism, as he knows, is the obverse of suffering; it is the desire to assert boldly, not equivocally, to opt for

> The hap-hollow hallow-ho
> Of central things . . .
> The blood-red redness of the sun . . .
> The red bird most and the strongest sky.   (*CP*, 243–244)

The tum-ti-tums, the hoobla-hoos, and the hap-hallow hallow-hos are hardly Stevens' best inventions, and redness betrays him into overathletic postures.

It is quite clear that the beginning of "Mr. Burnshaw and the Statue" is satiric (and comic, as Stevens delivers the crushing Marxist remark on the marble horses, "These are not even Russian animals"). The authenticity of the horses is denied entirely; they never did have any connection with reality, they are purely mental confections, fantastic grown-up toys.[14] But no one who has read *Notes*, with its serious assertion about the major man that "the hot of him is purest in the heart," its characterization of the poet as a "hot, dependent orator," and its injunction "plainly to propound," would say that this passage was satiric:

> The statue seems a thing from Schwarz's, a thing
> Of the dank imagination, much below
> Our crusted outlines hot and huge with fact,
> Ugly as an idea, not beautiful
> As sequels without thought. In the rudest red
> Of autumn, these horses should go clattering
> Along the thin horizons, nobly more
> Than this jotting-down of the sculptor's foppishness
> Long after the worms and the curious carvings of
> Their snouts.   (47)

The brutality of the wormy snouts, sculptors of the corrupting brain, becomes a joy if one is a true revolutionary untainted by nostalgia. But when Stevens flogs himself into these revolutionary attitudes his language proves obstinate, and gives itself instead to a "red" and "hot" naiveté of the primitive.

From the vantage point of Africa, the Statue seems different: not meaningless, as it seems to the Old Woman, not a confection totally unreal, as it seems to the revolutionary, but a tame, domestic thing. Among jaguars and serpents, what are horses? Africa, in its symbolic role, represents the primitive as hated and feared, but acknowledged, not repressed. Neither the revolutionary welcome nor the conservative sadness in nostalgia produces Africa; rather it is the elegist as fatal prophet who sees the Green Blackness, or the Black Greenness. And when this elegist views the Statue from the African perspective in the light of his own necessary prophecy, he sees it not as the energetic thrusting verb of the first poem but as a static noun, an outline of "edges" and "surfaces," a thin shape, a tamed beast of burden deriving from a more wintry climate:

> But could the statue stand in Africa?
> The marble was imagined in the cold.
> Its edges were taken from tumultuous wind
> That beat out slimmest edges in the ear . . .
> Its surfaces came from distant fire; and it
> Was meant to stand, not in a tumbling green
> Intensified and grandiose, but among
> The common-places of which it formed a part . . .
> There it would be of the mode of common dreams,
> A ring of horses rising from memory
> Or rising in the appointments of desire,
> The spirit's natural images, carriers,
> The drafts of gay beginnings and bright ends,
> Majestic bearers or solemn haulers trapped
> In endless elegies.
>   . . . It came
> If not from winter, from a summer like

A winter's noon, in which the colors sprang
From snow, and would return again to snow,
As summer would return to weazened days.   (56–57)

The reserved approval of this passage is not unkind, but rather indulgent of the Statue in its proper climate, that transitional climate so native to Stevens, reminding us of the "whisked and wet" summers of his North in the *Comedian*, but so pallid to the tropics where memory moves on leopards' feet and desire appoints messengers clawed and sopped with sun.

The diplomats in the tropics are indifferent to any aesthetic meaning the Statue might have; in their eyes it is simply a piece of furniture in the plaza, a relic of the past, of the "cruel" colonizers, serving to remind the workers of their present bliss under socialism. Ananke too is indifferent to the Statue, but he looks on Africa with the same impartial chill, as he shines alike on the just and the unjust, gathering all things mortal with cold immortal hands.

We are given one last perspective on the Statue before the final view: the perspective of the enthralled devotee. Though we might expect Stevens' tone here to be unequivocal, it is not. He yearns, it is true, toward a reverse primitivism, a return to the Eden untouched by doubt, before the obsolescence of the Statue was foreseen, before the pang of nostalgia entered aesthetic response. In this yearning there are two extreme points of strain: the attempt to recapture the ecstasy of ignorant response, and the worship of the artist as the creator of the immortal, transcending perceived change. It is age looking for the lost voice of youth, experience speaking the syllables of innocence, as we meet again the accents of religious ecstasy (in which the spectators, the Statue, and the sculptor are one), modulating into lines which become violently uneasy as they tell the sculptor's achievement in the past:

In this he carved himself, he carved his age,
He carved the feathery walkers standing by,
Twitching a little with crude souvenirs
Of young identities, Aprilian stubs.
Exceeding sex, he touched another race,
Above our race, yet of ourselves transformed,
Don Juan turned furious divinity,
Ethereal compounder, pater patriae,
Great mud-ancestor, oozer and Abraham,
Progenitor wearing the diamond crown of crowns,
He from whose beard the future springs, elect.
More of ourselves in a world that is more our own,
For the million, perhaps, two ducks instead of one;
More of ourselves, the mood of life made strong
As by a juicier season; and more our own
As against each other, the dead, the phantomesque. (64–65)

In *Notes*, Stevens will ascribe the making of art to our foreignness in the world, and to our desire for a compensatory native world made by poetry:

From this the poem springs: that we live in a place
That is not our own and, much more, not ourselves.

(*CP*, 383)

But in *Owl's Clover* he claims that the artist gives us an extrapolation of this world, a world more our own, more of ourselves — a claim in actuality, not a description of a wish. To reconcile us to the world (the function of the poet in "Asides on the Oboe") is not the same as to transform the world or create the future.

The claim in this passage from *Owl's Clover* is once again Shelleyan — that from the artist's beard the future springs, elect. Stevens is not natively or naturally so bold. The bearded creator exudes a fertility exceeding sex, but still a furious fertility, in a juicier season. This fertility, like all spawning in Stevens, wears an aura of the precious and the disgusting at once: the artist as Don Juan, oozer, mud-ancestor, and the Father of his country — a wholesale compound of Jehovah, Casanova, and George Washington — loses in poetic terms to the artist as Snow Man. In the end the reader of Stevens must see where the better poetry lies.

The Statue, then, is scrutinized in the light of several myths and also in the light of common day, changing shape and form as Stevens' various moods play over it. The poem, as we have come to expect in Stevens, is a study in change. One final perspective is given us:

> The statue in a crow's perspective of trees
> Stands brimming white, chiaroscuro scaled
> To space . . .
> The statue stands in true perspective. Crows
> Give only their color to the leaves.   (70–71)

For a moment we pause in winter, in the January of "No Possum, No Sop, No Taters," where

> The crow looks rusty as he rises up.
> Bright is the malice in his eye . . .

> One joins him there for company,
> But at a distance, in another tree.   (*CP*, 294)

Whatever tone this is, in both these excerpts, it is not elegiac as we usually understand the word. This tone, peculiar to Stevens, is not even stoic; its cold gaiety and its bright chill lightly touch the final dry resignation of *Owl's Clover*, felt in the perspective of hum-drum space. The poem quickly returns then to its elegiac farewells, where Stevens sketches the nucleus of what will become a greater poem, "The Plain Sense of Things," where he can sustain the vision only glimpsed in *Owl's Clover*:

> After the leaves have fallen, we return
> To a plain sense of things. It is as if
> We had come to an end of the imagination,
> Inanimate in an inert savoir.
>
> It is difficult even to choose the adjective
> For this blank cold, this sadness without cause.
> The great structure has become a minor house.
> No turban walks across the lessened floors.
>
> The greenhouse never so badly needed paint.
> The chimney is fifty years old and slants to one side.
> A fantastic effort has failed, a repetition
> In a repetitiousness of men and flies.
>
> Yet the absence of the imagination had
> Itself to be imagined. The great pond,
> The plain sense of it, without reflections, leaves,
> Mud, water like dirty glass, expressing silence
>
> Of a sort, silence of a rat come out to see,
> The great pond and its waste of the lilies, all this
> Had to be imagined as an inevitable knowledge,
> Required, as a necessity requires.   (CP, 502–503)

Owl's Clover is conventional in its framework of temporal decay. Everything declines in time, even the work of the imagination; in cultural terms, certain types of beauty become obsolete in the evolutionary scheme, just as General Du Puy or the colonizers of Africa had a style now anachronistic. This attitude makes the poet a passive spectator of the worms at Heaven's gate, taught by ruin to ruminate that time will come and take his love away. In a flat way, ruminations of ruin determine the close of *Owl's Clover*:

> The spring is hum-drum like an instrument,
> That a man without passion plays in an aimless way.
> Even imagination has an end,
> When the statue is not a thing imagined, a stone
> That changed in sleep.   (71)

In the face of this hum-drum season, this wasted figure with an instrument propounding blank final music (*CP*, 362), even the Subman concedes and halts his flow of imagery:

> Even the man below, the subverter, stops
> The flight of emblemata through his mind.   (71)

As the Subman is extinguished, all imaginative energy comes to a standstill.

The case is entirely different in "The Plain Sense of Things," where the Subman, far from being inert, is represented as engaging in the most strenuous activity of all — actively imagining his own annihiliation. Although the poem begins in inertia, it pulls itself together with immense effort to assert the life, not the extinction, of the imagination:

> Yet the absence of the imagination had
> Itself to be imagined.

This, the central statement of Stevens' poetry, puts the "blame" for the obsolescence of art strictly on consciousness itself, and offers, instead of a rather facile panorama of cultural change, a metaphysical statement about interior necessity. Ananke, an external force disposing of the Statue as he likes, is replaced by an internal requirement of the poet's being, and the spectator, weeping to have that which he fears to lose, is metamorphosed into the compelled destroyer. In this late poem, Stevens does not even take the middle position of acknowledging a complicity with time, but rather takes exclusively on himself the entire responsibility for "this blank cold, this sadness without cause." "The Plain Sense of Things" begins with an elegiac catalogue of familiar things, and the spectator names his sadness:

> The great structure has become a minor house.
> No turban walks across the lessened floors.

The essence of romantic elegy is grieving comparison — "then" compared to "now," a view of the decay of nature — and Stevens is a notable elegist in this vein. But he stops short and turns on the very things he has been regretting, calling them "a fantastic effort, a repetition/ In a repetitiousness of men and flies."

In this special vocabulary of meaninglessness known to us from "Jouga" and other poems, Stevens allows a disgust for his elegiac subject to intrude, and prepares for his revelation that some part of himself is responsible for decay. The second catalogue in the poem, matching the earlier elegiac one, tries to decide, in an oscillation of the sort Stevens loves, whether the present state of the pond represents an austere beauty or a primeval chaos:

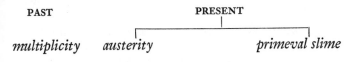

PAST   PRESENT

multiplicity   *austerity*   *primeval slime*

> The great pond,
> The plain sense of it,
>   without

reflections,

> leaves,
> mud,
> water like dirty glass

expressing silence of a sort,
silence   of a rat come out to see,
the great pond   and   its waste of the lilies
     All this had to be imagined.

(CP, 503)

The noticeable difference here from the first catalogue is that this list is nowhere comparative in the elegiac sense except in the phrase "without reflections." The nostalgic comparing of present with past, as we saw it in the first half of the poem, has been largely abandoned, and the landscape is being seen almost "pure," with no overtones of misery, seen with the eyes of the Snow Man. Such a "purifying" of the elegiac into the visual, which may be called by several names, is perhaps best described here as a return to surfaces,[15] since that is Stevens' metaphor in this poem — one sees no reflections, only the glassy plain of the water, only the mud, the leaves, the lily pads. The pathos of the description culminates in the paradoxical "waste of the lilies," transforming the pond into a desert. The suppression of the elegiac in describing "the nothing that is" can never be complete, and the attempt to see "nothing that is not there" is always a heroic impossibility. Nevertheless, in "The Plain Sense of Things," we can see the direction of Stevens' late work.

But *Owl's Clover* cannot rest in the fervent conviction that bare night is best. After arriving at hum-drum space, it asserts violently that absence is in reality a presence, and the most positive of presences at that (Jocundus) as well as the most common (the medium man). Stevens has taken this direction before and will take it again, notably in "The Latest Freed Man"

(*CP*, 204–205), linked to *Owl's Clover* in both subject and rhetorical direction. At moments of feeling that resemble each other, Stevens often takes up similar grammatical and rhetorical turns: one of these (which he uses for parallel ends in *Owl's Clover*, "The Latest Freed Man," and "The Man on the Dump") is the series of infinitives, a free-floating series of verbal impulses, we might say, conveniently unattached (or if attached, almost casually so) to a central verb — the impression to be gained, ideally, being one of extreme spontaneity, freedom, and continuing action temporally unchecked.[16]

> To be without a description of to be,
> For a moment on rising, at the edge of the bed, to be,
> To have the ant of the self changed to an ox
> With its organic boomings, to be changed
> From a doctor into an ox.   (*CP*, 205)

> Is it peace . . . one finds
> On the dump? Is it to sit among mattresses of the dead,
> Bottles, pots, shoes and grass and murmur *aptest eve*:
> Is it to hear the blatter of grackles and say
> *Invisible priest*; is it to eject, to pull
> The day to pieces and cry *stanza my stone*?   (*CP*, 203)

The man on the dump proposes what may be called an antielegy: that is, he keeps the comparative basis of the elegiac form (an apt eve versus the evening on the dump, heavenly canonical choirs versus the blatter of grackles, the unity of poetry versus the fragments of daily life) but he refuses to make the requisite comparisons, and simply defies the present nothingness by calling it by the names of the best he has known, asserting a countervalue which he at the same time identifies with the sordid present, since all "truths" are equal. There is no such thing, he declares, as *the* truth, and who ever put such a delusion in our minds?

In "The Latest Freed Man" and in the conclusion of *Owl's Clover* the dump is simply ignored, mentally obliterated from the landscape, as the speaker "turn[s] away from the abominable farewells." The latest freed man has escaped from the notion that somewhere "the" truth exists: the old doctrine of the landscape is not present even as junk; nor are the severed heads of the ruined horses in view at the end of *Owl's Clover*. This may seem cavalier: what has happened to the dump, to the Trash Can at the End of the World? We are not told, only offered a choreography of floating infinitives:

> To flourish the great cloak we wear
> At night, to turn away from the abominable
> Farewells and, in the darkness, to feel again
> The reconciliation, the rapture of a time
> Without imagination, without past
> And without future, a present time, is that
> The passion, indifferent to the poet's hum,
> That we conceal? A passion to fling the cloak,
> Adorned for a multitude, in a gesture spent
> In the gesture's whim, a passion merely to be
> For the gaudium of being, Jocundus instead
> Of the black-blooded scholar, the man of the cloud, to be
> The medium man among other medium men.

By a grammatical modulation, the active infinitives ("to flourish," and so forth) turn into infinitives of state (to be) and then in the conclusion, active existence extends into passive infinitives, actualized by an agent never explicit:

> The cloak to be clipped, the night to be re-designed,
> Its land-breath to be stifled, its color changed.

And the final union, which we are expecting since the passive infinitives become accomplished in the past participle "changed," takes place in the timeless world of the present participle,

> Its color changed,
> Night and the imagination being one. (71)

These verbal transformations, imitating the process they describe, are comparable to modulations in Stevens' other apotheoses. This is an apotheosis, Absence apotheosized into Presence, just as the latest freedman is apotheosized (primitive though the notion of *theos* may be here) into an ox. The heaping of phrase upon phrase, the loosening of syntax, the smaller appositions within larger appositions, have their logical end here. It all depends, as Stevens says, on "turning away" from the farewells, refusing to look at the dump, the severed heads. In later poems like "The Plain Sense of Things," Stevens will assert that if the dump did not exist he would have had to invent it — a far cry from this refusal to contemplate it.

Jocundus is conceived here at too great a cost, the cost of being "indifferent to the poet's hum." Stevens seems scarcely to remember, at the end of the poem, that those who turned away from elegiac farewells had taken to composing Concertos for Aeroplane and Pianoforte and to complacent drinking in cafés, praising fromage and cognac. And Jocundus turns away not only from the Solitary Urn but also from Africa — as if a poem could obliterate so quickly myths so drastically imagined. Just as the *Comedian* expressed the pious wish that each man's relation might be so "clipped," *Owl's Clover* wants the cloak of night to be "clipped," and the night "re-designed," a domestic effort which ignores the serpentlike Ananke with the frost glittering on his face and hair (*CP*, 152).

The tragic threat of the African fertility and the savagery of the million is not met in the "gaudium" of the final lines, but

117

perhaps no reconciliation embracing so much was possible to Stevens in the thirties. What *Owl's Clover* did do was to enfranchise large tracts of Stevens' imagination which the compressed form of *Decorations* had necessarily repudiated, to serve as a catchall for the new leanings toward the hum-drum (the day's news) even though his style could not yet be hum-drum itself, to free him to try the satiric, the social, and mythical all combined, and to reveal to him, even if negatively, the limits of his rhetoric and the limits of the topical. It was not in the day's news but in the rainy streets of New Haven that Stevens would find the quotidian, but it was probably impossible, in the thirties, to pass over the relation of the poet to the convulsions of the social order, just as it would be impossible, in the forties, for Stevens to ignore the war. Neither theme suited him, and between these two "social" periods he tried other forms, the first a return to the ballad and the folk, via *The Man with the Blue Guitar*.

V. A Duet with the Undertaker

To live in war, to live at war,
To chop the sullen psaltery.

In *The Man with the Blue Guitar* (1937) [1] Stevens returns, after the elaborations of *Owl's Clover*, to a deceptive open plainness — not to the classic verticals of *Thirteen Ways of Looking at a Blackbird* or the riddles of *Like Decorations in a Nigger Cemetery*, but to the airiness of folksong. The thirty-three cantos of the guitarist are Stevens' nearest approach to "lyrics" in the old sense: many are in the first person; most use a forthright direct address precluding high oratory; and in tone — forsaking runes and epigrams alike — they are usually loose, explicit, even colloquial. For a change, Stevens seems to write an "easy" poem, a structure of expansions and contractions, of affirmation balanced by reservation, asserted for the most part by a single speaker. Stevens will never again use the expedient of the one lyric voice to unify a long poem, and even here he requires his more detached third-person reference to frame the poem and to resolve it. The single voice, suggesting a consistency of ultimate utterance and attitude, can hardly embrace Stevens' earnest seriousness combined with volatile irony, and the man playing the blue guitar is too persistently present to be simultaneously diminished in Stevens' usual mode of double vision. Like *Thirteen Ways of Looking at a Blackbird*, *The Man with the Blue Guitar* is an attractive poem, but Stevens is constricted by it, and the habitué of Stevens misses in it the leisure and elbow room of *Notes*. The reader remembering the efforts to include a wide social scene in *Owl's Clover* might also bring a charge of narrowness against the poem.

The myths in *Owl's Clover* taken all together compose a pantheon and cosmos: Ananke the god above, the Subman the god below, the Portent in the sky, the Hades at the end of the world, the group of ineffectual angels, and the vast Greenest Continent. In the *Man with the Blue Guitar*, the gods are annihilated, and the third dimension which they represent is eliminated. A strict two-phase system is all that remains, as the mind alone confronts the world alone, without any sacred parental presences. The music of the guitar is abrupt, staccato, far from the rapturous nostalgia of empty heaven and its hymns. But in a few cantos of the poem Stevens permits himself to remember those detached ethereal symbols he had loved precisely for their elusiveness:

> Now
> I stand in the moon, and call it good,
> The immaculate, the merciful good,
>
> Detached from us, from things as they are.   (vii)

Stevens worships the moon because it is immaculate, detached, a merciful maternal light free of the grossness of this life, the mother as virgin. But in this poem he realizes the equivalence of this worship with a desire for death: when everything becomes as elusive and detached from him as the moon, he will be dead, and a chill descends on the poem:

> It is the sun that shares our works.
> The moon shares nothing. It is a sea.
>
> When shall I come to say of the sun,
> It is a sea; it shares nothing;

The sun no longer shares our works
And the earth is alive with creeping men,

Mechanical beetles, never quite warm?
And shall I then stand in the sun, as now

I stand in the moon, and call it good,
The immaculate, the merciful good,

Detached from us, from things as they are?
Not to be part of the sun? To stand

Remote and call it merciful?
The strings are cold on the blue guitar.   (vii)

When Stevens wrote to Hi Simons about this canto, he paraphrased it and then disavowed his own paraphrase: "I have a
sense of isolation in the presence of the moon as in the presence
of the sea. If I could experience the same sense in the presence
of the sun, would I speak to the sun as I so often speak to the
moon, calling it mercy and goodness? But if I could experience
the same sense in the presence of the sun, my imagination grows
cold at the thought of such complete detachment. I do not desire to exist apart from our works and the imagination does not
desire to exist apart from our works. While this has a *double
entendre*, still its real form is on the page . . . A poem of symbols exists for itself. You do not pierce an actor's make-up: you
go to see and enjoy the make-up; you do not bother about the
face beneath. The poem is the poem, not its paraphrase" (*L*,
362). The differences between paraphrase and poem here are
significant. The paraphrase is put as a hypothesis ("If I could
experience this, would I speak so?") while the poem is put as
a deathly intimation of the future ("When shall I come to say
this, and shall I then call the sun good?"). The poem ends as
the guitar falls silent in apprehension, while the paraphrase ends

with a firm and flat assertion: "I do not desire to exist apart from our works and the imagination does not desire to exist apart from our works." The effect of isolation on the poet's view of men is dropped entirely from the paraphrase, but we feel behind the poem Stevens' desolate truth, that life for him was not an affair of people, and that was the trouble.

With this unwilling realization that a total worship of the elusive would make men, already partly unreal, seem like mechanical beetles, Stevens settles into a new accommodation to the real, but without disguising his hostility. It is war, or so it seems, between himself and the world, an eternal struggle for power between two adversary principles. In the *Comedian*, the world was a chastening and educative presence, in itself parental, a curriculum for the marvelous sophomore. Crispin's role was to be docile, and the innate foolishness of that state of tutelage provoked in the poem Stevens' unremitting irony of surface. Here, the sophomore has grown up, and takes on the world as an equal. If it is a monster, he will be a monster; if it is antagonist, he is protagonist; if it is discord, he will be chord; if it is oppressor, he will be rebel; if it is land, he is ocean. This resolute equality gives the total poem its character as a declaration of independence, a brusque coming-of-age. (It makes no difference that Stevens is over fifty when he writes *The Man with the Blue Guitar*; if he was a sophomore at forty-two in the *Comedian*, we can judge the innately retrospective quality of his poetry.) Stevens will never write again in such an abrupt and self-assertive way, nor put to himself so many troubled and unequivocal questions:

> Tom-tom, c'est moi. The blue guitar
> And I are one.
>
> I know that timid breathing. Where
> Do I begin and end?   (xii)

Things as they are have been destroyed.
Have I?   (xv)

The poem has a mould. But not
Its animal. The angelic ones

Speak of the soul, the mind. It is
An animal.   (xvii)

It seems that these blunt sentences and questions are forced on
Stevens by his adversary position, and by a wish to rough out
his actual stand in brief notations, to keep himself from lapsing
back into the fatal euphonic seductions of memory or prophecy.
It is euphony, rather than rhetoric, that the poem forsakes, but
Stevens cannot, in the end, forget entirely his yearning to escape
the two-dimensional world he has adamantly presented:

                        The bread
Will be our bread, the stone will be

Our bed and we shall sleep by night.
We shall forget by day, except

The moments when we choose to play
The imagined pine, the imagined jay.   (xxxiii)

In those moments of playing the imagined on the guitar, Stevens
will remember the dream and the moon. But except for those
evasions, he will contend with his adversary, the world of
"things as they are."

The shearsman-tailor-guitarist is once again Stevens as *faux
naïf*, though not so archly simple as some of the personae in
Harmonium (notably St. Ursula and the girls plotting against
the giant), but with remnants of that technique of artlessness

artfully concealing art. Naiveté is only one of several stances taken in the poem, but the controlling figure with his reductive guitar (a harmonium is at least an organ, even if a puny one) is incapable of the vastnesses explored by the later long poems, and at times, with his narrow range, introduces a certain silliness:

> A million people on one string?
> And all their manner in the thing,
>
> And all their manner, right and wrong,
> And all their manner, weak and strong?   (iv)

On the other hand, *The Man with the Blue Guitar* seems humane and accessible by comparison with the ostentatiously stylized long poems preceding it. Our semi-Wordsworthian notions of the poet as a man speaking to men are satisfied by *The Man with the Blue Guitar*, just as our inherited notions of the rapturous poetic are satisfied by *Sunday Morning*.

After indulging in the grandiose paragraphs of *Owl's Clover*, Stevens seems to have set himself the problem (exaggerated even more in the opening of *Description without Place*) of making a long poem out of the fewest possible words, a challenge resembling the tour de force of the single image with variations that he had carried out in looking at the blackbird or the seasurface full of clouds. The monotonous continuo of a strumming guitar appears in the repetitive downbeat of "things as they are" and "the blue guitar" (with all their variations) as well as in the insistent resurgence of other talismanic phrases. The technique of the minimal vocabulary, though it dominates the poem, is nowhere carried so near the utmost edge of intelligibility as in the twentieth canto:

> *What is there in life except one's ideas,*
> *Good air, good friend, what is there in life?*

Is it *ideas* that I *believe?*
Good air, my only friend, believe,

Believe would be a brother full
Of love, *believe would be a friend,*

*Friend*lier than *my only friend,*
Good air. Poor pale, poor pale guitar.   (xx)

The italicized seventeen words, or twenty-one syllables, are varied, repeated, and expanded into an eight-line poem. No poet could keep this up for long, but it nevertheless represents the central process of the man with the guitar, and represents as well a continual rhetorical temptation to Stevens. It shows a stubborn unwillingness to progress, as Crispin had done, by a multitude of metaphors all referring roughly to the same tenor (in Crispin's case, his surrounding soil).

There is an insistence here on the single word, unadorned, as sufficient: what varies is the position or relation of the word. The nineteenth canto, for instance, operates on the adequacy of the word "monster" for ten of its twelve lines before it concedes a name — "the lion" — to the monster. Set over against the monster is the self, which is also kept pure of any variation until the last couplet. The variety (since it is not allowed to penetrate the nouns) comes in the envisaged relation — in predicative metaphors of relation — rather than in adjectival description:

That I	may reduce	the monster
to myself		
and then	may be	
myself	in face of	the monster
	be more than part of	it
	more than	

the monstrous	player of one of	its monstrous lutes
	not be alone	
	but reduce	the monster
	and be two things	
	the two together as one	
	and play	of the monster
and of myself	or better [play]	
not of myself at all		but of that
	as its intelligence	
	being	
the lion in the lute	before	the lion locked in stone.

The poetic energy is spent here in examining relationships, pass-ing from the most egotistic ("to reduce the monster to myself") to the least egotistic (to play "not of myself at all"). This canto is, in genre, a puzzle-poem, resembling the newspaper puzzles which transform one five-letter word into another in four steps, changing one letter each time. In its severity of means, it re-sembles the deliberate impoverishment of vocabulary in the canto quoted earlier.

These separate illustrations confirm our impression that in *The Man with the Blue Guitar* Stevens was restricting him-self on purpose. Yeats's injunction to himself could serve as epigraph for Stevens here:

> Hands, do what you're bid:
> Bring the balloon of the mind
> That bellies and drags in the wind
> Into its narrow shed.[2]

A pure dualism (a "series of antitheses" as Stevens said of one canto — *L*, 360) gives *The Man with the Blue Guitar* a philo-sophical structure as stringently limited as its vocabulary and its syntax: we are presented with things as they are, unmodified by adjectives, versus the blue guitar, a music unenhanced. We might call this the soil versus man's intelligence. Yet in *The Comedian as the Letter C* Stevens gave himself freedom to display the soil in all its variety, to shift from landscape to landscape, from one manifestation of the soil to another — land to sea, storm to cabin, wife to babies. Now the canvas has been greatly simplified: there is the monster and there is myself. Or there is the sea and there is myself. Though the metaphors for the adversary are multiple in the poem, they are "thin" metaphors, not adjectivally enriched for their own sake as the storm and the sea and the babies were. The adversary may wear different faces — a lion here, an icicle there — but those masks are diaphanous, and serve only to identify the type of resistance that the adversary is marshaling this time. Behind the mask, we know those eyes.

There are innumerable possible relations between two antagonists, and Stevens rings many changes on them:

> A is annihilated by B, or vice versa   (iii, x, xiii, xxvii)
> The battle remains perpetual   (xvi)
> A is subjugated to B, becomes a servant, or vice versa   (xxv)
> A is incorporated into B, becomes a part of him   (xi)
> A discovers that he "is" B — father-son, twin, mirror image
> (vi, ix, xix, xxix, xxx)
> They kill each other   (xi)
> They unite and marry   (xxii)
> Their clashing of swords, seen by a spectator, seems to him
> a harmony, not an antagonism; a dance, not a battle;
> a balance, not a struggle   (viii, xxiii, xxvi)

All of these outcomes, and probably more, are expressed in the poem. Though at its most benign, the relation can be called "the universal intercourse" (xxii), in general this poem, with its imagery of war or helplessness before an alien adversary, is a form of Stevens' gigantomachia, taking place in an element of antagonisms.

At one extreme is the joyful domination of the world, where the poet plays with reality as if it were his toy, and the world, unconscious of the manipulation of its parts, offers no resistance, and strictly speaking is no adversary at all. The poet here is Jocundus; the meter, as we might expect, is markedly dance-like; the language is deliberately primitive, the rhymes frequent, the sentences tumbling on each other, linked in childish "ands." The literary prototype of all this is "And the green grass grew all around, all around, all around," together with Stevens' importations from the Pennsylvania Dutch:

> He held the world upon his nose,
> And this-a-way he gave a fling.
>
> His robes and symbols, ai-yi-yi —
> And that-a-way he twirled the thing.
>
> Sombre as fir-trees, liquid cats
> Moved in the grass without a sound.
>
> They did not know the grass went round.
> The cats had cats and the grass turned gray
>
> And the world had worlds, ai, this-a-way:
> The grass turned green and the grass turned gray.
>
> And the nose is eternal, that-a-way.   (xxv)

This is the poet of "Ploughing on Sunday," and "Earthy Anecdote," the poet as folk-composer, barefoot and rude, for all his robes and symbols. Though Stevens, much later, called this poet a great personage (*L*, 793), the language is nevertheless the idiom of the nongreat, in fact the idiom of children, to suit the euphoria of the lines.

At the other extreme from this exhilaration is the moment when the mind is annihilated by nature, as it is when Stevens takes Emerson's frolic architecture of the snow and makes it into something far more satiric:

> It is the sea that whitens the roof.
> The sea drifts through the winter air.
>
> It is the sea that the north wind makes.
> The sea is in the falling snow.
>
> This gloom is the darkness of the sea.
> Geographers and philosophers,
>
> Regard. But for that salty cup,
> But for the icicles on the eaves —
>
> The sea is a form of ridicule.
> The iceberg settings satirize
>
> The demon that cannot be himself,
> That tours to shift the shifting scene.   (xxvii)

Just when geographers (and their interior equivalent, philosophers) think they have accurately mapped the world, the multiform sea, Stevens says, confounds them in its allotropic forms of encrusting snow and ice. New and unexpected contours arise. Geographers and philosophers, in Stevens' metaphor, are demons that cannot be themselves, that cannot let the landscape alone, but tour the world trying to rearrange it in an orderly way, not realizing that the world, ironically enough, is always in the process of rearranging itself.

Such a paraphrase of the poem does not reveal its mode, which is the depressed opposite to the persiflage of ai-yi-yi. The poem is not tragic, but drawn and wry, spoken not by the struggling guitarist, but by a preceptor well versed in ennui, with his frenchified "Regard." Rhythm is practically abrogated; rhyme is prohibited; syntax seems reduced to the simple declarative sentence; rhetoric is cramped to simple indication. (Only in the final sentence, and there solely in imitation of the futile tours of map-makers, does the syntax become more than primitive.) "And" is dropped from the language. The sentences stand like epitaphs, in strict autonomy:

> It is the sea that whitens the roof.
> The sea drifts through the winter air.
>
> It is the sea that the north wind makes.
> The sea is in the falling snow.
>
> This gloom is the darkness of the sea.

In one of Stevens' earlier poems, "Sea-Surface Full of Clouds," emphasis fell on the variety and pleasure of a cruise among sea-settings; here, the encrusting brine of a solitary basic element, the sea, stands, in all its variations (snow, icicles, icebergs, salt), for all the "shifting scenes." The earlier poem relished change of contour, this poem finds man mocked by it as he discovers the same blank element underneath it all: the exuberance of *Harmonium* is paid for by the repression of this canto.

Even in such puritanism of statement, Stevens, as always, manages artifice nevertheless. The declarative sentences, weighted with monotony as they are, nevertheless are all syntactically different, and these variations are anything but accidental. In the opening line, for instance, the sea, a predicate nominative, is an agent of active change through its transitive predicate; in the second line, it is the subject and the verb is intransitive; in the third, the sea is the object created in its aerial form of mist by the north wind; in the fourth, the sea is located in snowy space; and in the fifth, it is a remote and gloomy genitive. The use of "is" differs in each instance: only once (l. 9) is it the copula of definition, and elsewhere it functions as an expletive or as a verb of causation. In short, Stevens is really no less "rhetorical" here than in the excesses of *Owl's Clover*; he uses a less obvious rhetoric, that is all, managing a neutral verb with the cunning he had earlier expended on panache.

In the extreme of annihilation represented by this victory of nature, a dry, arid, even acrid tone always dominates. This tone of finality, of flat statement, can be simply factual, as it is in the canto on the sea, or elegiac, or apprehensive, as it is in the seventh canto, where the antithesis is insisted on in a speech approaching blank muteness:

> It is the sun that shares our works.
> The moon shares nothing. It is a sea.
>
> When shall I come to say of the sun,
> It is a sea; it shares nothing;
>
> The sun no longer shares our works.   (vii)

"My imagination grows cold," as Stevens wrote to Hi Simons about this canto, "at the thought of such complete detachment. I do not desire to exist apart from our works" (*L*, 362). That chill of the imagination is always enacted by a repressed syntax, but it can take on the vivacity of irony:

> The employer and employee contend,
>
> Combat, compose their droll affair,
> The bubbling sun will bubble up,

Spring sparkle and the cock-bird shriek.
The employer and employee will hear

And continue their affair. The shriek
Will rack the thickets.   (xxxi)

Whatever its tonal range, the shrunken commentary which is
the whole poem brings us the voice of the dead man using the
inhuman skeleton of language, perhaps brightened by a lively
diction as it is in the tale of employer-employee, but still "vitally
deprived" (*OP*, 94), the reflection, always, of a mood in which
the summer sea can seem nothing but "a tiara from Cohen's"
(*OP*, 72). This is no more a "natural" language than the afflatus
of earlier poems, since Stevens never was, and never would be,
in any of his manifestations, a poet of the illusion of natural
speech.

Despair, in the flat poems, prompts not only the denial of the
gaiety of language, but also a denial of the validity of metaphor.
The natural world wears masks; and as we are reduced to simile,
all we can do is "To say of one mask it is like,/ To say of another it is like." The old tendency to metaphor, and to its poetic
corollary the pathetic fallacy, dies hard, but it must grudgingly
be suppressed, and only the simile, with its Gradgrind insistence
on the unmagical, can be permitted:

The earth is not earth but a stone,
Not the mother that held men as they fell

But stone, but like a stone, no: not
The mother, but an oppressor, but like

An oppressor that grudges them their death
As it grudges the living that they live.

The poet has no choice but

> To live in war, to live at war,
> To chop the sullen psaltery,
>
> To improve the sewers in Jerusalem,
> To electrify the nimbuses.   (xvi)

These sullen infinitives, implying in their untensed eternity a
perpetual bondage for the poet, are first sad, then ironic, then
satiric, as they comment, by the reminiscence of their grammatical form, on Stevens' "blissful" infinitive series of the sort that
appeared in "The Latest Freed Man" and in the conclusion to
Owl's Clover. There is a "blissful" series in *The Man with the
Blue Guitar*, too, but it is a violent one:

> Ah, but to play man number one,
> To drive the dagger in his heart,
>
> To lay his brain upon the board
> And pick the acrid colors out,
>
> To nail his thought across the door,
> Its wings spread wide to rain and snow,
>
> To strike his living hi and ho,
> To tick it, tock it, turn it true,
>
> To bang it from a savage blue,
> Jangling the metal of the strings . . .   (iii)

This is the companion poem to the canto where the poet held
the world upon his nose, or rather its logical predecessor: this
is the whipped-up manifesto, while the other, in its past tense,
is the accomplishment; this shows the adversary as serio-comic
cadaver, the other shows the adversary as subjugated toy. A

third set of infinitives in *The Man with the Blue Guitar* is more moderate, more like the infinitives of "The Man on the Dump," a tired proposal, an attempt (doomed, as we know from *Notes toward a Supreme Fiction*) to achieve balances, not to wait for them to happen:

> So it is to sit and to balance things
> To and to and to the point of still,
>
> To say of one mask it is like,
> To say of another it is like,
>
> To know that the balance does not quite rest,
> That the mask is strange, however like.   (xxix)

This program for action is prompted by a sense that all things exist in an opposition which is potentially a balance, and the secular scholar, reading his lean Review in the vaults of the cathedral, opposes in his being both the religious past (for all the nostalgia of his location) and the festival of Jocundus, while the celibate cathedral is balanced by what is outside it, nuptial song.

Granted all the inadequacies of the masks, the poem faintly insists that only opposition defines, and that the Franciscan don knows his ascetic self only by looking in the fertile and swarming mirror of the world. The parallels of these personae — both scholar and ascetic Franciscan monk — to Stevens himself are only too clear, and his sense of estrangement from the physical, of course, solicits this exhausted and sedentary distributive justice.

Since the joy of "playing man number one" is possible only in prospect, not in accomplishment, the happier moments in *The Man with the Blue Guitar* come in a sense of interaction with an enemy who, while keeping his alien nature, nevertheless suddenly engages in a partnership. The relation to the monster, quoted above, is a case in point, ending as it does with a mirror image of perfect symmetry,[3] reinforced by parity of rhythm and deliberate alliteration, as Stevens proposes

> To be the lion in the lute
> Before the lion locked in stone.

A simpler moment of cooperation comes in Stevens' remarkable attempt to mimic a duet (xxiii):

<table>
<tr><td></td><td colspan="2">A few final solutions
like a duet with</td></tr>
<tr><td></td><td>the undertaker:</td></tr>
<tr><td>a voice in the clouds</td><td>another on earth,</td></tr>
<tr><td>the one a voice of ether,</td><td>the other smelling of
drink,</td></tr>
<tr><td>the voice of ether prevailing,</td><td>the swell of the undertaker's
song in the snow
apostrophizing wreaths,</td></tr>
<tr><td>the voice in the clouds serene and final,</td><td>next the grunted breath
serene and final</td></tr>
<tr><td>the imagined   and</td><td>the real</td></tr>
<tr><td>thought   and</td><td>the truth</td></tr>
<tr><td>Dichtung   und</td><td>Wahrheit,</td></tr>
<tr><td colspan="2" align="center">all confusions solved.</td></tr>
</table>

Though the images are contrastive, they are placed in identical apposition, and since the natural tendency of apposition is the equation of the things listed, the lulling of the duet, as it proceeds from its initial "solutions" to its concluding "solved," becomes ever less oppositional,[4] until both voices, in identical modification, become equally serene and final. Also, they become equally lofty: the "low" undertaker, grunting and smelling of drink, has been raised to the dignity of Wahrheit, and perfect parity is attained between the adversaries, not only in social and syntactic levels, but in rhythm too, as the lines become crypto-dimeters:

> The imagined and the real,
> Thought and the truth,
> Dichtung und Wahrheit,
> All confusion solved.

The poetic forms of conflation (appearing in the poems about mirror images, duets, or paradoxical identity) differ from the forms taken by cantos describing a "universal intercourse" between reality and the mind. That interchange demands a rhetoric which depends, not on balancing the opponents "to and to and to the point of still," but on giving a sense of their fruitful interaction, as they go about increasing store with loss and loss with store. The movement between imagination and its objects can be thought of, Stevens suggests, either as the journey of imagination into nature or as nature's discovery of space in the imagination.

The winging of imagination into reality is the subject of one of Stevens' best-known lyrics, one which he himself paraphrased at length in a letter to Hi Simons in 1940:

> Poetry is the subject of the poem,
> From this the poem issues and
>
> To this returns. Between the two,
> Between issue and return, there is
>
> An absence in reality,
> Things as they are. Or so we say.
>
> But are these separate? Is it
> An absence for the poem, which acquires

Its true appearances there, sun's green,
Cloud's red, earth feeling, sky that thinks?

From these it takes. Perhaps it gives,
In the universal intercourse.   (xxii)

Stevens' paraphrase is an abstract one, and could be applied very widely: "Poetry is the spirit, as the poem is the body. Crudely stated, poetry is the imagination. But here poetry is used as the poetic, without the slightest pejorative innuendo. I have in mind pure poetry. The purpose of writing poetry is to attain pure poetry. The validity of the poet as a figure of prestige to which he is entitled, is wholly a matter of this, that he adds to life that without which life cannot be lived, or is not worth living, or is without savor, or, in any case, would be altogether different from what it is today. Poetry is a passion, not a habit. This passion nourishes itself on reality. Imagination has no source except in reality, and ceases to have any value when it departs from reality. Here is a fundamental principle about the imagination: It does not create except as it transforms. There is nothing that exists exclusively by reason of the imagination, or that does not exist in some form in reality. Thus, reality = the imagination, and the imagination = reality. Imagination gives, but gives in relation" (*L*, 363–364). The subject of Stevens' commentary is, properly speaking, the principle of which the poem is an instance, rather than the poem itself, which exists as much by its own strategies as by the principles that underlie it.

Given the apparent simplicity of this canto, strategy may seem an elaborate word to use, but beneath its carefully diagrammatic reciprocity, peculiar underground transformations are at work to confirm the apparently artless statement. Stevens' first notion is to reverse the usual question-answer form of a preceptorial, and give the answer unequivocally in the opening lines. But the question it provokes is implicit in the terminology of that first, apparently solid, statement. We are told that the poem issues from and returns to its proper subject — poetry; this *motion*, offered in verbs, is then nominalized, given a fixed point to stand on, so to speak, made countable as two things — *an* issue, *a* return. These two things are then located firmly in space, and in the space between them there is a third thing, also a nominalization, called *an* absence. Since an issue, generally speaking, is perceptible and therefore "real," and a return is likewise "real," so by inference the absence is equally visible, like the "nothing" that nevertheless "is" in "The Snow Man." There is also a hidden attempt to make us equate the entire phrase "an absence in reality" with "things as they are": that is the natural way to take the apposition. Only the single word "reality" is logically in apposition with "things as they are," but the pressures of syntax work against logic here. With the next question, "But are these separate?" the logic becomes even more clouded, since the antecedents of "these" are at best dubious: absence versus issue and return? or poetry versus reality? Even the contestants are left vague, the better to further their mutual implication. In fact, the whole purpose of the poem is to make fluid things solid, to make verbs into nouns, shifting phenomena into stationary objects, in order to permit the vaporous poem to take on the satisfying solidity of the natural world.

The "true appearances" which the poem is said to take on, as they are detailed one by one, seem at first only assumed garments — sun's green, cloud's red — tones like the colors of the natural world, only surrealistically changed. But then the series of appearances begins to claim substantially more than color: the poem takes on "earth feeling," and finally the vastest object, sky. Sky that thinks, earth feeling, are earth and sky given mind and soul, added to, made ampler than they are. From the modest assumption of a superficial color, the poem has gone on to claim for its aggrandizement the great natural bodies, earth and sky. "From these it takes," says Stevens, and again the antecedent is difficult to identify. Clearly, the poem "takes" from the sun, the cloud, the earth, and the sky, but these are not present as unqualified nouns to act as antecedents; they are present only in their already modified form. So we have been prepared, by the taking which is an enlarging, for the final statement, richer than the sentence preceding it — "Perhaps it gives" — not "gives to these" as it "takes from these," but "gives," in the pure absoluteness of the verb. There is a general benefaction, a universal largesse, reflected in the final grand language that claims a "universal intercourse" in the cosmos.[5] The interaction is made plausible both by Stevens' solidifying of the moving poem, and by his lightening of reality into "absence," so that insubstantial words can weigh fairly against things as they are.

In another canto of interaction (xxvi), the imagination is represented as the fluid environment or lodging of the solid world, the sea which encompasses the land; the intercourse between the two becomes the tidal music of earth and ocean at the shore, as the imagination in its ebb and flow washes over reality. As we imagine Utopia the imagination flows; it ebbs as we fail to bring Utopia about, and become nostalgic about what might have been.[6] Nature here is diminished by being located always against a larger, if more nebulous, encompassing medium.[7] The solidity of the world is syntactically referred always to the generating multiform vapor, as the world becomes

the relic	of	farewells,
rock	of	valedictory echoings
a bar	in	space
sand	heaped in	the clouds
giant	against	the murderous alphabet
		the swarm of thoughts
		the swarm of dreams.

The consequent music of interaction, though disembodied, is

nevertheless mountainous and solid because of the equal force of the adversaries, the gigantic land and the omnipresent ocean. As Stevens imagines "inaccessible Utopia,"

> A mountainous music always seemed
> To be falling and to be passing away.

The rhythm of the whole canto imitates a tidal ebb and flow, with every precaution taken against predictable stress.

An ironic single instance of the same ebb and flow occurs earlier in the *Blue Guitar* (xi). First there is the flow of a new synthesis of vegetable and mineral, of men and the world:

> Slowly the ivy on the stones
> Becomes the stones. Women become
>
> The cities, children become the fields
> And men in waves become the sea.

But the untruthfulness of the harmony, once it is achieved, causes revulsion:

> It is the chord that falsifies.

The ebb of dissonance begins, and its motion is syntactically the motion of the flow, but in reverse, as the old formulas, no longer fruitful, become merely traps for the living:

> The sea returns upon the men,
>
> The fields entrap the children, brick
> Is a weed and all the flies are caught,
>
> Wingless and withered, but living alive.

It is true that the chord had falsified, but the discord is no better, as it rises in a cacophony of disintegration:

The discord merely magnifies

or, as Stevens said, "Discord exaggerates the separation between its elements" (*L*, 363). The only hope for a new thesis leading to a new synthesis is time, the only sure fact in the shifting scene:

Deeper within the belly's dark
Of time, time grows upon the rock.

The single four lines of flow, the single four lines of ebb, punctuated by the momentary stasis of chord and discord, summed up in the final couplet by a permanent gestation of time by time, make up a canto typical of *The Man with the Blue Guitar*, a rigid and flawless structure imitating the strict Necessity of its subject, the locked eternal confrontation of man and nature.

The thirty-three cantos as a whole show a sharply limited aspect — the warlike one — of Stevens' central subject, the relation between sense and consciousness. What he said (*L*, 360) about one canto is true of the poem as a whole: it is "a series of antitheses." If economy is the virtue of the poem, thinness is its vice, and fragmentation the risk it runs. We feel that this poem, like the earlier *Decorations* but unlike *Notes* and *The Auroras of Autumn*, could be rearranged internally without loss, and that Stevens has yet to find a surer form for the long poem, one which will survive a possible deliquescence into component parts. The human verve of the poem, its seductive rhythms, its spareness of line, and its discipline are its chief attractions; *Owl's Clover* looks elephantine beside it. And yet there is no single creation in *The Man with the Blue Guitar* with the moving power of the Statue, the Old Woman, or Africa. There must be, we feel, a way of mediating between the unwieldy elaboration of *Owl's Clover* and the slender images of *The Man with the Blue Guitar*; there should exist a middleman between the poet as solemn hierophant and the poet as simple shearsman.

The poet as solipsist aesthete is of course a possibility, but less of a one than Stevens' earlier critics imagined. The aesthete makes a single odd but yearning appearance in a memorable passage of *The Man with the Blue Guitar*:

> The pale intrusions into blue
> Are corrupting pallors . . . ay di mi,
>
> Blue buds or pitchy blooms. Be content —
> Expansions, diffusions — content to be
>
> The unspotted imbecile revery,
> The heraldic center of the world
>
> Of blue, blue sleek with a hundred chins,
> The amorist Adjective aflame . . . (xiii)

Though the passage begins by regretting the days when the pale intrusions of ideas and beliefs would not have been corrupting to the imagination, it shores itself up by repudiating art as a rite or as a sacred trust, and hails the adjective as its own excuse for being, fat, content, aflame, as fertile and as central as it likes. Blue is the color of amorists young and full of bravado, a bravado imitated in the comic assonance of the last line, but their blue, corrupted by pallor, will die down to "the basic slate, the universal hue." The relish Stevens shows here for the imagination's Latin, its copious declensions and conjugations, depends on asking no more from its expansions and diffusions than a rich fertility. There are no grand claims made here for poetry; it is an imbecile revery, and the aesthete is its prophet. This fervent adjectival namer, resembling a pasha with his hundred chins, is the Argus of the sensual body, with chins serving in place of eyes. (The Argus of the natural world will appear in *New Haven*, xxx, in the "hundreds of eyes" of the tree squirrels.) But the aesthete, or dandy, as it is generally understood, is one of Stevens' minor, though authentic, personae. In the later poems a more desolate and more commanding voice takes the stage. Before that voice appears, however, Stevens will be touched by the war, and will once again try a liaison between the poet and man, man revealed by war as the "common hero."

VI. Abecedarium of Finesoldier

> Make a model
> Of this element, this force. Transfer it
> Into a barbarism as its image.

The uncertainty of purpose in Stevens' next volume, *Parts of a World* (1942), springs from a cause more corrosive than the obtrusive fact of war. Stevens seems to have come close, at this time, to an ultimate disbelief in decoration. The paradigm for poetry becomes, as it sometimes became for Thoreau, the laboratory notebook, a certification in the driest terms of the truth of accurate observation, while the restless tendency of the eye to cast "ground obliquities" on the plum is relegated to a comic limbo of the spidery grotesque lit by a "mignon, marblish glare." These two poles — a methodical recording and an eccentric fancy — are mutually exclusive: in poems where either exists alone, the tone can be harmonious, but combined they disturb each other profoundly, as they do in *Examination of the Hero in a Time of War* (1942),[1] the long scrutiny in which all the poems in *Parts of a World* culminate.

Stevens' "laboratory experiments" can be either positive or negative, a clearing of the air or a reduction to the subhuman, but in either case the flat identities remain arrogantly declarative and angular, and all visions seen fancifully aslant are tamped down. The new painting has to be sculpture, as Stevens declares in his little manual for pedagogues, "A Study of Two Pears,"

since the painterly illusion of two dimensions masquerading as
three falsifies as much as any indulgent and evasive simile might:

I
The pears are not viols,
Nudes or bottles.
They resemble nothing else.

II
They are yellow forms
Composed of curves
Bulging toward the base.
They are touched red.

III
They are not flat surfaces
Having curved outlines.
They are round
Tapering toward the top.

IV
In the way they are modelled
There are bits of blue.
A hard dry leaf hangs
From the stem.

V
The yellow glistens.
It glistens with various yellows,
Citrons, oranges and greens
Flowering over the skin.

VI
The shadows of the pears
Are blobs on the green cloth.

> The pears are not seen
> As the observer wills.   (196–197)

Not even this poem can be purely visual, and Stevens permits unobtrusive metaphors in the flowering yellows and the shadows as blobs, not to speak of the hint of purposeful composition in the word "modelled" and in the spontaneous alliterations telling us that the pears are "composed of curves/ Bulging toward the base. . . . / Tapering toward the top." [2] The negatives in the poem reveal the strong hostility toward decoration prompting Stevens' unequivocal denials, but they also reveal a counterforce which revenges this limiting of man's imaginative powers by an equally flat (but this time destructive) anatomy, not of pears but of the city:

> That's the down-town frieze,
> Principally the church steeple,
> A black line beside a white line;
> And the stack of the electric plant,
> A black line drawn on flat air.
>
> It is a morbid light
> In which they stand,
> Like an electric lamp
> On a page of Euclid.
>
> In this light a man is a result,
> A demonstration, and a woman,
> Without rose and without violet,
> The shadows that are absent from Euclid,
> Is not a woman for a man.
>
> The paper is whiter
> For these black lines.

It glares beneath the webs
Of wire, the designs of ink,
The planes that ought to have genius,
The volumes like marble ruins
Outlined and having alphabetical
Notations and footnotes.
The paper is whiter.
The men have no shadows.
And the women have only one side.   (221)

In the midst of this "pen-and-ink drawing," as Michel Benamou
has described it,[3] the one normative resentment leaps to significance: the planes "ought to have" genius, but they do not. The
poem of sorry verities disappoints, and though the extraordinary
ought to be able to arise out of the common, it does not; only
the fitful fantasy of the imagination could cast rose and violet
into the morbid Euclidean light, but those colors would be at
once snuffed out by the one-dimensional constriction of the
glaring paper. From the two-dimensional world of *The Man
with the Blue Guitar*, we have been brought to this lethal world
of single lines.

Rebelliously, the imagination continues its chromatisms, but
by now Stevens is living in distrust of its variegation, and senses
a possible madness resulting from a wholesale and licentious
imaginative dispensation, where anything is beautiful if you
say it is, and oak leaves are hands, if the poet chooses to make
that metaphor about them. Irresponsibility in imaginative fes-
tooning leads to a hysteria of tempo, the *vivace* of a neurotic
woman, sustained in her bizarre confections only by "the very
will of the nerves." She stops in the common dirt, like the ordinary women in their catarrhs, to imagine a feverish and sur-
real elegance cum vulgarity, allied (by her fretful porpentine
ways) to the ambience of the simpering Byzantines in "Peter
Quince at the Clavier":

Under the eglantine
The fretful concubine
Said, "Phooey! Phoo!"
She whispered, "Pfui!"

The demi-monde
On the mezzanine
Said, "Phooey!" too,
And a "Hey-de-i-do!"

The bee may have all sweet
For his honey-hive-o,
From the eglantine-o.

And the chandeliers are neat . . .
But their mignon, marblish glare!
We are cold, the parrots cried,
In a place so debonair.

The vocabulary of grotesque fancy yields to absolute delusion as the duchess, so to speak, orders her servant Hans to bring lunch, an elegant white wine coupled with the metal food of madness:

The Johannisberger, Hans.[4]
I love the metal grapes,
The rusty, battered shapes
Of the pears and of the cheese

And the window's lemon light.

But she acknowledges, in the last hardened phrases of the poem, that her dogma, "Anything Is Beautiful if You Say It Is," cannot prove true; she admits at last what she exerts and what she sees; her last "I love" is directed to

The very will of the nerves,
The crack across the pane,
The dirt along the sill. (211)

The last kiss, as Yeats once said, is given to the void. When
Stevens writes, in this mood, of the "pure" and decorative
imagination, he gives it a trivial, decadent, and hallucinatory
vocabulary, perversely arch and insectlike, sexually ambiguous,
inhuman, unreal, superficial, and self-limiting. The aim is to suggest that as the Imagination approaches Fancy, to use Coleridge's
terms, it becomes no longer revelatory but nonsensical, embodied in absurd and fabulous creatures like Lady Lowzen.

Flora Lowzen is first of all an oak tree, as Frank Doggett
has suggested,[5] waving leaves that look like hands to the poet,
stretching roots down into the earth, brushing acorns from her
branches, brooding on the past when she was in flower. But in
this riddle poem, as Doggett calls it, she is not so much the self,
as he would have it, but yet another version of the female and
the One of Fictive Music, an inhuman version this time, and a
bridge to later versions of more sinister import, like Madame
La Fleurie, the cannibal bearded mother. Once, Lady Lowzen
had been Flora, the goddess bestowing fertility; even longer
ago she had been a figure like the Indian death goddess Kali;[6]
but now she is a sequined decorator. The whole poem seems in-
nocently enough motivated by the poet's idle noticing that oak
leaves look like hands, but even such a commonplace metaphor
is satirically repudiated by Stevens' new Puritanism as he describes the eternal demon-woman — deceptive, evasive, glittering, deadly, elegiac, trivial — the demon who tours to shift the
shifting scene:

Oak Leaves are Hands

In Hydaspia, by Howzen,

Lived a lady, Lady Lowzen,
For whom what is was other things.

Flora she was once. She was florid
A bachelor of feen masquerie,
Evasive and metamorphorid.

Mac Mort she had been, ago,
Twelve-legged in her ancestral hells,
Weaving and weaving many arms.

Even now, the centre of something else,
Merely by putting hand to brow,
Brooding on centuries like shells.

As the acorn broods on former oaks
In memorials of Northern sound,
Skims the real for its unreal,

So she in Hydaspia created,
Out of the movement of few words,
Flora Lowzen invigorated

Archaic and future happenings,
In glittering seven-colored changes,
By Howzen, the chromatic Lowzen.   (272)

In becoming "the chromatic Lowzen," undignified by first
name or title, this Lamia of rainbow sortilege is trivialized.[7] From
her grave form in Stevens' earlier poems as sister and mother
and diviner love, she develops into a bachelor of fairy mas-
querade, skimming the surface of reality because she wants
always the rainbow changes of the unreal. At the end of the

poem the fable comes full circle, its last line echoing its beginning in an ironic mimicry of Lady Lowzen's inability to effect
any real change:

> In Hydaspia, by Howzen,
> Lived a lady, Lady Lowzen . . .
> So she in Hydaspia created . . .
> Flora Lowzen invigorated
> Archaic and future happenings . . .
> By Howzen, the chromatic Lowzen.

This is the monumental silliness of parody, in this case a parody
of "Kubla Khan." It is also, in its skeletal form, a parody of the
blank repetitions in "Jouga." Despair of substantial meaning in
language makes Stevens turn either to jingle or to heavy reiter-
ation, and he reaches both extremes in his repudiation of metaphor throughout *Parts of a World*. The particular queerness of
Stevens' language in "Oak Leaves are Hands" forbids any easy
statement to the effect that Flora Lowzen represents, in Northrop Frye's suggestion, "the original maternity of nature." [8] On
the contrary, she is the image-making faculty at its most autistic
and therefore least effective.

Certain questions about the choice of words are put very
forcibly by this poem. Why, for instance, is Lady Lowzen said
to be metamorphorid (instead of metamorphic, or — to preserve the pun on "metaphor" — metamorphorical)? Why is
she a bachelor? Why does Stevens invent the word "feen" and
what does it mean? Where did Lady Lowzen and her location
get their names? Some possible answers arise from dictionaries.
The suffix -id, for instance, is no longer a living one, but the
words in which it appears are mostly heavy ones (languid, tor-
pid, turgid, stolid, torrid, stupid, and so on); not even vivid
and florid are vivacious words. Also, as a suffix it occurs in
biological descriptions — ephemerid, arachnid — which might

suggest that Lady Lowzen is a subhuman many-legged species. At any rate, the word is sinister and anything but glittery or chromatic. "Bachelor," in a use now obsolete, meant a single woman, but there is probably also a pun (since Lady Lowzen is a "poet"), on *bacca lauri*, the laurel berry (O.E.D. s.v. *baccalaur*). "Feen," as Marie Borroff has pointed out to me, is first of all a phonetic spelling of the French *fine*, making Flora Lowzen a "Bachelier de Fine Masquerie"; it may also be formed from *fée* and -en on the analogy of "golden," meaning fairylike; the French noun *fée* (to sort with "bachelier" and "masquerie") is perversely given a germanic suffix, another mimesis of Lady Lowzen's ambiguous status. As for the proper names, aside from Hydaspia they seem purely invented, but even though they may be subliminally dictated, some choice of sound or meaning always does occur; Marie Borroff adds that *Laub* (leaf) and *lösen* (to let fall, as of leaves) may have combined to suggest "Lowzen," as *hausen* (to house, dwell) may have suggested Howzen. Mac Mort serves to place Flora's parentage and to suggest the imagery of Flora as Black Widow spider but is probably chiefly effective in its relentlessly final sound.[9]

In this poem (and, I think, everywhere that Stevens uses this purposely demented language), metaphor and the extraordinary "feen masquerie" to which it leads are relegated to a realm of Gothic excess. There follows, in direct contrast, an attempt to espouse the common. "The guerilla I," reads the manifesto of the ordinary, "should be booked/ And bound. Its nigger mystics should change/ Foolscap for wigs." The caps of folly once off, the decorations in nigger cemeteries once repudiated, the poet can conceive "the diviner health disclosed in common forms" (195). Speech too has its common forms, and they seem, even when they are not, totally anti-rhetorical, informational, and verifiable. The seductions of science woo Stevens in *Parts of a World*, as division, definition, accurate description, and discrimination become the axes of his poetic world, voiced in a new slanginess, a will to reduce all curves to geometrically describable forms, and a hatred not only for metaphor but even for the similes he allowed himself in *The Man with the Blue Guitar*. It is Stevens' second quest for the barbaric: what he had thought to find sexually in "that alien, point-blank, green and actual Guatemala" (241), he now hankers after in the masculine common life. The female jungle, that "green barbarism turning paradigm" (31) of Crispin's voyage becomes, in *Parts of a World*, the barbarism of the hero, in the image of "the man-like body of a primitive" (277). The hero (who in *Transport to Summer* will be given the slightly different emphasis of "major man") is the source of Stevens' new preoccupation with the common language and its common forms; and the framing of a poetry out of the speech of the million presents him with a linguistic problem analogous to the creation of a hero from the common soldier: the materials (theoretically) are unpromising in each case, but out of prosaic commonness the mysterious hero and his special poetry can presumably arise.

But they can arise only when fact and the imagined become one, when the earth seems all of paradise that we shall know, to use the more lofty speech of *Sunday Morning*. Stevens presents the central problem of *Parts of a World* in the statement on poetry and war which in the original edition followed *The Examination of the Hero*. In war, he proposes, the scale of events is so huge that fact alone can for once satisfy, in its grandiose scope, that hunger of the mind which is generally appeased only by the imagination:

> The immense poetry of war and the poetry of a work of the imagination are two different things. In the presence of the violent reality of war, consciousness takes the place of the imagination. And consciousness of an immense war is a consciousness of fact. If that is true, it follows that the poetry of war as a consciousness of the victories and

defeats of nations, is a consciousness of fact, but of heroic fact, of fact on such a scale that the mere consciousness of it affects the scale of one's thinking and constitutes a participating in the heroic.

The equation here of the large (or the communal) with the heroic seems debatable, and for a poet of lyric rather than epic ambitions, it might lead to an unprofitable aesthetic, the one uneasily proposed later in "Paisant Chronicle" (334). But Stevens qualifies his statement. It is not enough to participate in the (undesirable) heroic of war; we need a desirable heroic not of conflict but of satisfactions to allay the appetite for bliss:

> It has been easy to say in recent times that everything tends to become real, or, rather, that everything moves in the direction of reality, that is to say, in the direction of fact. We leave fact and come back to it, come back to what we wanted fact to be, not to what it was, not to what it has too often remained. The poetry of a work of the imagination constantly illustrates the fundamental and endless struggle with fact. It goes on everywhere, even in the periods that we call peace. But in war, the desire to move in the direction of fact as we want it to be and to move quickly is overwhelming.
> Nothing will ever appease this desire except a consciousness of fact as everyone is at least satisfied to have it be.[10]

The first part of the statement implies a rhetoric of the everyday; the second, as we have come to expect, a rhetoric of the envisioned, a dialogue ending only when the two are one.

As usual, Stevens' program is rather simpler than its execution, and the putatively common soldier of *Examination* speaks the first lines not in the common tongue but in a voice straight from "The Sun This March." "Cold is our element and winter's air/ Brings voices as of lions coming down," Stevens had written in the earlier poem (134). The soldier says:

> Force is my lot and not pink-clustered
> Roma ni Avignon ni Leyden,
> And cold, my element. Death is my
> Master and, without light, I dwell.   (i)

The poem begins, in other words, in a lyric strain nearer to Stevens than to his plain hero, and the commentary on the hero's embrace of his lot is pure Stevens of *Sunday Morning*:

> Passions of rain, or moods in falling snow;
> Grievings in loneliness, or unsubdued
> Elations when the forest blooms; gusty
> Emotions on wet roads on autumn nights; . . .
> These are the measures destined for her soul.   (67)

> The brightness
> Of arms, the will opposed to cold, fate
> In its cavern, wings subtler than any mercy,
> These were the psalter of their sybils.   (i)

This resemblance can be explained by an equation appearing in one of the rejected stanzas for *An Examination of the Hero*, where Stevens decides that "The self-same rhythm/ Moves in lamenting and the fatal,/ The bold, obedience to Ananke" (*OP*, 83). This is to say that the same feeling underlies both the elegiac and the stoic; but the formulation was made before Stevens had found a stoic style to substitute for his elegies, and the elegiac strain found in this first canto persists through a great deal of *Examination of the Hero*.

In the pastiche of the second canto, the elegiac finality is dropped, and we see in this poem the strain on Stevens' language as soon as he envisages the pull to transcendence starting up from the mass and not down from the soul. He invokes first the archaic belief in a providential God, a belief which once drew up to heroism men like his Pennsylvania Dutch ancestors — "The Got whome we serve is able to deliver/ Us"; but he then speaks as the guitarist for whom belief would be a friend:

> Good chemistry, good common man, what
> Of that angelic sword?

or "Good air, good friend, what is there in life?" (175). The angelic sword, now debased to the convulsive chemistry of dynamite, gives way to a heroic masculine figure, described in language very much like the language used to evoke Lady Lowzen, a magician of the imagination who delivers us from the diabolic insinuations of meaninglessness. This deliverer is

> Captain, the man of skill, the expert
> Leader, the creator of bursting color
> And rainbow sortilege, the savage weapon
> Against enemies, against the prester,
> Presto, whose whispers prickle the spirit.   (ii)

This conjuror, summoned in familiar heapings of appositions, is an old survivor, but he is hardly a native of the austere world in which the pears are not nudes or viols or anything else: in the world of the Hero he is in fact an interloper. The hero's ultimate exaltation must be in soberer colors than rainbow sortilege. The nonsense syllables of distrust which Stevens uses to name the captain's opposite ("the prester/ Presto"), like the names of Lady Lowzen by Howzen, conclude the over-rhetorical bubble of praise. It seems that a hero must be made not by flashy prestidigitation, but by stricter practice based on a commoner discipline, outlined in the fourth canto.

Once one has spent the morning practicing exercises, scales, arpeggios, and chords; once the afternoon is spent reading about music and the evening in reflecting on it; then and only then it may be that virtuosity, based on that very hum-drum routine, can arise of itself, in an effortless mastery. Stevens' claim is that the process of creation is not miraculous, but can be laid out quite as flatly, as colloquially, and as scientifically as a recipe:

> At the piano, scales, arpeggios
> And chords, the morning exercises,
> The afternoon's reading, the night's reflection,
> That's how to produce a virtuoso.

This recipe is followed by a tone poem in which the piano mimics a submarine voyage in a fantastic cascade of notes, but there is no primitive wonder expressed at the mimesis. The closing comment is the cool remark of the connoisseur of notes who "places" the virtuoso's effort: "The mountain collapses. Chopiniana." (iv)

No speculative connoisseurship, in the end, can substitute for the admiration Stevens wants to express lyrically for the hero, and yet religious overtones are forbidden to his search for "the neutral centre, the ominous element,/ The single-colored, colorless, primitive" (242). He makes repeated essays in possible languages of admiration, trying on each one, so to speak. Before the summary training recipe above, he had tried mathematical proportion statements in awkward combination with words of the sublime:

> These sudden sublimations
> Are to combat what his exaltations
> Are to the unaccountable prophet or
> What any fury to its noble centre. (iii)

After his recipe, he proceeds to the injunctions of taste, taken from the book of interior decoration:

> . . . Devise. Make him of mud,
> For every day. In a civiler manner,
> Devise, devise, and make him of winter's
> Iciest core, a north star, central
> In our oblivion, of summer's
> Imagination, the golden rescue:
> The bread and wine of the mind, permitted
> In an ascetic room, its table
> Red as a red table-cloth, its windows
> West Indian. (vi)

This sculptor's program, too elaborate and too laden with the superlative, provokes in Stevens a series of speculations on cultural fashions, on the classic hero of war versus the bourgeois hero of peace, speculations in which Stevens tries the offhand and casual tone of an experienced journalist, a collector of types:

> *Gazette Guerrière.* A man might happen
> To prefer *L'Observateur de la Paix*, since
> The hero of the Gazette and the hero
> Of *L'Observateur*, the classic hero
> And the bourgeois, are different, much.
> The classic changed. There have been many,
> And there are many bourgeois heroes. (vii)

For this worldly surveyor, heroes are "things for public gardens,/ . . . men suited to public ferns." And even the concession to the imagery of a romantic tryst is given a denatured slant: the hero-to-be goes to his destiny like a lover, true, but this lover is "mumbling a secret, passionate message," incapable of the high declamation of drama native to the tragic and aristocratic hero.

Because his admiration is not yet harmonious, Stevens, appearing now as a skeleton, flagellates himself into gaudy enthusiasm. There is no irony in the unqualified endorsement of a "robust" parade for his hero, since it puts flesh, he tells us, on the skeleton's bones, and provides a new religious experience as the aesthete feeds on the common:

> But a profane parade, the basso
> Preludes a-rub, a-rub-rub, for him that
> Led the emperor astray, the tom trumpets
> Curling round the steeple and the people,
> The elephants of sound, the tigers
> In trombones roaring for the children,
> Young boys resembling pastry, hip-hip,
> Young men as vegetables, hip-hip,
> Home and the fields give praise, hurrah, hip,
> Hip, hip, hurrah. Eternal morning . . .
> Flesh on the bones. The skeleton throwing
> His crust away eats of this meat, drinks
> Of this tabernacle, this communion,
> Sleeps in the sun no thing recalling.   (xi)

A-rub, a-rub-rub, and tum-ti-tum and ohoyaho, ohoo, and hip hip hurrah are to the common mass what rainbow sortilege is to the elite, or so Stevens likes to think, and the transformations of the *profanum vulgus* into vegetables and pastry, food for the skeleton even though expressed in a comic "lingua franca," do not differ in principle from the rejected transfigurations of the emptily hyperbolic "imagination's Latin" in the tenth canto:

> And if the phenomenon, magnified, is
> Further magnified, sua voluntate,

Beyond his circumstance, projected
High, low, far, wide, against the distance
In parades like several equipages,
Painted by mad-men, seen as magic,
Leafed out in adjectives as private
And peculiar and appropriate glory,
Even enthroned on rainbows in the sight
Of the fishes of the sea, the colored
Birds and people of this too voluminous
Air-earth — Can we live on dry descriptions,
Feel everything starving except the belly
And nourish ourselves on crumbs of whimsy?   (x)

At this point in the poem, Stevens can apparently dismiss his whimsical exaltations but not his hurrahing profanities — those he cherishes in his courtship of "the real" and the anonymous. The celestial additive "more" [11] and its comparative accompaniments are applied not to heavenly enchantment, as they once were (in Stevens' frequent phrases like "diviner love," "beyond the genius of the sea," "ghostlier demarcations, keener sounds"), but to the less-than-human; the emblem of the hero seems

To stand taller than a person stands, has
A wider brow, large and less human
Eyes and bruted ears: the man-like body
Of a primitive. He walks with a defter
And lither stride. His arms are heavy
And his breast is greatness. All his speeches
Are prodigies in longer phrases.   (ix)

This is the remembered comparative of Stevens turned inside out, the goldener nude of a later day become aborigine. In *Notes*, Stevens will derisively repudiate this accommodation to the primitive and common, this submersion of the discriminative self into the crowd at the parade:

> To sing jubilas at exact, accustomed times,
> To be crested and wear the mane of a multitude
> And so, as part, to exult with its great throat,
>
> To speak of joy and to sing of it, borne on
> The shoulders of joyous men, to feel the heart
> That is the common, the bravest fundament,
>
> This is a facile exercise.   (398)

It is in fact the facilest exercise, as the next facile is to detach oneself from the crowd chorus and sing or play a solo on one's instrument, attempting a personal enhancing of the hero to supplement mob veneration.[12] The "difficultest rigor" is to do neither but to rest in the moment untransformed, yet to be shaken by it as if it were.

Stevens' various attempts to evoke a hero — the visionary less-is-more of the primitive, the offhand tone of the man of the world judging judiciously between heroes, the training manual, the book of decorative taste, the appositions of sortilege, and the hypnotic rhythms and feminine endings of the fourteenth canto — all are subordinate to the larger rhetorical frame of the poem, which governs its discrimination, logic, and study. The aesthetic of the common finally demands a sober rational statement of just what a hero is and is not, and of how he arises. To this end, Stevens' generative chains of logic are forged in a succession of sequential topic sentences:

> To grasp the hero, the eccentric
> On a horse, in a plane . . . (iv)

The common man is the common hero.
The common hero is the hero.
Imprimatur.   (v)

Unless we believe in the hero, what is there
To believe?   (vi)

              . . . The classic hero
And the bourgeois are different, much.   (vii)

The hero is not a person.   (viii)

If the hero is not a person, the emblem
Of him . . . seems
To stand taller than a person stands.   (ix)

And if the phenomenon, magnified, is
Further magnified . . .
              — Can we live on dry descriptions?   (x)

It is not an image. It is a feeling.
There is no image of the hero.
There is a feeling as definition.   (xii)

              . . . The hero
Acts in reality, adds nothing
To what he does.   (xiii)

After the hero, the familiar
Man makes the hero artificial.
But was the summer false? The hero?   (xvi)

These topic sentences preserve, as core, a steady quasi-rational progress quite different from the narrative motion of *The*

Comedian as the Letter C, the moody undulations of *Owl's Clover*, the strict riddling links of *Decorations*, or the series of antitheses in *The Blue Guitar*. These hypotheses of pseudo-logical statement will serve Stevens very well in the future as a meditative armature for long poems, as a check on his impulse toward the purely decorative, and as an incentive to that plain propounding so intrinsic to his later style:

> . . . Instead of allegory
> We have and are the man, capable
> Of his brave quickenings, the human
> Accelerations that seem inhuman.   (xii)

Stevens never abandoned these strings of topic sentences as a method of making a poem: the late notes for a projected poem in eleven stanzas, to be called "Abecedarium of Finesoldier," resemble the sentences excerpted above: [13]

I
I am bound by the will of other men.

II
Only one purpose exists but it is not mine

III
I must impale myself on reality

IV
Invisible fate becomes visible

V
Cry out against the commander so that I obey

VI
In the uproar of cymbals I stand still

VII

They are equally hapless in the contagion innate in
    their numbers

VIII

The narrative stops . . . Good-bye to the narration.

IX

As great as a javelin, as futile, as old

X

But did he have any value as a person.

Although the last "sentence" is missing, the sense of outline
is very strong. Both *Credences of Summer* and *The Auroras
of Autumn* seem to be composed on this model, but the longer
late poems, though they contain such propositions, seem less
formally determined by them.

The outline of "Abecedarium of Finesoldier" (perhaps because it is just an outline) seems moving as it stands, but the
danger in the logical frame is a prosy flatness which Stevens does
not escape, notably in stanzas which read like the prose, however highly wrought, of *The Necessary Angel*:

> The hero
> Acts in reality, adds nothing
> To what he does. He is the heroic
> Actor and act but not divided.
> It is a part of his conception
> That he be not conceived, being real.
> Say that the hero is his nation,
> In him made one.   (xiii)

Even Stevens seems to have recoiled temporarily from this extreme imitation of philosophic discourse (though it will recur

in *Esthétique du Mal*), and he follows it with a flurry of feminine endings, musical rhythm, florid words, and incantation:

> A thousand crystals' chiming voices,
> Like the shiddow-shaddow of lights revolving
> To momentary ones, are blended,
> In hymns, through iridescent changes,
> Of the apprehending of the hero.   (xiv)

These uncertainties of effort succeeding each other in the poem make it one of Stevens' lesser claims to success in a long form, but in their discordance they refine our responses to the considerable number of different discourses Stevens permits himself.

In reading the best of Stevens, we sense how "things inward and outward [are] held/ In such an even balance," [14] how delicately his various tendencies are poised, when the stoic is not too harshly repressing the elegiac, when desire is not entirely delusive, when the imaginative is not violently sacrificed to the logical, or vice versa. Such a balance, a premonition of the greater poems to come, appears in the fine closing of *Examination of the Hero*. The stanza begins in bleak elegy of the heroic moment, now lapsed:

> Each false thing ends. The bouquet of summer
> Turns blue and on its empty table
> It is stale and the water is discolored.
> True autumn stands then in the doorway.

Reason draws the abstract moral from the saddened instances:

> After the hero, the familiar
> Man makes the hero artificial.

And then logic, with that hopeful lift that the fertile swarming of the mind always produces in Stevens, presses its alternatives:

> But was the summer false? The hero?
> How did we come to think that autumn
> Was the veritable season, that familiar
> Man was the veritable man?

The poet's mind, resentful at its own credulity in believing disillusion necessarily truer than admiration, reverts passionately to its summer experience, and the poem almost lapses into the superlative sentimentality of primitivism:

> So
>
> Summer, jangling the savagest diamonds and
> Dressed in its azure-doubled crimsons
> May truly bear its heroic fortunes —

But the motley streaked and sashed of the plus gaudiest vir is not to carry the day here: a more isolated and more somber hero rises in the last line, as summer

> May truly bear its heroic fortunes
> For the large, the solitary figure.   (xvi)

When Stevens moves freely and confidently back and forth among his intuitions, we sense a respect for all versions of experience: the claims of logic and the claims of metaphor, the vitality of observation and the vitality of fantasy, the pressure of accuracy and the resisting pressure of longing. The pitch is more natural here than anywhere else in the poem. In a fable like "Mrs. Alfred Uruguay" (248–250), the poetic persona splinters in two: into the nay-saying lady of the title who, like Nanzia Nunzio of *Notes*, wants bare reality; and the romanticized youth, "a lover with phosphorescent hair," who is attempting his own *Examination of the Hero*, creating out of the bones of martyred soldiers "the ultimate elegance: the imagined land." His easy victory includes no redemption of the lady, who is simply annihilated.

All through *Parts of a World*, one side or another of Stevens' expressiveness seems to be restrained, ignored, or falsified, in violent seesaws of effort: one moment he is the latest freed man, and the next he is the well-dressed man with the beard speaking his own epitaph — "It can never be satisfied, the mind, never" (247). Striking though these stances are, they are incomplete to readers who, knowing the entire sensibility of the volume, long to see all the variety collected together without indignity to any part. What we desire, Stevens desired, and found his way to — a long poem that incorporates the verbal flourishes of *The Comedian as the Letter C* with the myths of *Owl's Clover*, the taciturnity of *Decorations* with the simplicities of *The Blue Guitar*, the logical tones of *Examination of the Hero* with the fantasies of the romantic Flora Lowzen, and so on — "the complicate, the amassing harmony" achieved in *Notes toward a Supreme Fiction*.

VII. The Amassing Harmony

> It was not a choice
> Between excluding things. It was not a choice
> Between, but of.

The poems gathered under the title *Notes toward a Supreme Fiction* (1942) [1] seem hardly to need commentary, familiar as they have already become. We know the Arabian and the MacCullough and Canon Aspirin simply in their fated presences, and no longer question their ample existence. It takes in fact a conscious effort to imagine their nonexistence, their coming to be, their settling into place in the poem, just as it is a surprise to remember that those necessary and ever quotable propositions scattered through the poem were once inchoate. Stevens' great originality is lost in our long attachment to his resonance, and his poem, as it approaches the canonical prime of thirty years, is by now well on its way to acquiring the patina of acquaintance that smooths the surface of any remarkable work; it almost receives the bland nods we give to even the most arresting lines once they are aged a generation. Like the ephebe, we need to "become an ignorant man again," to see the poem new-born.

The flawless energy of *Notes* is matched by an unusual forthrightness, so that the poem feels at once both liberated and restrained: liberated in its fancifulness, its fables, its many manners, but restrained in its soberer forms of assertion and its more muted resolutions. Paradoxically, Stevens' willingness to abate the claims of imagination invigorates the verse; [2] the will that had, for so many years, strained toward an aspiring apotheosis is deflected now into an exhilaration of manner and a lightening of mood in all directions. Stevens is freed into equilibrium: released from protesting too much, he can vest himself in easier language and motion. No longer his own protagonist-comedian, he relinquishes his mantle to the new learner, his successor the ephebe, and instructs him concerning the Supreme Fiction under three broad, but stern, headings, which give the poem its extremely satisfactory triadic plan, so much firmer than the structures of its predecessors.

Notes is memorable not only for its personifications, as Frank Doggett has suggested,[3] but also for their attendant fables. It immortalizes not mythical objects, like the transcendent Statue, Serpent, or Trash Can of *Owl's Clover*, but rather objects which are quotidian, recognizable, accessible, or at least naturalized. One by one those significant figures are created: the Arabian, the Ephebe, the MacCullough, the Man in the Old Coat,[4] the President, General du Puy, the Planter, Nanzia Nunzio, the Blue Woman, the Lasting Visage, the Captain and Bawda, Canon Aspirin and his Sister, the Angel, the Fat Girl. Though they are allegorical, they represent the tangible rather than the desired, and they elicit that rueful mixture of feeling in which Stevens is most himself — a compound of scholarly irony, dry elegy, amusement, commiseration, respect, ethereality, and wryness. In the poem he pours forth, like the scholar of "Somnambulisma," "the fine fins, the gawky beaks, the personalia,/ Which, as a man feeling everything, were his" (304). His mind is fertile with illustrations named lightly and often humorously, but with a delicacy of feeling in which reasons for admiration are unassumingly put.

The Planter, for instance, is sparingly given us through his sense of place — his affectionate memory of the maternal pink land from which he came, his faithful cultivation of his blue island and its citrus trees, and his yearning for the lush southern island of ultimate sexual pineapples and bananas.[5] But the Planter is dead now, and the poem is suffused with a restrained mourning of the present neglect of his island:

> On a blue island in a sky-wide water
> The wild orange trees continued to bloom and to bear,
> Long after the planter's death. A few lines remained,
>
> Where his house had fallen, three scraggy trees weighted
> With garbled green. These were the planter's turquoise
> And his orange blotches, these were his zero green. (II, v)

After the setting, in this funerary inscription, there should follow the eulogy, and so it does, but not in those forced positive terms which we might have expected from Stevens' former incarnations of the heroic. Here in quadruple negatives Stevens offers the mildest comment, the most diffident praise:

> An unaffected man in a negative light
> Could not have borne his labor nor have died
> Sighing that he should leave the banjo's twang.

Put positively, it might become: "He lived in a positive light, a man deeply affected by his islands, and therefore he could bear his labor, and could die, in spite of exile and desire, sighing that he should have to leave even so simple and small a pleasure as his banjo's twang." [6]

Stevens' tact in his negative praise is also a tact in vision. The visionary moment is no longer described in high-pitched affirmations, but is quieted to a more human tone:

> Perhaps there are moments of awakening
> Extreme, fortuitous, personal, in which

We more than awaken, sit on the edge of sleep,
As on an elevation, and behold —

Behold what? A voluminous master folded in his fire? or a great
bosom, beard and being, alive with age? Not in this poem: rather
we behold a dissolving, not a presence; a loosening of strictures,
not a revelation; we

> . . . sit on the edge of sleep
> As on an elevation, and behold
> The academies like structures in a mist.

The choice Stevens makes — repetition over revelation, life's
nonsense over evangel — is reflected in the tendency, more visibly present in *Notes* than ever before, to close his poems on
a mitigation, a minor key, rather than on declaration or outright
dismissal. To this end, he takes up a favorite formula again, and
it becomes characteristic of the poem: not X (or Y or Z) but
A — in which X, Y, and Z are possible extremes (of canoniza-
tion, of repudiation, of immersion, of abstraction) and A is a
middle term, a mean which he proposes as a possible finality:

> It is of him, ephebe, to make, to confect
> The final elegance, not to console
> Nor sanctify, but plainly to propound.   (I, x)

Earlier affirmations are denied: "the air is not a mirror but bare
board" (I, iv); "it was neither heaven nor hell" (III, iv); and
new choices are made, as Canon Aspirin concludes:

> It was not a choice
> Between excluding things. It was not a choice
> Between, but of.   (III, vi)

The denial of antithetical extremes and the search for the middle accommodation preclude the mythical, whether celestial or demonic, and bring Stevens not only to his concluding mitigations but also to his long search, pursued throughout *Notes*, for the proper poetry of the middle term.

Poetry can no longer be a duet with the undertaker or a human song interpreting the inhuman ocean. Polarities are abandoned, at least theoretically, and in their place we find either a constant motion back and forth, as the hermit "comes and goes and comes and goes all day" (I, ii), or else a recurrent convergence. The poems embodying movement sometimes show it as perpetual oscillation "from that ever-early candor to its late plural" (I, iii), but in one of the best versions of change Stevens prefers to show us, in anticipation of the ancient Omega of *New Haven*, the last stages of senescence in "a lasting visage in a lasting bush," the inching toward exhausted repetitiousness which precedes the energetic return of the primitive. As a whole, the canto exists thematically in a gross imbalance, as seventeen lines of stony sleep are countered by four lines of resurrection:

> A lasting visage in a lasting bush,
> A face of stone in an unending red,
> Red-emerald, red-slitted-blue, a face of slate,
>
> An ancient forehead hung with heavy hair,
> The channel slots of rain, the red-rose-red
> And weathered and the ruby-water-worn,
>
> The vines around the throat, the shapeless lips,
> The frown like serpents basking on the brow,
> The spent feeling leaving nothing of itself,
>
> Red-in-red repetitions never going
> Away, a little rusty, a little rouged,
> A little roughened and ruder, a crown

The eye could not escape, a red renown
Blowing itself upon the tedious ear.
An effulgence faded, dull cornelian

Too venerably used. That might have been.
It might and might have been. But as it was,
A dead shepherd brought tremendous chords from hell

And bade the sheep carouse. Or so they said.
Children in love with them brought early flowers
And scattered them about, no two alike.   (III, iii)

This vision of the adamant but overthrown Jehovah is a survival, by way of "Ozymandias," of Stevens' view of the statue in Africa. Jahweh in the burning bush is metamorphosed into "a carved king found in a jungle, huge/ And weathered" (*OP*, 108), and the colossus is ominously unnamed. It is not *the* head of a known sovereign, but *a* head, shapeless, half overgrown, obscure, generalized like a fallen Mayan statue.

The poem becomes a play on articles, definite and indefinite, so that in spite of the grand structure of imbalance between the long sentence describing the dead god and the short sentence describing the Orphic Christ, there is nevertheless a balance occurring between the panoramic and the scrutinized:

A lasting visage in
a lasting bush
a face of stone in
an unending   red
                    red-emerald
                    red-slitted blue

a face of slate
an ancient forehead hung
    with heavy hair   *the* channel slots of rain
                    the red-rose-red and weathered and
                    the ruby-water-worn,
                    the vines around
                    the throat

```
                              the shapeless lips
                              the frown like serpents basking on
                              the brow

                              the spent feeling leaving nothing of itself
                              red-in-red repetitions never going away
a little                      rusty
a little                      rouged
a little                      roughened and
                              ruder
a crown                       the eye could not escape
a red renown blowing
    itself upon               the tedious ear
an effulgence faded,
              dull cornelian too venerably used.
```

Stevens begins (via the indefinite article) in an overview of the head, darts momentarily closer in an attempt to define its redness, returns heavily to the heavy face, and then (with the definite article), peers minutely at the statue, detailing in turn its channels, its redness, its vines, throat, lips, frown, and brow. The poem then examines with equal definiteness its own abstraction of the statue; instead of nouns like "lips" and "throat" we have nouns like "feeling" and "repetitions." As Stevens said in his commentary: "Adoration is a form of face to face. When the compulsion to adoration grows less, or merely changes, unless the change is complete, the face changes and, in the case of a face at which one has looked for a long time, changes that are slight may appear to the observer to be melodramatic. We struggle with the face, see it everywhere & try to express the changes" (*L*, 438). The changes are first expressed psychologically in close perspective, as feelings and repetitions, but later they are distanced, and are expressed metaphorically in relation to the actual statue, which has been removed once again to a generalized perspective by the indefinite article: "a crown, a red renown . . . an effulgence." The definite article, at this point, has been appropriated by the perceiver — *the* eye, *the* ear. The bridge between the long predominance of the definite article in the middle of the poem and the new reappearance of the indefinite article in "*a* crown" is the false "indefinite article" in the adverbial groups "*a* little rusty," "*a* little rouged," "*a* little roughened."

There are several meanings played off against each other in the poem. The intent of the poem is certainly, as Stevens said (*L*, 438), to show the necessity of improvisation. The statue, *usée* (Stevens puns on the French sense in saying the statue is "too venerably used"), brings about, at the end, its own counterforce. The difficulty with this resurrective "meaning," one might say, is that the shepherd, so carefully introduced with an indefinite article to parallel the lasting visage, is a much less successful invention than the colossal head, which is, whatever its debt to Shelley, remarkable. So the second "meaning" emerges: a study of deity in decline. Stevens's best interest is concentrated on this long one-sentence description, which is itself dual: what the deity looks like, and how his decline feels to us. These two motions, the objective and the subjective, are themselves each composed of definite and indefinite parts, making them mirror images of each other. In short, though the poem as a whole tilts out of balance, with very little space given to resurrection, the first long sentence, describing the fallen god, is in itself perfectly symmetrical. Though this canto could be called, then, from its superficial form, a poem of adversaries, it seems more truly a poem interested in definition of a single pole by closer and closer approximations, with each slight shift of emphasis marking a further advance in precision.

The improvisation of newness in decline which Stevens illustrates rather weakly in the end of the canto concerning the colossal head is treated much more stringently in the famous poem on birdsong (II, vi), which is, for all its bizarre nature, one of the best cantos in *Notes*. Here, the intervention of the dead shepherd is represented by the intervention of the poet-sparrow in his coppice, but instead of ending with a flowery and pastoral new dispensation, Stevens foresees the eventual staleness of any heavenly sound. Stevens' remark about this canto is equally true of the lasting visage: "In this monotony the desire for change creates change" (*L*, 438). Here, the monotony refers to the sound made by all birds but the sparrow: they say "ké-ké" while the sparrow says "bethou me." On the other hand, as Stevens said earlier, the "tutoie-moi" of the sparrow is equally tedious: "All this insistent tutoyant becomes monotonous and merges into a single sound. So faces tend to become one face as if they had met a glass blower's destiny; as if a glass blower, for all the bubbles he blows, blows only one, and so he does" (*L*, 435). There cannot be any naive stance taken, at this moment, toward the sparrow, since this new sound he makes has in it the potential for monotony just as surely as did the previous sounds. The poem, in short, is a forcibly intellectual one, in which the mind is not for one moment allowed to disregard its knowledge of previous tedium and subside into a simple, momentary, and forgetful enjoyment of a new sound. In intellectual, though not experiential terms, the poem illustrates Keats's bitterness to Reynolds:

> It is a flaw
> In happiness, to see beyond our bourn, —
> It forces us in summer skies to mourn,
> It spoils the singing of the nightingale.

"Bethou," says Stevens in a prose *post facto* assent to his sparrow, "is the spirit's own seduction" (*L*, 438), but the violence of his Shelleyan model probably accounts for some of Stevens' violence in the poem. Though it is all very well for him to give ornithological explanations for his adjectives (the wren is bloody because "wrens are fighters") these bits of natural history do nothing to explain the feeling that leads him to apply the most defamatory epithets he can find to the singing birds. The hatred he feels for the decline into monotony of their "ké-ké" also accounts for his libels on bishops, choristers, and glass-blowers, anticipated in "Parochial Theme":

> The voices
> Have shapes that are not yet fully themselves,
>
> Are sounds blown by a blower into shapes,
> The blower squeezed to the thinnest *mi* of falsetto.   (191)

The sparrow begins his call in pure self-congratulatory eminence, but by stealthy increments joins the petrified singers.

> Bethou me, said sparrow, to the crackled blade,
> And you, and you, bethou me as you blow,
> When in my coppice you behold me be.
>
> Ah, ké! the bloody wren, the felon jay,
> Ké-ké, the jug-throated robin pouring out,
> Bethou, bethou, bethou me in my glade.

"Bethou is intended to be heard; it and ké-ké, which is inimical, are opposing sounds," says Stevens (*L*, 438); but already, by its proximity to the robin's ké-ké as well as by its insistence, "bethou" loses its ingratiating quality. Nevertheless, the distinction between the two sounds appears again:

> There was such idiot minstrelsy in rain,
> So many clappers going without bells,
> That these bethous compose a heavenly gong.

Bethous, then, are celestial, "heavenly"; but there is something vaguely ecclesiastical and perhaps "heavenly" about those idiot bells. As we are told that the bloody wren and felon jay are putatively celestial choristers, exegetes, and bishops, the two domains of self-regarding divinity begin to fuse:

> One voice repeating, one tireless chorister,
> The phrases of a single phrase, ké-ké,
> A single text, granite monotony,
>
> One sole face, like a photograph of fate,
> Glass-blower's destiny, bloodless episcopus,
> Eye without lid, mind without any dream —
>
> These are of minstrels lacking minstrelsy.

Monotony unites the separate sounds into one, as "a number of faces become one, as all fates become a common fate, as all the bottles blown by a glass blower become one, and as all bishops grow to look alike" (*L*, 438). These satiric exaggerations, though written after the poem, embody the cynicism directed earlier at the birds, and show the true center of revulsion in the canto, the anger at the inevitable exhaustion of religious myth. Though the celestial and ecclesiastical are theoretically used as metaphorical vehicles to illustrate the tedium of the natural, actually *they* are the true subject of the poem, and the call of the sparrow, just because it is so godlike, with its Shelleyan overtones of "Be thou *me*" as well as its overt "Be*thou* me," is all the more delusive just because it seems so heavenly at first. As soon as it is taken up by the masses, so to speak, it will take on its own dreadful monotony and petrify from myth to dogma. Stevens condemns its last rigidities:

> These are of minstrels lacking minstrelsy
> Of an earth in which the first leaf is the tale
> Of leaves, in which the sparrow is a bird

Of stone, that never changes. Bethou him, you
And you, bethou him and bethou. It is
A sound like any other. It will end.

It is no accident that the next poem in *Notes* begins, "We have
not the need of any paradise,/ We have not the need of any se-
ducing hymn," since by the end of the canto the birdsong "Bethou" has taken on a third meaning; the bird asks to be called
"thou" as God is called "thou" in hymns and prayers.

If bethou is the spirit's own seduction, the spirit can turn in
cruel reflexiveness and say, like Stevens in his great recantation,

> . . . He looked in a glass of the earth and thought he lived
> in it . . .
> It was only a glass because he looked in it. It was nothing
> he could be told.   (507)

The perfect comprehension of cyclical change and monotony
in a single poem, under the cold aegis of the too knowledgeable
mind, makes the innocent and spontaneous birdsong at once
vicious and idiot. For all its difficulty, the poem has the fascination of complete, if eccentric, self-possession both in its breadth
of view and in its final contemptuous dismissal of all sound.
Stevens will be glad enough of a tireless chorister in a later
poem, "Not Ideas about the Thing but the Thing Itself," but
for the moment the interchange between the celestial and the
earthly is no giving and taking but a perpetual delusion.

When, in *Notes*, centrality rather than motion asserts its cen-
tripetal magnetism, Stevens forsakes his metaphors of interchange, decay, or winged passage for the classic allegory of
unity, a marriage. Here, understandably enough in such a
heroic effort toward a planisphere for his antipodes, Stevens
fails:

There was a mystic marriage in Catawba,
At noon it was on the mid-day of the year
Between a great captain and the maiden Bawda.

It was their ceremonial hymn: Anon
We loved but would no marriage make. Anon
The one refused the other one to take,

Foreswore the sipping of the marriage wine.
Each must the other take not for his high,
His puissant front nor for her subtle sound

The shoo-shoo-shoo of secret cymbals round
Each must the other take as sign, short sign
To stop the whirlwind, balk the elements.

The great Captain loved the ever-hill Catawba
And therefore married Bawda, whom he found there,
And Bawda loved the captain as she loved the sun.

Or, two things equal to a third thing (the land, the sun) are equal to each other. The impersonality of the marriage is reflected in the final comment:

They married well because the marriage-place
Was what they loved. It was neither heaven nor hell,
They were love's characters come face to face.   (III, iv)

Presumably this may be read as an allegory representing the marriage in nature of reason and imagination. Stevens, ever suspicious of a potential incest in the reflexive operations of consciousness, here legalizes this union by the participation of both masculine and feminine principles in the phenomena of nature. But the marriage harks back in meaning to the high transcendence of other "mystic marriages" with the supernatural (to Christ, to Lady Poverty, and so on) and at the same time resorts in language to a spate of primitivisms: archaism, medievalism, simplistic narration.

It is one of the nostalgias, to escape the intricacies of self, and love someone else "in Christ," as the homilies put it, or "in Catawba," as Stevens has it. But the physical world of natural phenomena, as Stevens knew in his stricter accountings, has no sanctions of its own which can assuage the isolation of the mind: whatever the relations of the mind's faculties, only the mind itself can authorize them. The true command of the mind over its context is figured in *Notes* in another and happier use of the marriage figure (II, iv):

Two things of opposite natures seem to depend on one another, as

a man	depends on	a woman
day	on	night
the imagined	on	the real.

This is the origin of change.

Winter   and   spring
          (cold copulars)
                embrace

and forth the particulars of rapture come.

Music   falls on   silence
        like a sense
            a passion
        that we feel, not understand.

Morning	and	afternoon
	are clasped together, and	
North	and	South
	are an intrinsic couple, and	
sun	and	rain
	a plural.	

The rather coarse and stationary pledging of the Captain to Bawda is replaced here by a tentative and gradual merging of polarities, in which dependency becomes embrace, embrace becomes bringing-forth, and these partial or willed unions finally become necessary and intrinsic, as the opposites no longer consciously embrace but rather are clasped together and become a verbal identity in a dual noun — a couple, a plural.

It is only a step beyond that identity to a Wordsworthian communion in which "The partaker partakes of that which changes him," and where all relations — the filial, the obediential, the geographical — become one. The supremacy of the mind, which under all random associations can perceive the ideal of relation, then asserts itself confidently in its right to call all things by its own name, since it interacts with them all:

> Follow after, O my companion, my fellow, my self,
> Sister and solace, brother and delight.

The minimal but progressive nearings of relation as the lyric moves from line to line press on to warrant the identities at the close, and though this engulfing is perhaps not Stevens' most unforced version of the soul's place in the world, the gradual accelerations from hypothesis to feeling are not thrust on us bluntly, but strongly based and carefully prepared, and are, in their triple structure, exquisitely suited to the triads they inhabit.[7]

As I have said earlier about some of the canto endings in

Notes, the resolving term is often expressed after its negations — not X, nor Y, but Z. An expanded version of this formula gives some of the sections of the poem their firmness of form: there are long palinodes, for example, where Stevens hardens himself against some of his earlier addictions — participation in the communal, represented by mass parades; rhetorical transcendence like St. Jerome's (II, i); or the subtler addiction to metaphor, that impulse to variation which produced the kaleidoscope of "Sea Surface Full of Clouds." Now only memory, not invention, is allowed to assert its claim, and even dreams are not permitted to embroider on the world. There is a long restriction of desire in one canto (III, ii):

> The blue woman, linked and lacquered, at her window
> Did not desire that feathery argentines
> Should be cold silver, neither that frothy clouds
>
> Should foam, be foamy waves, should move like them,
> Nor that the sexual blossoms should repose
> Without their fierce addictions, nor that the heat
>
> Of summer, growing fragrant in the night
> Should strengthen her abortive dreams and take
> In sleep its natural form. It was enough
>
> For her that she remembered.

The options rejected by the conscious woman of blue phenomena are all the temptations of a superlatively capable soul which wishes at first to reduce the world to its linguistic, metaphorical, and intellectual mental presence — to make the cinquefoil bluish silver, like its French name, instead of yellow; to make the froth of clouds become frothy foam of waves; to cool down the sexual coral dogwood to the soul's reposeful tones. On the other hand, this blue woman is also tempted to deny her cool lacquered state and become primitive, to strengthen her own abortive dreams into a fantasy of heat.[8] These are the temptations of poetic identification, where the frothy clouds and the foamy waves are one, where etymology is reality as argentines become silver, where allotropic forms of water, like waves and clouds, are merged, and where the shrunken dimensions of reality can be filled out in the expansions of dream.

However, the blue woman's apprehension of "reality," after she has resisted the seduction of desire, is in itself radically metaphorical, and Stevens' poem declares itself as more than a simple yea-saying to "the real," whether in memory or in the present prospect. The will to change essences is denied, it is true, but in its place we find an indulgent humanizing of the argentines, coupled with a consciously fanciful, because purely verbal, identity between frothy clouds and frothy blooms:

> It was enough
>
> For her that she remembered: the argentines
> Of spring come to their places in the grape leaves
> To cool their ruddy pulses, the frothy clouds
>
> Are nothing but frothy clouds; the frothy blooms
> Waste without puberty; and afterward,
> When the harmonious heat of August pines
>
> Enters the room, it drowses and is the night.
> It was enough for her that she remembered.

The items in the landscape are allowed a self-fulfillment; the ruddy pulses of flowers are not willed into a coldness they do not feel; the frothy blooms are not forced to become sexual adjuncts, but waste without puberty; and the heat is not required to serve the blue woman's dreams but is permitted to drowse and darken into pure and imageless night. The motive for this indulgence is revealed in the solicitude of the pathetic fallacy, that Golden Rule of the imagination: the mind must do unto the world as it would be done by, in a policy of mutual forbearance and concession to separate selves.

As soon as the blue woman's concession is made, the self-sufficient and continuing preoccupations of the world become present to her vision and the poem moves from the past tense into a timeless present tense of memory and perpetuity. Once she has granted to the scene its own composition, she can take a last look, attaining finally the purely visual register which prescinds from both nature's tableau and her own. The new sight, not previously "arranged" by her private will and therefore not rebelliously "rearranged" by nature, is finally revealed as she sees

> The corals of the dogwood, cold and clear,
> Cold, coldly delineating, being real,
> Clear and, except for the eye, without intrusion.

Even in this final chill purity of line and color, the claim to a direct confrontation is qualified by the strict concession — "except for the eye."

The principle of construction animating the canto of the blue woman — a phase of denial, a phase of allowance, and a consequent phase of emancipation — rises naturally from Stevens' desire in *Notes* to see extremes meeting in a mean. In the earlier poems, a stylistic confusion often occurs when, in praising the mean, Stevens uses the language of one of the extremes. Even here, his eulogy of earth in the Catawba marriage is couched in orgiastic terms rather than in the terms of a "sensible ecstasy." The real triumph of *Notes* is to find, sometimes, a rhetoric at once celebratory and minimized, where climax becomes the assertion of anticlimax. When Stevens describes young poets, he first says of them:

> These are the heroic children whom time breeds
> Against the first idea — to lash the lion —

So far, an unexceptionable statement: poets are to dominate the violence of reality. But the mastery then takes a whimsical form, as the ephebe turns violence into circus play:

> — to lash the lion,
> Caparison elephants, teach bears to juggle.   (I, v)

This is at once triumph and deprecation, as Stevens uses the rhetoric of climax ("to do X, to do Y, to do Z") combined with the increasing absurdity of the actions, so uncelestial, so suited to the ironies of earth. Though Stevens has tried such anticlimactic climaxes before, they are the pre-eminent method of *Notes*, and of course tame into a new decorum the lines that precede them in any given poem. It would not do to have serious animals put into this circus, and so the sophistication of this ending is anticipated by the equivocal early descriptions of the animals as characters in a children's cartoon:

> The lion roars at the enraging desert,
> Reddens the sand with his red-colored noise,
> Defies red emptiness to evolve his match . . .

> The elephant
> Breaches the darkness of Ceylon with blares,

> The glitter-goes on surfaces of tanks,
> Shattering velvetest far-away. The bear,
> The ponderous cinnamon, snarls in his mountain.

These animals are blood brothers to the other cartoon personages in *Notes*, who sometimes seem at first to sort ill with the
maxims they illustrate. The Arabian and the hoo-ing ocean, for
instance, make up the cartoon half of a poem (I, iii) in which
the first half is pure lyric:

> The poem refreshes life so that we share
> For a moment, the first idea . . . It satisfies
> Belief in an immaculate beginning
>
> And sends us, winged by an unconscious will,
> To an immaculate end. We move between these points:
> From that ever-early candor to its late plural
>
> And the candor of them is the strong exhilaration
> Of what we feel from what we think, of thought
> Beating in the heart as if blood newly came,
>
> An elixir, an excitation, a pure power.
> The poem, through candor, brings back a power again
> That gives a candid kind to everything.

The blurrings of grammatical reference here are familiar, as
candor seems first to be one point, then both points, then a
quality of both points, then a means to both points, and so on.
The appositions and qualifications of power and candor become
ends in themselves, magical and incantatory manipulations of
two potent words, a ringing of changes on a will to change. But
the grotesquely contrastive conclusion of the poem, shocking at
first reading, is in effect a repudiation of the vatic language of
the first half:

> We say: At night an Arabian in my room,
> With his damned hoobla-hoobla-hoobla-how,
> Inscribes a primitive astronomy

Across the unscrawled fores the future casts
And throws his stars around the floor. By day
The wood-dove used to chant his hoobla-hoo

And still the grossest iridescence of ocean
Howls hoo and rises and howls hoo and falls.
Life's nonsense pierces us with strange relation.

The technique of the poem appears in miniature in the invention of "grossest iridescence": we have had twelve lines of iridescence, and now we are given eight lines of grossness. The allegorical "meaning" of the Arabian and the Dove and the Ocean dwindle in poetic importance beside the unexpected language in which they make their appearance. (The Wordsworthian Arabian astronomer-moon, like other astronomers in Stevens, is related to the dream imagination at its nightly work; the dove carries the simple primitive response of the senses to nature; the ocean becomes, as usual, the separate physical universe.) [9] The Arabian is described maniacally, the dove nostalgically, the ocean more matter-of-factly, but all grotesquely and primitively. In the first, we see the inchoate fancy, in the second, the inchoate senses, and in the third, the inchoate ground of being, not yet intelligible, still pure sound, pure non-sense.

So the elegant responsive triad of an immaculate beginning, a winged passage, and an immaculate end is grossly attached in retrospect to the triad of its causal stimuli in the vocables of nonsense: hoobla-how, hoobla-hoo, and hoo. The last line of the canto articulates the joining of physical stimulus and imaginative response: "Life's nonsense pierces us with strange relation." Because the language of this final epigram, with the exception of the word "nonsense" which gathers to itself the vocabulary of the second part, matches the lofty tone of the first part of the poem, the total effect of the whole canto is displaced toward intelligible meaning, not toward the randomness of the second part. The supralogical "rhyme" of "ocean" with "relation" emphasizes as a matter of course the conviction of form surpassing formlessness. In these blunt confrontations — of the exquisite and the guttural, the ephebe and the animals, the candor and the hoos — we are given primary clashes of speech, as the exquisite line is rudely married to the coarse cartoon and its howls.

The more general observance in *Notes*, however, is a civilized passage from tone to tone, with a flicker of grossness, a tinge of humor, a touch of logic or illogic, as Stevens moves within the various discourses of his ample harmonium. The variable atmosphere of these virtuoso pieces is set by the first poem, which requires a different set of descriptive terms for almost every triad. The fiction of instruction is maintained in the general address of this section, but the punning internal rhymes and repetition lighten the lesson:

> Begin, ephebe, by perceiving the idea
> Of this invention, this invented world,
> The inconceivable idea of the sun.

And the passion for grand statement — "The death of one god is the death of all" — is checked by the levity of the lullaby that follows this *Götterdämmerung*:

> Let purple Phoebus lie in umber harvest,
> Let Phoebus slumber and die in autumn umber,
>
> Phoebus is dead, ephebe.

These countermovements of matter and wit can hardly be called ironic except in the lightest sense; they act out the mind's suspicions of itself without centrally impugning in any way the doctrines of the proposed Supreme Fiction,[10] and yet without maintaining the relentless irony of the *Comedian*.

The most convincing affirmations in *Notes* are those made minimally and deprecatingly, but with a conviction that reaches into the arcana of language to articulate itself, as in the brilliant minimizings of the Supreme Fiction considered in relation to the weather (I, vi). Weather is the irradiating poetry of nature, the will to change that Stevens will celebrate later in *Notes* (II, x), that freshening volatility which corresponds to changes of taste, the irrational element in man and nature which is nevertheless, in a poetic sense, so "rational."[11] Stevens conjures up, at first, a vision of the Supreme Fiction all by itself, in abstraction, not in conjunction with either landscape or man:[12] though this is a clear impossibility, and though he deprecates it as "only imagined," he nevertheless hopes to imagine it well. As usual, there are three points of reference in the poem: the weather high up in the Northern blue sky; the landscape (birds, roofs, fruits, forsythia, magnolias); and the poet thinking in his roofed house.

The first effort is to convey the abstract in its abstraction from the human mind, and so Stevens names no perceiving subject, but gives us only the possible passive to an unnamed active, free from the enclosing chiasmus of perception:

> Not to be realized
>
>   because
>
>   not to be seen
>   not to be loved or hated
>
>   because
>
> not to be realized.

If we rearrange the passage chronologically, it tells us that we first see, then "realize," and only then can love or hate. "Realization" of phenomena is the first act of the mind; loving and hating are only its appurtenances.

After this formal absence of perception, Stevens looks to the weather, the bright *scienza* of alliterative spontaneous coherence:

> Weather by Franz Hals,
>
> Brushed up by brushy winds in brushy clouds,
> Wetted by blue, colder for white.

This is the first of the three positive statements in the five expository stanzas of the canto. The other two have also to do with the spring landscape, but just as Stevens required the negatives of privative consciousness (ll. 1–3) before the exuberance of the weather could burst on the scene, so he completes the denial of landscape before he can evoke it. The Supreme Fiction, in its abstraction, is "not to be spoken to" (a verbal bridge to the earlier restrictions of consciousness) and then it is said to be

> Without   a roof
> without   first fruits
> without   the virginal of birds.

This, Stevens continues, is nature seductive but not seduced, her "dark-blown ceinture loosened, not relinquished." Into this severe asceticism breaks the pretty landscape in a trill-like dilution of the windy sky:

> Gay is, gay was, the gay forsythia
> And yellow, yellow thins the Northern blue.

The devastating musical charm of this interpenetration of flowers and sky is quickly refused by the poet, who reverts to his strictness of privative description: the abstract fiction is

> Without   a name
>   and
> Nothing   to be desired
>   if
> only   imagined.

However, just as the weather is subject to change from the birdsong babyishness of forsythia,[13] so is the poet's house subject to modification both from the sky ("My house has changed a little in the sun") and from the landscape ("The fragrance of the magnolias comes close,/ False flick, false form, but falseness close to kin").

The Supreme Fiction, not yet embodied, is "not to be seen" — its first condition — and is therefore invisible. On the other hand, it is only known to be present by its changes, and so is "visible." But these final paradoxes do not bear much elucidating, and are not meant to, lightly phrased as they are. The closing triad persists at first in the deprecatory and minimizing formulation as it tries to bring the real and the abstract together:

> The weather and the giant of the weather,
> Say the weather, the mere weather, the mere air.

Even the last affirmation, though positively put, is itself equivocal; the Supreme Fiction is "An abstraction blooded, as a man by thought." In this conclusion, the human enters only as illustration, a function suitable to this poem in which the perceiver is repeatedly eliminated. The weather (or the Supreme Fiction, since by this time they are indistinguishable) is called "an abstraction blooded," in a phrase distilled from the earlier lines concerning "thought beating in the heart, as if blood newly came" (I, iv), but the colorlessness of the conclusion is perhaps too remote after the energetic beginning.

Notes toward a Supreme Fiction contains many familiar turns, but what is new in its cantos, besides Stevens' insistence on equilibrium and centrality, and his rapidly changing tones, is a consistently dazzling manipulation of objects in action, especially in the more extended fables, like the fable of the bees (II, i–ii). We experience an assault of "violets, doves, girls, bees, and hyacinths," not to mention seraphs, jonquils, bandeaux, chronologies, and mothers. The sheer profusion of properties is bewildering:

> The old seraph, parcel-gilded, among violets
> Inhaled the appointed odor, while the doves
> Rose up like phantoms from chronologies.
>
> The Italian girls wore jonquils in their hair
> And these the seraph saw, had seen long since,
> In the bandeaux of the mothers, would see again.
>
> The bees came booming as if they had never gone,
> As if hyacinths had never gone.

We recognize Stevens' constant polarities — the celestial (seraph, gilt, doves, violets); the natural (bees and hyacinths); and the human (the girls and their mothers) — and these are linked in their similarities (purple violets and hyacinths, yellow gilt and jonquils, rising doves and bees). But it is unusual to have such a flurry of décor at each pole. The sense of "a glass aswarm with things going as far as they can" arises more often in Stevens from the deliberate confusions of syntax than from multiple points of reference. But here Stevens insists on lavish imagery as well as on rapid "logic":

> We say
> This changes and that changes. Thus the constant
>
> Violets, doves, girls, bees and hyacinths

> Are inconstant objects of inconstant cause
> In a universe of inconstancy.

After this airy summary, reflectiveness masters the scene as Stevens holds up his images in criticism and scrutinizes them in their withering declensions one by one: the possible bestial Saturnalia of the seraph,[14] the doves transmuted to clattering pigeons, and the seductiveness of Italian girls mingling with the odor of flowers to produce an acidic erotic perfume:

> This means
>
> Night-blue is an inconsistent thing. The seraph
> Is satyr in Saturn, according to his thoughts.
> It means the distaste we feel for this withered scene
>
> Is that it has not changed enough. It remains,
> It is a repetition. The bees come booming
> As if — The pigeons clatter in the air.
>
> An erotic perfume, half of the body, half
> Of an obvious acid is sure what it intends
> And the booming is blunt, not broken in subtleties.

Stevens' expertise in presenting several images at once, first in their repetitiveness and then in their change, can hardly be matched. The paralyzing sameness of a relentless spring in "a world/ Whose blunt laws make an affectation of mind" (519), the despair latent in attributing the emotions of love to pre-destined chemical changes of obvious acids, the crassness of a yearly obligatory mechanical resurrection — all easily senti-mentalized — are etched by acrid language until the dying fall of the final phrase. The speaker is hypnotized in the repetition around him: he "forgets" that he has said ten lines earlier that "the bees come booming as if they had never gone," and begins to say it again, "The bees come booming/ As if —" but breaks off, only to recur once again to that interminable sound as the last index of distaste: "And the booming is blunt, not broken in subtleties."

In the continuation of this fable there is a kindred swell of related images, and the poems, together, are an instance, taken seriously, of Stevens' axiom "Anything is beautiful if you say it is." Even the droning of the bee is beautiful, rightly seen, and the flat conclusions of the first poem beget four restless questions, as we are given that rejuvenating lift of the mind that changes perspective. The first question doubts that the resurrection is in fact mechanically ordained by Ananke:

> The President ordains the bee to be
> Immortal. The President ordains. But does
> The body lift its heavy wing, take up,
>
> Again, an inexhaustible being, rise
> Over the loftiest antagonist
> To drone the green phrases of its juvenal?

The second question expresses resentment of this perpetual and pointless reincarnation-order, a joke of the President of the Immortals on us:

> Why should the bee recapture a lost blague,
> Find a deep echo in a horn and buzz
> The bottomless trophy, new hornsman after old?

Because "no politician can command the imagination" (*NA,* 28), the metaphysical President cannot control the dazzling energy of windblown banners, even though he can direct the decorous placing of his own indoor curtains:

The President has apples on the table
And barefoot servants round him, who adjust
The curtains to a metaphysical t

And the banners of the nation flutter, burst
On the flag-poles in a red-blue dazzle, whack
At the halyards.

Whatever our determinist metaphysics, in other words, the experience of energetic free feeling flaunts its own truths, as spring, however predictable in theory, brings golden furies rising in us. This paradox prompts the third and fourth questions: why make comparisons with past springs? and what is reality if not what we feel?

Why, then, when in golden fury

Spring vanishes the scraps of winter, why
Should there be a question of returning or
Of death in memory's dream? Is spring a sleep?

The consciousness poisons its own springs of feeling by these speculations on repeated tropisms from past to present, but Stevens decides to "vanish" [15] the scraps of winter, ignore the rumblings and discontents of memory, and assert the ever new primacy of love:

This warmth is for lovers at last accomplishing
Their love, this beginning, not resuming, this
Booming and booming of the new-come bee.

It is only at the end of this brilliant stanza that we realize the pun on existence: the new-come bee is the new be-come and the new-come being. We realize it so late precisely because Stevens' brisk scenes dominate over his allegorical intent, while never concealing it.

One last, new, and striking effect in *Notes* comes at the end, in Stevens' adoption of the lyrical "I." Though he had spoken briefly in the first person in the prologue to the poem and in a line or two elsewhere, only the last three cantos of "It Must Give Pleasure" use the "I" as a continuing figure, and the singularity is not repeated in the other long poems. The "I" of the *Blue Guitar* is a dramatized character, a guitarist, but the "I" of *Notes* is Stevens himself, or a voice as close to his as the genre permits. In Stevens' continuing hesitation over a proper pronominal voice, this is one experiment, one finally to be discounted, since in the later long poems extraordinary efforts are made to avoid all first-person voices, plural as well as singular. Perhaps in an effort to justify his own reluctance toward the first person, Stevens had written in 1940, "The poet confers his identity on the reader. He cannot do this if he intrudes personally." [16] However, in *Notes*, the risk of the personal voice is undertaken in a remarkable sequence which aims at bringing the whole edifice to perfection in a complex reconciliation of tones. The final trinity of cantos is preceded by the most desperate moment in the whole poem. Repetitive, accumulative, and hysterical affirmations mount in a crescendo conveying the fear which is their origin:

> To impose is not
> To discover. To discover an order as of
> A season, to discover summer and know it,
>
> To discover winter and know it well, to find,
> Not to impose, not to have reasoned at all,
> Out of nothing to have come on major weather,
>
> It is possible, possible, possible. It must

Be possible. It must be that in time
The real will from its crude compoundings come,

Seeming, at first, a beat disgorged, unlike,
Warmed by a desperate milk. To find the real,
To be stripped of every fiction except one,

The fiction of an Absolute —

In the midst of these paroxysms, we may doubt the materialization of an Angel who "solves" the poem:

> — Angel
> Be silent in your luminous cloud and hear
> The luminous melody of proper sound.   (III, vii)

The anxious insistence of the questing present infinitives, the tempting slip into the perfect infinitive which evisages the quest as already completed, the final dubious decline into the passive infinitive as the quest becomes a stripping undergone, not an active accomplishment — these renderings of doubt cast a pall over the Angel and over Stevens' too easy "proper sound."

In the three cantos that follow, the insights of depression are not so easily repudiated. The first (III, viii), after a heroic expansion, turns despairingly on the mind's ramifying extrapolations and evasions, and ends in disgust:

> These external regions, what do we fill them with
> Except reflections, the escapades of death,
> Cinderella fulfilling herself beneath the roof?

But before this dismissive recoil, there has been a nobility of hypotheses, a "fantastic effort" which has failed. "What am I

to believe?" Stevens begins, and then embroiders in his hypo-
thethical verbs (here italicized) all yearnings and possibilities:

> If the angel in his cloud,
> Serenely *gazing* at the violent abyss,
> *Plucks* on his strings *to pluck* abysmal glory,
>
> *Leaps* downward through evening's revelations, and
> On his spredden wings, *needs* nothing but deep space,
> *Forgets* the gold centre, the golden destiny,
>
> *Grows* warm in the motionless motion of his flight,
> Am I that imagine this angel less satisfied?
> Are the wings his, the lapis-haunted air?
>
> Is it he or is it I that experience this?

The implied answer, "It is I who experience the experience of
the creatures of my imagination," provokes another question,
this time not about the "accessible bliss" of pleasure, but about
the "expressible bliss" of creation:

> Is it I then that keep saying there *is* an hour
> Filled with expressible bliss, in which I *have*
>
> No need, *am* happy, *forget* need's golden hand,
> *Am* satisfied without solacing majesty.

This parallel, imitating the spate of verbs in the angelic experience, yields the final human hypothesis evoked by the initial
angelic one:

> And if there is an hour there is a day,

> There is a month, a year, there is a time
> In which majesty is a mirror of the self.

The majesty that solaces is expendable; an expressible majesty replaces it, and the impoverished but regal self can make its Jehovah-like assertion:

> I have not but I am and as I am, I am.

The brief moment (no month, no year) of self-sustaining majesty collapses at once. The colors deepen and grow small, and Cinderella's finery returns to rags as the mind turns on its own self-adorning "escapades." [17]

The Icarus of these celestial explorations becomes the diminished "I" of the ninth poem of "It Must Give Pleasure," engaged, not in leaps through space, but in the final circularity of motion. The celestial leaps of the Angel disappear in favor of the apparently childlike pleasures of merely circulating, of stopping short in preludes rather than trying to reach codas. Singing, not finishing the song, is the purpose of the birds of the poem; but in claiming such anonymity of action Stevens must forsake the authoritative "I" of the preceding poem and yield to a common "we" which modulates into a detached observation of the "man-hero," at the farthest possible remove from the self-sufficient boast, "I can do all that angels can," which begins the poem.

There is a resemblance in subject of this canto (III, ix) to "The Pleasures of Merely Circulating," but Stevens changes advocacy here. In the earlier poem, there had been a wry celebration of man's willingness to believe in general order and periodicity in spite of both the dark intimations of particular dooms and the playful vagaries of chance:

> The garden flew round with the angel,

The angel flew round with the clouds,
And the clouds flew round and the clouds flew round
And the clouds flew round with the clouds.

Is there any secret in skulls,
The cattle skulls in the woods?
Do the drummers in black hoods
Rumble anything out of their drums?

Mrs. Anderson's Swedish baby
Might well have been German or Spanish,
Yet that things go round and again go round
Has rather a classical sound.   (149–150)

"The Pleasures of Merely Circulating" is about arbitrary chance versus our liking for order — as in fact many of Stevens' poems are. But the carousel giddiness of the first stanza (in charming alliance with its mobile-like gardens and angels and clouds) and the reductive tone of the last stanza (since no "philosophical" argument could survive the introduction of that baby) together with the hint, once voiced by Reuben Brower, that "classical" has overtones here of "classy," put the poem straight into a very queer genre of its own, rather like a sophisticated version of the alarming and energetic religious minatory rhymes for infants in the eighteenth and ninetenth centuries. Even the sinister hints are embraced by the animated dance movement and the patent rhymes, until the whole cosmos is picked up and sent round with the final shrug.

By the time Stevens comes to write *Notes*, the circular movement has changed to something infinitely more laborious, a treadmill rather than a merry-go-round, and the rhythm, constantly broken by commas, retards and contradicts the "pleasurable" sense:

> . . . These things at least comprise
> An occupation, an exercise, a work,
>
> A thing final in itself, and, therefore, good:
> One of the vast repetitions final in
> Themselves and, therefore, good, the going round
>
> And round and round, the merely going round,
> Until merely going round is a final good.

These hesitating and minimal urgings, combined with the drab-ness of the birds in the poem — a too weedy wren, a forced cock-bugler, and a robin practicing mere repetitions — remove the poem entirely from the first fine careless rapture of bird song. A change of style, as Stevens was fond of saying, is a change of subject (*OP*, 171). In the light of this canto, routine is the final good, and the exceptional seems merely monstrous:

> Perhaps,
> The man-hero is not the exceptional monster,
> But he that of repetition is most master.   (III, ix)

This deadened statement is one version of a belief in the com-monplace which recurs rather often in the last volumes, but it is only later that Stevens can lend elevation to his conjectures on the value of repetition. In the homage to the last days of San-tayana, routine will be apotheosized into the actual grandeur of the minimal still-life:

> The bed, the books, the chair, the moving nuns,
> The candle as it evades the sight, these are
> The sources of happiness in the shape of Rome . . .
>
> It is a kind of total grandeur at the end,

> With every visible thing enlarged and yet
> No more than a bed, a chair and moving nuns,
> The immensest theatre, the pillared porch,
> The book and candle in your ambered room.   (508, 510)

The view in Rome is double, with the illumined large and the veritable small coexisting without tension in a reciprocal dignity, both plainly established, neither refuting the other, as the poet takes his stand on the Pisgah threshold from which he confronts two realities at once.

Notes never quite stops upon that particular point of vantage, and therefore Stevens cannot rest in a total concession to repetitive routine, however humane. The last poem proper of *Notes* attempts a naturalistic apotheosis: earth is to be no terra paradise, no very varnished green, but a green and fluent mundo, incarnated in a terrestrial Muse. Stevens' mode of address to the interior paramour (though the Spanish "mundo" harks back to the quasi-Spanish primitivism of the *Blue Guitar*) is neither primitive nor worshipful like his address to the One of Fictive Music; rather by turns it is idyllic, ironic, peremptory, tender, and detached, as Frank Doggett has so finely shown: Stevens "is expressing in his conclusion, then, the genesis of a poem from the imagination of it pictured in procreant terms ("Fat girl, terrestrial, my summer, my night") through the evasions and transformations of its conception, with the arduous work of composition ("Bent over work, anxious, content, alone") to the realization of his conception in language (calling it by name), when it is fixed in the crystal of a poem." [18] The poem is one of Stevens' successes by his own criterion; it resists the intelligence almost successfully, in its elusive changes:

> Fat girl, terrestrial, my summer, my night,
> How is it I find you in difference, see you there
> In a moving contour, a change not quite completed?

You are familiar yet an aberration.
Civil, madam, I am, but underneath
A tree, this unprovoked sensation requires

That I should name you flatly, waste no words,
Check your evasions, hold you to yourself.
Even so when I think of you as strong or tired,

Bent over work, anxious, content, alone,
You remain the more than natural figure. You
Become the soft-footed phantom, the irrational

Distortion, however fragrant, however dear.
That's it: the more than rational distortion,
The fiction that results from feeling. Yes, that.

They will get it straight one day at the Sorbonne.
We shall return at twilight from the lecture
Pleased that the irrational is rational,

Until flicked by feeling, in a gildered street,
I call you by name, my green, my fluent mundo.
You will have stopped revolving except in crystal.   (III, x)

The poem is all the more touching because Stevens had begun
Notes in a professorial role, instructing the ephebe in his own
Sorbonne. The effect of this canto is an abandonment of the
preceptorial role (though he is tempted to that role in the wish
to name his paramour flatly, wasting no words, checking her
evasions). The intent of the poem is not to resolve theoretical
difficulties but to evoke some of the hues controlling Stevens'
relation to the "untrue" mundo, as it seems from moment to
moment celestial, familiar, exasperating, solacing, pleasing, and
irrational. In the suavity of the last five lines, the poet is already,

even before the stability to come, in control of his images, not beset by them: he will be pleased, not solaced or exalted; he will be flicked by feeling, not moved by passion; and the final civilized calling-by-name will take place not under a tree but framed in crystal in a gildered street, as the green primitive is at last seen for what it is — a beginning leading to the crystal, not an end in itself.

After the fine fluidities of the last canto the epilogue to *Notes* is something of an anticlimax, repeating earlier material and resting on the rather too simply put interdependence of the man of action and the man of words. It dwells chiefly on the poet's war and its contribution to active life, never giving equal time poetically to what the soldier might give the poet. Also, it moves away from the special first-person speech of the last three cantos into Stevens' elegiac tone, and perhaps would not have been appended to *Notes* if the war had not made some external justification of poetry seem necessary. In any event, it is not the true ending of the poem, which comes only in the poet's reconciliation, not with the active life, but with his own ever changing images of desire. Stevens is always in danger of becoming sentimentally regretful about the "untrue" ornamentation our feelings bestow on the world, and his most facile tone is one of some self-pity at the necessary consciousness intervening between himself and "reality." *Notes toward a Supreme Fiction* is a strenuous exploration of every possible escape from that self-pity and its literary forms — nostalgia and elegy. In spite of its sometimes forced or hectic direction away from those familiar past grooves, it remains, in its wide embrace of extremes into a center, and in its massively solid structure, the most harmonious expression of Stevens' late-flowering genius.

VIII. The Metaphysical Changes

> . . . the air, the mid-day air, was swarming
> With the metaphysical changes that occur,
> Merely in living as and where we live.

Notes toward a Supreme Fiction is deceptively placed in the *Collected Poems*, since in separate publication (1942) it preceded *Transport to Summer* (1947), the volume it now appears to crown. The significant long poems of *Transport to Summer* are *Esthétique du Mal* (1944) and *Description without Place* (1945).[1] (I postpone *Credences of Summer*, 1947, to place it with its companion piece, *The Auroras of Autumn*, 1948.)

Both *Esthétique* and *Description* are experimental poems, and keep something of the awkwardness of experiments, seem in fact to be a regression after the self-confident finish of *Notes*. *Description* especially comes close to dying of an excess of its own style, much as *Owl's Clover* did, but in the direction of aridity rather than of exuberance. *Esthétique* presents a more opaque surface: its fifteen cantos are violently unconnected in tone, and even the formal stanzaic alignments of *Notes*, which were so congenial to Stevens, are not observed. *Esthétique du Mal* is at once the most random and the most pretentious of Stevens' long poems. Later, in *An Ordinary Evening in New Haven*, he will say that in order to prove the theory of poetry to be the theory of life, some "more severe, more harassing master" would be needed. The ambitious attempt to link evil and aesthetics was prompted conceivably by the same defensiveness toward "life" which produced the epilogue to *Notes*, Stevens' most notorious attempt to prove that poetry and life are interdependent. With equal defensiveness, we are likely to fall gratefully on *Esthétique du Mal* as a direct testament to Stevens' feelings about the great questions of war, suffering, skepticism, and death. The social and communal reference of *Examination of the Hero* is discarded here for a more lyric examination of the evil most tempting for Stevens — the evil of nostalgia and self-pity, the appetite for sleek ensolacings — or worse, a "scholarly" interest in his own pain. It is with the second temptation — the refusal to feel — that the poem begins: "His book made sure of the most correct catastrophe." But this polite chilliness never returns, and in the rest of the poem the battle is joined between two possible attitudes toward unhappiness in a world deprived of parental presences: self-pity on the one hand, and on the other, the sense that such privative exacerbations teach us our own "essential savor."

Stevens' self-pity shows itself doubly, and unsympathetically. First, it is briefly blamed, in Nietzschean terms, on "a too, too, human god, self-pity's kin/ and uncourageous genesis" (iii). Stevens' tone is querulous, even petulant:

> The fault lies with an overhuman god,
> Who by sympathy has made himself a man . . .
>
> If only he would not pity us so much,
> Weaken our fate, relieve us of woe both great
> And small, a constant fellow of destiny.

Alternatively, the self-pity in the poem takes on the falsely moving accents of consolation, but without letting go the nostalgia for the past. The proposed argument of canto v, for instance, is a rejection of the mythological for the actual, but in fact all the trappings of the mythological — elegiac and religious

diction, the celestial "more," the parental and familial images —
are defiantly, even confusedly, present. No sense of poetic difference between the actual and the visionary is preserved; rather
the actual is forced to act the visionary role:

> Softly let all true sympathizers come,
> Without the inventions of sorrow or the sob
> Beyond invention. Within what we permit,
> Within the actual, the warm, the near,
> So great a unity, that it is bliss,
> Ties us to those we love. For this familiar,
> This brother even in the father's eye,
> This brother half-spoken in the mother's throat,
> And these regalia, these things disclosed,
> These nebulous brilliancies in the smallest look
> Of the being's deepest darling, we forego
> Lament, willingly forfeit the ai-ai
>
> Of parades in the obscurer selvages.
> Be near me, come closer, touch my hand, phrases
> Compounded of dear relation, spoken twice,
> Once by the lips, once by the services
> Of central sense, these minutiae mean more
> Than clouds, benevolences, distant heads.   (v)

While this may, and does, appeal on first reading, it wears very
thin. As Stevens said, the most superficially palatable is often
finally the most evanescent, and in this mawkish votary of love
we hardly recognize the Stevens of "Sur Plusieurs Beaux Sujets"
who comments truthfully on his own impersonal affinities: "For
myself, the indefinite, the impersonal, atmospheres and oceans
and, above all, the principle of order are precisely what I love;
and I don't see why, for a philosopher, they should not be the
ultimate inamorata. The premise to Storrs [with whom Stevens

is here disagreeing] is that the universe is explicable only in terms of humanity" (*OP*, xxxii–xxxiii). Stevens' wish to assuage self-pity by consolatory familial sympathy leads to the final disparity between matter and manner. He asserts that we are "exquisite in poverty" and "wholly human" but he uses these conclusions as almost negligible brackets to an effusion of incantatory reminiscence of a more opulent time:

> These are within what we permit, in-bar
> Exquisite in poverty against the suns
> Of ex-bar, in-bar retaining attributes
> With which we vested, once, the golden forms
> And the damasked memory of the golden forms
> And ex-bar's flower and fire of the festivals
> Of the damasked memory of the golden forms,
> Before we were wholly human and knew ourselves.   (v)

Just as human condolences and love evoke a slackened poetry in Stevens, so does the elegy for the unknown soldier (vii), who is meant to represent, in his wound, the common human fate. The canto begins with a self-conscious, sentimental, and repellent "devotional" conceit, "How red the rose that is the soldier's wound," and goes on progressively obscuring its denotation by repetition and interweaving, by uneasy logic, and by another rhythmic *berceuse transatlantique*. Whatever the attitude of mind which can produce, in the twentieth century, the original conceit, it surely means that Stevens has averted his mind from the visual scene and has fixed it not on experience but on pious value. It is a betrayal of Stevens' most ambitious aesthetic to name death a summer sleep, to call a wound a rose, to palliate finality by a stroking hand, and to blur the tragic outline by a spell of Parnassian language.[2]

A canto like this elegy for the soldier, though it works on us in certain decorative ways, makes us ask what place we give it, finally, in Stevens' work. If we judge his verse in the light of his greatest and most individual poems, we ask, with him, that he should "be in the difficulty of what it is to be." The love of grandeur leads him into ornate loftiness; the wish that life could be a comedy of superior amusement, and no more, leads him into brittleness; and either road is easier than the severe refinement he asks from himself at his best. Though Stevens may remain a memorable poet of nostalgia, he himself hoped for a different niche in the history of poetry — one reserved for the poet, writing the poem of earth, who had passed beyond the need to console or sanctify. This major struggle for a proper speech is enacted in its most overt way in the course of *Esthétique du Mal*, as each of the possible styles asserts its own glamour. The elegiac mode rises to its finest lines when it is tinged with scorn of the quotidian:

> The genius of misfortune
> Is not a sentimentalist. He is
> That evil, that evil in the self, from which
> In desperate hallow, rugged gesture, fault
> Falls out on everything: the genius of
> The mind, which is our being, wrong and wrong,
> The genius of the body, which is our world,
> Spent in the false engagements of the mind.   (iv)

The alloy here of bitterness and praise yields the point and railing of the final phrase, which uses to advantage, like some other closings in the poem, a resolution by anticlimax, as the social triviality of the mind's "engagements" puns on the other more serious meanings of the word — whether by English suggestions of solemn promises or French overtones of moral undertakings. Even the deservedly praised ending of *Esthétique* does not match the firm ongoing momentum of this passage, and the bitter pressure of its tone.

At the end of the poem, Stevens describes his own paralysis:

> The greatest poverty is not to live
> In a physical world, to feel that one's desire
> Is too difficult to tell from despair.   (xv)

In a passage looking back, in conceit and later in diction, to *Sunday Morning*, Stevens imagines a tableau rather like Rossetti's invention in "The Blessed Damozel," as nonphysical people in a nonphysical paradise look down in yearning on the green corn gleaming on earth, and feel, in their hopeless longing to touch it, a minor version of what Stevens and others like him now feel in their conscious separation from their animal being. The perfect unity of man and nature is one of our Supreme Fictions, and in our imagination "The green corn gleams and the metaphysicals/ Lie sprawling in majors of the August heat,/ The rotund emotions, paradise unknown." This wishful panorama of the primitive is the unattainable desire too difficult to tell from despair. And the qualified praise of the present which closes the poem takes on, not a tone of sufficiency, but a note of rather plaintive acquiescence, as, in phrases which keep canceling their predecessors, the good is balanced off against the concessives to evil:

> One might have thought of sight, but who could think
> Of what it sees, *for all the ill it sees?*
> Speech found the ear, *for all the evil sound,*
> *But the dark italics it could not propound.*
> And out of what one sees and hears and out
> Of what one feels, *who could have thought* to make
> So many selves, so many sensuous worlds,
> *As if* the air, the mid-day air, was swarming
> With the metaphysical changes that occur,
> *Merely* in living as and where we live.   (italics mine)

To put off the elegiac in this elegiac way is hardy to establish a "third world without knowledge,/ In which no one peers, in which the will makes no demands" (xii). Stevens saw this more clearly than any of his readers, and he knew as well that games of logic, with their assemblages of categories, brought him no closer to that world, that any "extreme of logic would be illogical" (xiv). Nevertheless, he goes to that extreme:

> He disposes the world in categories, thus:
> The peopled and the unpeopled. In both, he is
> Alone. But in the peopled world, there is,
> Besides the people, his knowledge of them. In
> The unpeopled, there is his knowledge of himself.
>
> . . .
>
> Is it himself in them that he knows or they
> In him? If it is himself in them, they have
> No secret from him. If it is they in him,
> He has no secret from them.   (xii)

It was passages of this sort that irritated some of the first readers of *Transport to Summer*, lines in which a false construct is established by sophistic logic at the expense of all exigencies of feeling. Stevens, in "Crude Foyer," agreed:

> Thought is false happiness: the idea
> That merely by thinking one can,
> Or may, penetrate, not may,
> But can, that one is sure to be able —
>
> That there lies at the end of thought
> A foyer of the spirit in a landscape
> Of the mind.   (305)

The way to the third world is not by teetering hypotheses or theoretically unassailable deductions any more than it is by opiate rhythms to dead soldiers.

It remains for us to ask where *Esthétique du Mal* finds its surest footing: if not in its initial detachment, not in its hypnotic melodies, not in its peccably impeccable disposition of logic, not in its sentimental consolations, not in its miracles (ix), then where? If the flawed was painful to Stevens, it was also attractive, and the most original and confident passage in the poem is one where Stevens tells an indulgent parable of the yellow sun and its parasitic bird, both insatiable. The opening is both sympathetic and comic, as each sentence rises and then sprawls in collapse:

> The sun, *in clownish yellow*, but not a clown
> Brings the day to perfection *and then fails*. He dwells
> In a consummate prime, *yet still desires*
> *A further consummation*. For the lunar month
> He makes the tenderest research, intent
> On a transmutation which, when seen, appears
> To be *askew*. And space is filled with his
> *Rejected years*. (italics mine)

The last two debacles are all the more visible because they head lines of verse, and we linger between humor and affection for this awkward sun. Against all these elaborate efforts of the sun stands one bony sentence:

> A big bird pecks at him for food.

The sentence is bony, of course, because the bird is:

> The big bird's bony appetite
> Is as insatiable as the sun's.

And so they are blood brothers, the sun and the bird, in their appetite.

This dramatic and fabular presentation of the didactic text is the method that *Notes* had used so simply and well. Stevens' philosophic interests, which could lead him into miasmas of abstraction, are both tamed and freshened by the simplicities of a tale. Here we have a children's story of mirror images — the expanding sun, the pecking bird: the sun is spurred on by the inevitable downward spin of each cycle (hourly, daily, monthly, seasonally, yearly, by eras) while the bird, eating the sun-as-fruit, is spurred on by its divinations of perfections better than its present food:

> The bird
> Rose from an imperfection of its own
> To feed on the yellow bloom of the yellow fruit
> Dropped down from turquoise leaves. In the landscape of
> The Sun, its grossest appetite becomes less gross,
> Yet, when corrected, has its curious lapses,
> Its glitters, its divinations of serene
> Indulgence out of all celestial sight.

To conceive of reality (the researching sun) as sharing our spiritual appetite for transcendence is a piece of splendid panache believable only in the context of meticulous reportage and schematic neatness with which Stevens' tale is told. Day leads properly to month, month to year; later, hour yields to season and season to era; the sun "still desires" (1.3) and at the same time "still promises"; every movement has its countermovement in this poem of programmatic symmetry. If something ascends, then it falls; if research is begun, then it goes askew; as the bird rises, the fruit drops; as the fruit ripens, the bird downwardly revolves, and so on to the end:

The sun is the country wherever he is. The bird
In the brightest landscape downwardly revolves
Disdaining each astringent ripening,
Evading the point of redness, not content
To repose in an hour or season or long era
Of the country colors crowding against it, since
The yellow grassman's mind is still immense,
Still promises perfections cast away.   (vi)

This poetic law of conservation of energy accounts for the un-
predictable and satisfying close of the canto. At first Stevens
had seemed (partly because of the large space allotted to the
bird) to endorse the questing of the bird's appetite above everything else, but just as the moment when the descent downward
would become irrevocable, the poem (with the bird) pulls out
of its plunge, and we are told that the bird's eternal restlessness
is really a conversion to the sun's point of view, a celestial dis-
satisfaction in an earthly appetite. The poem ends as it began,
with a mixed view of the sun, part admiring, part indulgent.
Everything is tempered and insatiable at once, in this willing
accommodation both to gross appetite and to intimations of unattainable immortality. The Wordsworthian desire for celestial
light is seen as a relapse into an appetite too gross, more gross
than the appetite for reality, but this desire for the heavenly is
finally acceptable because it is stimulated, after all, by reality.
The divination of something out of sight here becomes only a
quirk of the human personality, a curious lapse, a predictably
recurring discontent which motivates the next spurt of activity
toward the real. The equilibrated and restrained language keeps
the appetites "corrected" and Stevens' central view — that interaction is, above all, interesting — prevails.[3]

The single attempt at myth in *Esthétique du Mal* (x) is more
honest than its counterparts in *Owl's Clover*, and in it Stevens
tries to go beyond the invention, lovely in itself, of the "fat girl,

terrestrial," who had assuaged his restlessness in *Notes*. To combine that fat girl with the wicked cannibal queen of "Madame La Fleurie" (507) and to declare her essential innocence at the same time is perhaps too ambitious a program, but over and over Stevens asks the essential nature of the female, thinking perhaps of Whitman's "savage mother" as well as of his own interior paramour. There is at first a jaunty informality and self-deprecation in the introduction of his vaguely cartooned "mother":

> He had studied the nostalgias. In these
> He sought the most grossly maternal, the creature
> Who most fecundly assuaged him, the softest
> Woman with a vague moustache and not the mauve
> *Maman*. His anima liked its animal
> And liked it unsubjugated.

But the myth cannot maintain its own flippancy, and it moves on to imitate Whitman and then to play with its own fantasy:

>   . . . Home
> Was a return to birth, a being born
> Again in the savagest severity,
> Desiring fiercely, the child of a mother fierce
> In his body, fiercer in his mind, merciless
> To accomplish the truth in his intelligence.
> It is true there were other mothers, singular
> In form, lovers of heaven and earth, she-wolves
> And forest tigresses and women mixed
> With the sea. These were fantastic.

But to make a whole out of the moustached woman, the fierce mother, and mermaids is to ask too much, and the myth ends with a piece of theorizing which will take on new life in *The Auroras of Autumn*, and will, as Stevens predicts, free him from easy consolations. This is the theory of the innocence of event, which will become, in *The Auroras of Autumn*, the theory of the impartiality of nature, as grim as it is benevolent.

> The softest woman,
> Because she is as she was, reality,
> The gross, the fecund, proved him against the touch
> Of impersonal pain. Reality explained.
> It was the last nostalgia: that he
> Should understand. That he might suffer or that
> He might die was the innocence of living, if life
> Itself was innocent. To say that it was
> Disentangled him from sleek ensolacings.

The rest of *Esthétique du Mal* gives us nothing particularly new. It is a redoing of earlier poems, from *Le Monocle de Mon Oncle* (ix) all the way down to *Notes* (iii), with pieces in between from *The Man with the Blue Guitar* (viii), *Owl's Clover* (xiv), and "To the One of Fictive Music" (v).

In short, *Esthétique du Mal* seems a poem enumerating old themes in old modes or else applying itself to a new theme — evil and pain, explicitly so named — without a corresponding energy of new perceptions. *Description without Place*, as if in revulsion against the insistence on "serious content" in *Esthétique du Mal*, puts an equally perverse but more congenial emphasis on appearance, and therefore on manner. The two are linked by a passage in the third canto of *Description without Place*:

> There are potential seemings turbulent
> In the death of a soldier, like the utmost will,
>
> The more than human commonplace of blood,
> The breath that gushes upward and is gone,

And another breath emerging out of death,
That speaks for him such seemings as death gives.

As Stevens became convinced that poetry, even in world wars, need not be topical or social, so he became convinced that the reality of poetry was not given to it by the newspapers but by the self, and was engendered by its adjectives, whether the amorist Adjective aflame of his earlier poems or the more mitigated commodious adjective of the later ones. *Description without Place* is an ode to the Adjective, and its subject is the connection between the adjectival and the verbal modes, or, to put it in terms of *Notes*, the moment when the characters of the author take on for a moment life of their own, as his adjectives become the principles of their action. The theoretical center of the poem is its manifesto in canto iii:

> Things are as they seemed to Calvin or to Anne
> Of England, to Pablo Neruda in Ceylon,
>
> To Nietzsche in Basel, to Lenin by a lake.

Though, strictly speaking, we can verify no system of value, all our motivation nevertheless arises from our notion of the past, our judgment on the present, and our vision of the future, or, as Stevens said, "We live in the description of a place and not in the place itself" (*L*, 494).

To justify the ways of the mind to man is the polemic aim of the poem, but its rhetorical aim is a queerly hypnotic one. We take leave of sense here, not in the flighty perversities of "Oak Leaves Are Hands" or "Anything Is Beautiful If You Say It Is," but rather in a steady guitarlike hum of reiterated syllables, aiming by and large not for the forcible enhancings of transfiguration, but for the intricate pulse and steadiness of self-involved major and minor premises:

It is possible that to seem — it is to be,
As the sun is something seeming and it is.

The sun is an example. What it seems
It is and in such seeming all things are.

Thus things are like a seeming of the sun
Or like a seeming of the moon or night

Or sleep. It was a queen that made it seem
By the illustrious nothing of her name.

Her green mind made the world around her green.
The queen is an example . . . This green queen

In the seeming of the summer of her sun
By her own seeming made the summer change.

In the golden vacancy she came, and comes,
And seems to be on the saying of her name.

Her time becomes again, as it became,
The crown and week-day coronal of her fame.   (i)

If this is not the unspotted imbecile revery, it is not far from it.
The aim, like the aim of some stanzas in *The Man with the Blue
Guitar*, is to preserve the appearance of logic while the incessant
vagaries of repetition confuse logical distinctions, the whole
being enclosed in a kind of baby talk in which the complicated
and abstract philosophical vocabulary usual to such arguments
is deliberately replaced by its simplest and most primitive substitutes, as "appearance" becomes "seeming," "reality" becomes
"the sun," "imagination" becomes "a queen," and so on. Stevens'
queens and rabbits and firecats are all more complex in reference

than their Grimm Brothers prototypes, but they bring a putative simplicity to his theme, matching the putative transparency of his logic. To think that the ostentatious speaker of *The Comedian* could come to this innocent lisping is astonishing.

But this is no manner that can be sustained, even though Stevens shows increasing attachment, in some later poems, to a childlike tone of confiding filial trust. He does sustain this tone through the second canto of *Description*, but later other manners supervene. One is a lapsing back to the old dazzles of *Owl's Clover*, with the same recognizable manipulation of tenses to yield apocalypse, as conjecture ("might") becomes hypothesis ("would"), and hypothesis is hypostatized to a visionary present tense, the whole complicated by high hazy references to "a point in the fire of music where/ Dazzle yields to a clarity":

> There might be, too, a change immenser than
> A poet's metaphors in which being would
>
> Come true, a point in the fire of music where
> Dazzle yields to a clarity and we observe,
>
> And observing is completing and we are content,
> In a world that shrinks to an immediate whole,
>
> That we do not need to understand, complete
> Without secret arrangements of it in the mind.   (iii)

Those secret arrangements in the mind are finally more interesting to Stevens than his forced faith in an instinctual beatific vision, and after his first sketchy historical instances of the pressure of the mind on reality (Calvin, Pablo Neruda), he elaborates on two illustrations, Nietzsche and Lenin, in the most interesting and new part of the poem, a forecast, in some ways, of the later eulogy on Santayana:

Nietzsche in Basel studied the deep pool
Of these discolorations, mastering

The moving and the moving of their forms
In the much-mottled motion of blank time.

His revery was the deepness of the pool,
The very pool, his thoughts the colored forms,

The eccentric souvenirs of human shapes,
Wrapped in their seemings, crowd on curious crowd,

In a kind of total affluence, all first,
All final, colors subjected in revery

To an innate grandiose, an innate light,
The sun of Nietzsche gildering the pool,

Yes: gildering the swarm-like manias
In perpetual revolution, round and round . . .

Lenin on a bench beside a lake disturbed
The swans. He was not the man for swans.

The slouch of his body and his look were not
In suavest keeping. The shoes, the clothes, the hat

Suited the decadence of those silences,
In which he sat. All chariots were drowned. The swans

Moved on the buried water where they lay.
Lenin took bread from his pocket, scattered it —

The swans fled outward to remoter reaches,
As if they knew of distant beaches; and were

> Dissolved. The distances of space and time
> Were one and swans far off were swans to come.
>
> The eye of Lenin kept the far-off shapes.
> His mind raised up, down-drowned, the chariots.
>
> And reaches, beaches, tomorrow's regions became
> One thinking of apocalyptic legions.   (iv)

Though Nietzsche and Lenin are, for Stevens' purposes, trans-figured to mythic proportions and made visible chiefly in their imaginative stress, enough historical variety is attached so that the equivocal manner-of-being of the green queen does not disturb us in these two flesh-and-blood creatures.

The repetitive sonorities of the first two cantos of *Description without Place* are maintained, but the vocabulary no longer borders on the childish, and the sentences are no longer primitive. In fact, the imitative action here, as Nietzsche creates a new coloration of the world, is a deeper and deeper sinking-in toward the object of vision as it becomes the visionary object. "The mind of one man, if strong enough," as Stevens said, "can become the master of all the life in the world" (*L*, 360). The first of the two sentences describing Nietzsche imitates Nietzsche's own submersion into the pool:

> Mastering the moving
>   and the moving of their forms
>   in the much-mottled
>   motion of blank time.

The second sentence continues, in a much ampler form, this elongation from its subject in a deep engulfing, returning at the end to a reminder of the solar presence, the conferring mind of the visionary, "the sun of Nietzsche gildering the pool." The chain of appositions themselves depending on appositions composing this second sentence is Stevens' golden string — a chain of links from Nietzsche's revery to the human shapes and manias transformed in his thoughts. The other imitative principle in the passage is the oscillation of rhythm, beginning conventionally and accelerating to the short phrases in the fifth couplet as the shapes appear all first, all final. These accelerations and hesitations seem to evoke for Stevens the reversions and urges of the philosophical mind, and they will later be put to exquisite use in his elegiac ode "To An Old Philosopher in Rome."

The second experience retold in this canto, the experience of the active political man rather than the philosophic radical, is a different matter. Lenin's response to the lake is not Nietzsche's descent deeper and deeper into revery; it is the brusque evaluation of the revolutionary, impatient of European decadence, even though he is dressed in its keepings. The scenic sentences are curt:

> Lenin on a bench beside a lake disturbed the swans.
> He was not the man for swans.
> The slouch of his body and his look were not in suavest keeping,
> The shoes, the clothes, the hat suited the decadence of those silences in which he sat.
> All chariots were drowned.
> The swans moved on the buried water where they lay.

One quick action breaks the tableau:

> Lenin took bread from his pocket, scattered it —

And then the verse changes to a feast of internal rhyme, as Lenin precipitates a new order:

> The swans fled outward to remoter reaches,

As if they knew of distant beaches,
    And were dissolved.
The distances of space and time were one
And swans far off were swans to come . . .
And reaches,
Beaches,
Tomorrow's regions
Became one thinking of apocalyptic legions.

The suggestion of frivolity in the feminine rhymes is not accidental; humor infuses Stevens' vision of peremptory revolutionary planning as Lenin's mind in one breath "raises up, down-
drowns, the chariots" in a private Red Sea, and disposes of the
old order by a comic public-park version of the feeding of the
multitude. Set over against each other, Nietzsche and Lenin
become the rapidly sketched imitative metaphors of all description without place, whether philosophic or political.

Though Stevens has used, as examples of description without
place, the syntheses of the past (in Nietzsche and Lenin), the
presidings of myth (the green queen), the zeitgeist of an age
(ii), and the individual artistic effort (iii), the most beautiful
passage in the poem, the fifth canto, uses our sense of the natural
world, different each hour and each day, as the paramount case
of "delicate clinkings not explained." Cantos v and vi, taken
together, remind us of "To the One of Fictive Music," invoking,
in the words of the earlier poem, "the difference that heavenly
pity brings," and praying that our description will be like, "yet
not too like." As Stevens will say later, in *An Ordinary Evening
in New Haven*, the point of vision and desire are the same, and
by his poem of desire (canto v) he brings about his poem of
vision, which he calls here revelation (canto vi). The two cantos
rest on several archetypes of desire and fulfillment, as Stevens
evokes the rainbow-arc of God's covenant, the wanderings of
the Israelites, the messianic day-star of the prophets, the word-

made-flesh of St. John, the dove of Pentecost, and the final apocalypse. Revelation, when it comes, must be visible,

> Yet not too closely the double of our lives,
> Intenser than any actual life could be,
>
> A text we should be born that we might read,
> More explicit than the experience of sun
>
> And moon, the book of reconciliation,
> Book of a concept only possible
>
> In description, canon central in itself,
> The thesis of the plentifullest John.   (vi)

The metaphor central to the earlier ode to the Muse has been radically changed: there, the image had been music, but here it is far drier — an explicit text, a concept, a canon, a thesis. Doctrine has replaced melos, as Stevens acknowledges his own abstraction. The "difference" is no longer conferred by heavenly pity, but is self-born, as we refer to each other the different seemings things have, as each summer day seems different from every other. Description without place is a sense of things:

> It is a sense
>
> To which we refer experience, a knowledge
> Incognito, the column in the desert,
>
> On which the dove alights. Description is
> Composed of a sight indifferent to the eye.
>
> It is an expectation, a desire,
> A palm that rises up beyond the sea,

A little different from reality:
The difference that we make in what we see

And our memorials of that difference,
Sprinklings of bright particulars from the sky.

Stevens gives us characteristic flourishes of imagery in the midst of definition, his pages of illustrations for each axiom. The plain column, dove, and palm give way as illustration to the evanescent "sprinklings of bright particulars," whatever they may be. Blake's "minute particulars" and Shakespeare's "bright particular star" of *All's Well That Ends Well* (I, i, 97) gave Stevens the phrase, and Shakespeare's star perhaps called up the cycle of Hesper-Phosphor which Stevens, abandoning theory for imagery, uses to end the canto:

The future is description without place,
The categorical predicate, the arc.

It is a wizened starlight, growing young,
In which old stars are planets of morning, fresh

In the brilliantest descriptions of new day,
Before it comes, the just anticipation

Of the appropriate creatures, jubilant,
The forms that are attentive in thin air.   (v)

Like the bright particulars, the appropriate creatures and the attentive forms are halfway between image and idea. Stevens may have learned this language of intermediate forms from the greater species of it in Wordsworth:

There, darkness makes abode, and all the host
Of shadowy things work endless changes, — there,

As in a mansion like their proper home,
Even forms and substances are circumfused
By that transparent veil with light divine,
And, through the turnings intricate of verse,
Present themselves as objects recognised,
In flashes, and with glory not their own.

(*Prelude*, VI, 598–605)

In any case, Stevens' attenuations of image into incorporeality serve him, like his necessary angel, superlatively well, in these prophetic and attentive presences.

But the poem struggles violently and unsuccessfully to find a mode of conclusion in a jumble of styles. The last canto begins (except for its fourth line) in the gnostic, philosophical, and self-involved copulative style:

Thus the theory of description matters most.
It is the theory of the word for those

For whom the word is the making of the world,
The buzzing world and lisping firmament.

It is a world of words to the end of it,
In which nothing solid is its solid self.

The canto then takes on the manner of Crispin, the speech he used when he declared in his prolegomena that

The man in Georgia waking among pines
Should be pine-spokesman . . . .
Sepulchral senors, bibbling pale mescal . . .
Should make the intricate sierra scan.   (38)

Here, the "hard hidalgo"

Lives in the mountainous character of his speech;

And in that mountainous mirror Spain acquires
The knowledge of Spain and of the hidalgo's hat.

From this bluff instance, the poem lapses into prestidigitation
to end in portentousness. The theory of description matters most,
Stevens concludes,

> Because everything we say
> Of the past is description without place, a cast
>
> Of the imagination made in sound;
> And because what we say of the future must portend,
>
> Be alive with its own seemings, seeming to be
> Like rubies reddened by rubies reddening.   (vii)

"Redden" is one of those verbs of progressive action which
Stevens finds immensely useful in his desire to guarantee the
future. Like other verbs which lean into the time to come (his
favorites are "become" and "change" and "transform"), verbs
of progressive change, like "darken" or "deepen" or "spread,"
draw us into the future with them. One peculiarity of these
verbs is that they are generally both transitive and intransitive,
with the intransitive sense historically secondary.[4] "To redden"
can mean, and presumably originally meant, "to make red."
However, "rubies reddening" clearly means "rubies becoming a
deeper red," an action which is self-contained and self-limiting.
It is a grammatical zeugma, in other words, for rubies to be
reddened by the intransitive action of other rubies reddening,
and yet the latent transitiveness of "redden" allows Stevens his
luminous colorings. The burden of the final couplet is that
whatever we say of the future must have more verbal energy

than it needs for its own purposes, have a diffusing radiance to share merely in saying what it says. Prediction, in other words, should have prophetic beauty. We are accustomed to this notion in respect to poetry itself — that its resonance is, in terms of information, redundant; but Stevens is proposing here a doubled intensity, it would seem, coming perhaps from what he called in *Adagia* the poetry of the idea as well as the poetry of the words. The means he uses are perhaps too transparent for comfort, especially the outright tautologies of the last couplet. At any rate, the repetitiveness of vocabulary found in *Description without Place* will never again be the raison-d'être of an entire long poem. What will serve for a canto of the *Man with the Blue Guitar* is not viable for a whole poem — the reliance on a minimal number of counters (as in "good air, good friend") or on a multiplication of relations between the two stationary poles, seeming and being (the monster in the lute versus the monster locked in stone).

Even though *Description without Place* has a relatively short span, its deliberately copulative structure of definition impoverishes the poem, as it did *Examination of the Hero*. Nevertheless, it is hard to understand the great falling-off in power from *Notes toward a Supreme Fiction* in both *Esthétique du Mal* and *Description without Place*. We might say that they represent extremes in Stevens: *Esthétique du Mal* is Stevens at his least ironic, least humorous, most sentimental, and even most platitudinous, while *Description without Place*, is Stevens at his most impersonal, his most logical, his most "objective," his most theoretical. *Esthétique du Mal*, in spite of its title, is, as Stevens said, a collection of aperçus (*L*, 469), and took upon itself what was, for Stevens, an uncongenial subject, the problem of pain and evil. Stevens' own definition of his proper subject comes in a letter to José Rodríguez Feo, in a reference to another writer: "I very much wish I could read more exactly the essay of Aníbal Rodríguez on the bases of *alegria*. His subject is a foot-

note to *felicidad*, which, after all, is the great subject" (*L*, 481).
The distinction Stevens makes is between pleasure and happiness,
but together they make up the "Paradise unknown" of emotion.
It makes no difference that Stevens generally writes about happiness from the point of loss: it still makes a different subject
from pain or evil. The two seasonal meditations on summer and
autumn which are to be Stevens' next essays in the long poem
will depart from definition and aesthetic theory in order to
turn more fully to panorama, and to personal immediacy.

IX. Douceurs, Tristesses

A blaze of summer straw, in winter's nick.

Wallace Stevens' late version of pastoral is a double one, embodied in two difficult poems — *Credences of Summer* (1947) and *The Auroras of Autumn* (1948).[1] The two poems are in effect the same day seen from two perspectives, Stevens' Allegro and his Penseroso, a day piece matched with a night piece (a night piece nonetheless auroral), his innocent Eden confronted by his true Paradise, where he finds the serpent. They are two, or rather twenty, ways (since each has ten cantos) of looking at middle age, when all moments of life are potentially overcast by memory or fear. A poem takes us, as Stevens said, from its "ever-early candor to its late plural," and *Credences of Summer* describes for us that late plural in all its harvest magnitude, while the chill that falls across *The Auroras of Autumn* springs, in contrast, from an austerity of mind not far from Keats's when he saw the Grecian urn as a cold pastoral. Though the scene of middle age remains unchanged, "the Eye altering, alters all."

No previous long poem in Stevens' collections had ever placed a lyric speaker firmly in a landscape of the present moment: all had used the haziness of a past distancing or the impersonality of an invented persona, whether a woman, a shearsman, or a comedian. In contrast, the confrontation of the present is insisted on over and over in these two poems; the eye is not allowed to stray, but is kept tightly bound by the repetitive "this" and "here" of successive lines:

This is the last day of a certain year.

This, this is the centre that I seek.

This is where the serpent lives, the bodiless.

Here, being visible is being white.

The scrutiny represented by the insistence on the demonstrative adjective and pronoun is a new mode for an expansive poem in Stevens. Though it is more evenly sustained in *The Auroras of Autumn* it is best described in *Credences of Summer*:

> Three times the concentred self takes hold, three times
> The thrice concentred self, having possessed
>
> The object, grips it in savage scrutiny,
> Once to make captive, once to subjugate
> Or yield to subjugation, once to proclaim
> The meaning of the capture, this hard prize,
> Fully made, fully apparent, fully found.   (vii)

This hard prize, so grasped and so exhibited, over and over, is the ever elusive present, so likely, like the ghost of Anchises, to evade embrace. These poems represent the wresting of Stevens' naturally elegiac style into a temporarily topographical poetry. Again, the result is happier in *The Auroras of Autumn*, where elegy and description are kept in a dissolving equilibrium, and present and past remain in a fluid focus. But in both poems, Stevens calls the present internal moment "this," and everything outside it in space and time "that," and the purpose of these two seasonal pastorals of inner weather is to find a relation between "this" and "that," a relation shadowed forth in an earlier poem, "This as Including That" (1944–45):

This rock and the dry birds
Fluttering in blue leaves,

This rock and the priest,
The priest of nothingness who intones —

It is true that you live on this rock
And in it. It is wholly you.

It is true that there are thoughts
That move in the air as large as air,

That are almost not our own, but thoughts
To which we are related,

In an association like yours
With the rock and mine with you.

But the assertion of relation, undermined by the same bitterness
we have seen in the rejection of Cinderella in *Notes*, collapses
in the final couplet:

The iron settee is cold.
A fly crawls on the balustrades.   (*OP*, 88)

"This" clearly does not include the complete "that," as the
settee and the fly stand outside the harmonious relation of
thoughts, the rock, and the poet with his interior paramour.
 The attempt to make "this" (the present moment) include
"that" is the soul of *Credences of Summer*, and is expressed in
the intellectual pivot of the poem: "One day enriches a year
. . . / Or do the other days enrich the one?" "The indifferent
experience of life," as Stevens said in *Two or Three Ideas* (1951),
"is the unique experience, the item of ecstasy which we have

been isolating and reserving for another time and place, loftier and more secluded." (*OP*, 213). Or, as he put it programmatically in *Notes*, the function of poetry is "forthwith,/ On the image of what we see, to catch from that/ Irrational moment its unreasoning." Stevens stands in the perfection of an August day in harvest, and asks whether this day in Oley, in its uniqueness, includes all others in the year, or whether it stands extrinsic to them. To fix the attention on the present is not at all a new idea in Stevens' verse; what is new is the expression of the idea in the present tense, in the actual scene, in the poetry of "this" and "here" and "now." *Notes toward a Supreme Fiction*, by its nature, had been a program for action, a Utopian poem, and had about it a marvelous note of expectancy, confidence, and buoyancy. *Credences of Summer*, as its title betrays, is the creed of the believer rather than the certain projection of the prophet or the divided commentary of the skeptic, but its intention cannot all command the strings. Its initial impetus of praise and involvement, resolutely kept in the original moment, is maintained through the first three cantos, but from then on the oneness with the here and now diminishes, until by the end of the poem Stevens is at an inhuman distance from his starting point.

Stevens is fully conscious of his wish to bask in the present and of the forces working against it, chiefly his natural asceticism and his equally natural intellectuality. As always, his protagonists represent aspects of himself, and so the vanishing present object is not only gripped in savage scrutiny by one Stevens, but also avoided by another:

> It was difficult to sing in face
> Of the object. The singers had to avert themselves
> Or else avert the object.

It is no longer enough to be an onlooker, as it was for the shearsman with the blue guitar, who wanted "to be the lion in the lute/

Before the lion locked in stone," his life spent in an eternal mirroring of the world. That spectatorship has turned into an immersion in the scene, a scene which is at once fully made by the poet, fully apparent of itself, and fully found, as if left, like Whitman's grass, designedly dropped. This mode of the this, the here, and the now, so remarkably difficult to maintain at any length, gives a suspense to the progress of both poems, as the tenuous identity of man and environmental moment is sought, precariously supported, and, finally, lost.

The identity dissolves, of course, with the entrance of the analytic mind, with the change from description to interrogation. This questioning occurs halfway through the ten cantos of *Credences of Summer*, and entirely pervades *The Auroras of Autumn*: in both cases the central question forces its way to the surface, almost against the speaker's will. In *Credences of Summer* the question, already quoted, asks the relation of the present to its context in time:

> One day enriches a year . . .
> Or do the other days enrich the one?

In *The Auroras of Autumn* the question looks for the relation of insight to sight, or the envisaged to the now:

> Is there an imagination that sits enthroned
> As grim as it is benevolent, the just
> And the unjust, which in the midst of summer stops
>
> To imagine winter?

After the question is put, a simple ease of landscape is never regained. The analytic is in the ascendant, as detachment, generalization, and removal from the scene take precedence over receptivity. The poems do not fail, but the human effort to rest in the present is predestined to collapse, at least for Stevens, who never was a poet formed to chant in orgy to the summer sun. Fifteen lines after he has asserted that the summer land is too ripe for enigmas, the central enigma of moment and context rises in him, and the hope of serenity is lost. But the end was foreshadowed in the elegiac and brutal claims for the land's ripeness with which the poem had begun:

> Now in midsummer come and all fools slaughtered
> And spring's infuriations over and a long way
> To the first autumnal inhalations, young broods
> Are in the grass, the roses are heavy with a weight
> Of fragrance and the mind lays by its trouble.
>
> Now the mind lays by its trouble and considers.
> The fidgets of remembrance come to this.
> This is the last day of a certain year
> Beyond which there is nothing left of time.
> It comes to this and the imagination's life.

All of Stevens' praise of summer is put in negative terms. There is "nothing left of time," and

> There is nothing more inscribed nor thought nor felt
> And this must comfort the heart's core against
> Its false disasters — these fathers standing round,
> These mothers touching, speaking, being near,
> These lovers waiting in the soft dry grass.

The scene is composed of details of warmth and feeling — the young broods, the fragrant roses, the mythical fathers, mothers, and lovers — but they emerge from the heavy toll of the mind's trouble, the disasters (even if false) of the heart's core, the fidgets of remembrance, the slaughtering, even of fools, and the repetitive knell of negative phrases. It is with all our memories of negative phrasing used pejoratively that we hear Stevens say "There is nothing more inscribed nor thought nor felt," and we feel the truth of deprivation in his paradoxes to come, when he will speak of "the barrenness of the fertile thing that can attain no more," and of "a feeling capable of nothing more." [2]

Credences of Summer, as I have said, turns on the difficult relation between the moment of satisfaction and "the waste sad time stretching before and after." Stevens attempts a Hegelian synthesis of the two in a triple invoking of a day, a woman, and a man, all raised above the norm into an embellishment, a queen, and a hero. He asks how they are related to that matrix which they resemble and from which they rise, and his answer falls into a logical scheme:

	One day enriches a year.
Thesis:	One woman makes the rest look down.
	One man becomes a race, lofty like him, like him perpetual.
	Or do the other days enrich the one?
Antithesis:	And is the queen humble as she seems to be, the charitable majesty of her whole kin?
	The bristling soldier . . . who looms in the sunshine is a filial form.
	The more than casual blue contains the year and other years and hymns and people, without souvenir.
Synthesis:	The day enriches the year, not as embellishment.
	Stripped of remembrance, it displays its strength — the youth, the vital son, the heroic power.

The extreme neatness of this processional resolution, in which the day, at the end, has metaphorically absorbed the queen (in the word "embellishment") and the soldier (in the word "heroic"), is not particularly convincing, since the permutations seem summoned not by feeling but by a too avid logic. After suggesting that a day in Oley can enrich a year as embellishment, Stevens makes the counterassertion that routine provides the necessary backdrop for the effect of this day: the other days, then, enrich the one, perhaps, if we are to speak justly. The final resolution — that this midsummer day *contains* all the rest, but without souvenir (rather as a concept contains, virtually, all its instances) — is an ingenious but frigid appropriation from logical abstraction. Its weakness is betrayed as Stevens has to buttress it by his gaudy language, always produced in moments of strain: the soldier who bristles and looms comes in phrases not flesh but fustian.

Because this blustering solution is a false one, the poem will have to begin all over again, resorting in turn to both self-enhancement and self-parody. Earlier, in the third canto, a visionary exaltation had been sketched in a tableau of height attained in the here and now:

> This is the barrenness
> Of the fertile thing that can attain no more.
>
> It is the natural tower of all the world,
> The point of survey, green's green apogee,
> But a tower more precious than the view beyond,
> A point of survey squatting like a throne,
> Axis of everything, green's apogee
>
> And happiest folk-land, mostly marriage-hymns.
> It is the mountain on which the tower stands,
> It is the final mountain . . .

> It is the old man standing on the tower,
> Who reads no book.

The tower, the mountain underneath it, and the old man above it, though drawn from Stevens' walks to the tower on Mount Penn,[3] are all emblems of the perfect day "in Oley when the hay,/ Baked through long days, is piled in mows." After the analytic questions about the day arise in the fifth canto, however, a different stance is needed: the tower and the old man are dispensed with, and the mountain is made to do duty for all three. The day had first been construed in pure greenness as green's green apogee, with its natural mountain base, its prolongation into the man-made tower, and its coronation with the human;[4] now in its self-enhancement it becomes at once purely "natural" without tower or man, and at the same time purely mythical and celestial, with only the most minor concessions to the original green. Metaphysics surmounts the physical:

> It is a mountain half way green and then,
> The other immeasurable half, such rock
> As placid air becomes.

Stevens had once admitted "This is the pit of torment, that placid end/ Should be illusion" (292), but here, for this brief moment of idealization, he sustains the immobility of his myth:

> It is the rock of summer, the extreme,
> A mountain luminous half way in bloom
> And then half way in the extremest light
> Of sapphires flashing from the central sky,
> As if twelve princes sat before a king.

The earlier old man has been enhanced into the sun-king, a Charlemagne surrounded by twelve peers; and the tower has been metamorphosed into the airy half of the mountain, previously seen in the "green" passage as a squatting throne, but here as a flashing beacon. It is a radiation upward of the entire original scene, and of course brings about its own downfall, or in literary terms its own parody. When we next see the tower, in the ninth canto, it has turned into a beanpole; the green mountain has been dwarfed to a weedy garden in decay, and the old man has degenerated into a cock robin perched on the beanpole, no longer garbed in a "ruddy ancientness" which "absorbs the ruddy summer" but instead huddled, waiting for warmth.

The imperatives with which Stevens will begin the scene in the salacious garden parody the confident imperatives of the second canto. There, action was paramount and insistent:

> Postpone the anatomy of summer . . .
> Burn everything not part of it to ash.
>
> Trace the gold sun about the whitened sky . . .
> And fill the foliage with arrested peace.

But like a fabliau coexisting with a miracle tale, the beast fable of the robin corrects this energetic and idealized perspective with a low and slackened demand:

> Fly low, cock bright, and stop on a bean pole. Let
> Your brown breast redden, while you wait for warmth.
> With one eye watch the willow, motionless.

That stopping, waiting, and watching while a complex of emotions falls apart into a soft decay is a psychological alternative to the active purging and redecorating of the second canto, just as the scarcely perceived sound made by the bird is an alternative to the marriage hymns of the natural greenery, and as the salacious weeds are an alternative to the fragrant roses of the opening. And both these "natural" extremes (of greenery or of weeds) are alternatives to the celestial possible: the luminous, the princely, the flashing sapphire stations before the king. Next to that aristocratic Round Table, the low primitiveness of the robin's utterance stands in a sinister guttural:

> This complex falls apart.
> And on your bean pole, it may be, you detect
>
> Another complex of other emotions, not
> So soft, so civil, and you make a sound,
> Which is not part of the listener's own sense.

Stevens has prepared us for this scrawny bird sound by the "green" marriage hymns and by two other passages in the poem — the choirs of the fourth canto and the trumpet of the eighth. These two are also mutual parodies, or, to speak more gently, sideglances at each other, mutual forms of critical reference. The choirs express final achieved polyphony, a primary which is not primitive but superbly complex, a primary free from doubt, as it was defined earlier in "Man Carrying Thing" (350). Things uncertain, indistinct, dubious, were there defined as secondary:

> Accept them, then,
> As secondary (parts not quite perceived
>
> Of the obvious whole, uncertain particles
> of the certain solid, the primary free from doubt . . .)
>   (350–351)

But here, in *Credences of Summer*, we are, in theory, confronted with "the obvious whole," "the certain solid," as Stevens assures us that the normally secondary senses of the ear, less immediate than the eye, swarm

> Not with secondary sounds, but choirs,
> Not evocations but last choirs, last sounds
> With nothing else compounded, carried full,
> Pure rhetoric of a language without words.

The earlier current of paradoxical negatives eddies through this fourth canto, as the thing that can attain no more, and the old man capable of nothing more, produce the music compounded with nothing else, full but without words. Stevens' aim is to disappoint us subtly as he pairs each word of potential, like "full" or "capable," with a negation of potential. All of *Credences of Summer*, in fact, may be seen as a meditation on that Keatsian moment in which the bees find that summer has o'erbrimm'd their clammy cells. Direction must either stop at the plenary season, or it imperceptibly conveys excess and decay, and Stevens' response is exactly that of the humanized bees: to think that warm days will never cease, or to follow a devious logic of wish.

> Things stop in that direction and since they stop
> The direction stops and we accept what is
> As good. The utmost must be good and is
> And is our fortune and honey hived in the trees
> And mingling of colors at a festival.

In the explicit critique of this passage in *The Auroras of Autumn*, Stevens will question his harvest credences:

> We stand in the tumult of a festival.

> What festival? This loud, disordered mooch?

But Stevens expresses perceptible dualities even within *Credences of Summer*, and can follow his celebratory polyphony with a single sharpened analytic clarion, forsaking the seductive lingerings of the last choirs for the peremptory fiats of the trumpet:

> It is the visible announced,
> It is the more than visible, the more
> Than sharp, illustrious scene. The trumpet cries
> This is the successor of the invisible.

And unlike those last choirs, which suppose nothing as they rise in the land "too serene" for enigmas, the trumpet is fully conscious. It knows that

> A mind exists, aware of division, aware
> Of its cry as clarion . . .
> Man's mind grown venerable in the unreal.

That venerable mind belongs to what Stevens will call the Omega in man, peering forever into distances. Credences of summer are only possible when that aspect of the mind is suspended by an effort, so that for a moment the present can suffice and the distant can "fail" the normally clairvoyant eye.

As Stevens has moved further and further away from the original gifted moment when the scene subdues the intellect and the mind lays by its troubles, he has approached a vantage point in which the mind, in a new ascendancy, more than half creates what it perceives. The final canto in *Credences of Summer* begins very coldly indeed, with the poet as a deliberate and distant manipulator of marionettes:

> The personae of summer play the characters
> Of an inhuman author, who meditates
> With the gold bugs, in blue meadows, late at night.
> He does not hear his characters talk.

The poem has passed from noon to night, and the gold bugs and blue meadows are the nighttime imitation of the gold sun and the blue sky of earlier stanzas. But as the puppet master sets his characters in motion, they achieve some life of their own: they bulge beyond his control, and they wear mottled costumes, wanting to take on the ideal self-forgetful ripeness of summer, but remaining personae nevertheless. To the end they remain fictions, and their costumes are moody, and they are free only for a moment. Even so, Stevens risks sentimentality in the ending,

> In which the characters speak because they want
> To speak, the fat, the roseate characters,
> Free, for a moment, from malice and sudden cry,
> Complete in a completed scene, speaking
> Their parts as in a youthful happiness.

No criticism of this passage, or of the entire stance of *Credences of Summer*, could be more pointed than Stevens' own later backward glance in "The Ultimate Poem Is Abstract," written about a day which also seems plenary, full of revelations, placid, blue, roseate, ripe, complete:

> This day writhes with what? The lecturer
> On This Beautiful World Of Ours composes himself
> And hems the planet rose and haws it ripe . . .
>
> If the day writhes, it is not with revelations.
> One goes on asking questions. That, then, is one
> Of the categories. So said, this placid space
>
> Is changed. It is not so blue as we thought. To be blue
> There must be no questions . . .

                    It would be enough
If we were ever, just once, at the middle, fixed
In This Beautiful World Of Ours and not as now,

Helplessly at the edge, enough to be
Complete, because at the middle, if only in sense,
And in that enormous sense, merely enjoy.   (429)

Credences of Summer, which begins "at the middle," is undermined by the difficulties made so bald in this later poem. To
be blue, there must be no questions. Stevens' desperate, if truthful, expedient with which to end the poem is the creation of the
inhuman author whose characters undergo spontaneous generation for a flicker of feeling. This inhuman author is the hermit
in the hermitage at the center, and he, not the senses, controls
the ending of the poem. Earlier, Stevens had denied that the
natural mountain depended in any way on the hermit:

                    It is not
A hermit's truth nor symbol in hermitage.
It is the visible rock, the audible.

But if the personae of summer are the author's creations, so perhaps is the rock of summer, and the poem, by posing what are
for Stevens the false poles of reality on the one hand and imagination on the other, diverts him from his truer subject: the variety
of several imaginative modes playing on any one thing. He is
never more uneasy than when he is trying to claim some autonomy for haymows in Oley, as he does earlier in the poem; it
forces him into his concluding evocation of a disembodied and
inhuman author as proper counterpart to the irremediably obdurate hay.

In *The Auroras of Autumn*, Stevens more suitably fixes his
shape-changing eye, not on the land, but on the huge cloudy

symbols of the night's starred face. In this wholly individual poem there is nevertheless scarcely a line not reminiscent of earlier volumes. Stevens' density of internal reference to earlier leitmotivs is greater here than in any other poem, so much so that almost nothing is unfamiliar in the images except the superb aurora borealis which dominates the whole. Stevens may have had Wordsworth's northern lights in mind, that manifestation which is "Here, nowhere, there, and everywhere at once" (*Prelude* V, 533). Wherever he found the symbol, whether in literature or in nature,[5] it corresponds perfectly to the bravura of his imagination, even more so than the slower transformations of "Sea-Surface Full of Clouds." And certainly these changing auroras match his solemn fantasia better than the effort, so marked in *Credences of Summer*, to hold the imagination still. Stevens' restless modulations need an equally restless symbol, and the lights (with their lord, the flashing serpent) are, like his poetry, "always enlarging the change."

For all its lingering glances at other poems, *The Auroras of Autumn* remains essentially the partner to its antithesis, *Credences of Summer*. Like the earlier poem, it begins, so unusually for Stevens in the long poems, by placing its speaker in the lyric present, declaring by that emphasis on the here and now a firm attempt to center the mind on the present, not to drift elegiacally back or press wishfully forward. But whereas Summer represented repose, immobility, static piled haymows and monolithic mountains, Autumn is compounded of Stevens' most congenial subjects — flux, rapidity, flickerings, and winds. For all the difference in state between the two seasons, it is characteristic of Stevens at this period to place himself in the same relation to each, as the poet attempting total absorption in the scene, refusing to distance himself from it until the poem is well advanced. The ostentation of the first canto of *The Auroras of Autumn* lies in its insistence on the formula "This is," repeated with different predicates, recalling the similar demonstrative beginning of *Credences of Summer*. And although Stevens begins at once his parable of father, mother, children, and scholar, the speaker's voice interpolates again and again references to "this" throne, "this" thing, "these" heavens, "these" lights, "this" imminence, and so on. The "thisness" of *The Auroras of Autumn*, in other words, is never allowed to lapse entirely, and in this way it is a poem more consistent than *Credences of Summer*. The narrator remains discreetly present in these recurrent demonstrative phrases.

The boreal serpent in his nest at the zenith, marking the north pole raised to the tip of the heavens, is clearly another variation on the old man on the tower or the robin on the beanpole, but where the old man reads no book and the robin takes no flight, the serpent is engaged in perpetual rapacious motion, wriggling out of its egg, sloughing its skin, gulping objects into itself, moving in the grass. There are at first two serpents, one on the earth and one in the sky, and the motion of the canto is a nervous ascent and descent and reascent and redescent, a vertiginous uncertainty expressed in antiphonal rhetoric:

> This is where the serpent
> lives, the bodiless.
> This is his nest.
>
> Or is this another wriggling
> out of the egg?
> These lights may finally attain
> a pole
> In the midmost midnight and
> find the serpent there,
> In another nest.
>
> This is his poison: that we
> should disbelieve even
> that.

Unlike *Credences of Summer*, which staved off interrogation as long as it could, *The Auroras of Autumn* encourages the anatomy of the season, and the analytic questions which form so strong a thread in the construction of the poem begin in the fourth line of the first canto. Stevens' demanding intellectuality stops in the midst of summer to imagine winter because it is natural to him to be reflective and abstract, even idly metaphysical, because he "likes magnificence/ And the solemn pleasures of magnificent space" (vi). But there are two manners of the analytic moment. One rests in the metaphor, say, of the serpent, and keeping the vehicle intact asks whether this moment is "another wriggling out of the egg"; the other sort departs from the original metaphor, and inventing surrogate poet-selves (like the inhuman author in *Credences of Summer* or his counterpart the spectre of the spheres in *The Auroras of Autumn*) uses these supplementary selves to pose the questions.

By the time Stevens reaches out to his disembodied spectre he has stepped considerably beyond the autumnal moment, and at the end, he converses with the rabbi in speculative and generalizing terms, juggling his combinations of happiness and unhappiness. With a wrench, at the end of the last canto, he returns to his original autumnal and auroral metaphors, and only retrieves his balance in the final tercet, where the spectre is violently set down to live all lives,

> That he might know
>
> In hall harridan, not hushful paradise,
> To a haggling of wind and weather, by these lights
> Like a blaze of summer straw, in winter's nick.   (x)

The energy of repudiation directed toward *Credence of Summer* in *The Auroras of Autumn* is nowhere clearer than in this igniting of the Oley hay mows. As they go up in flame, in a blaze of summer straw, they produce the streamers of the auroras, and the hushful paradise of August gives way to the hall harridan, a fit locale for "the harridan self and ever maladive fate" that went crying through the autumn leaves in *Owl's Clover*. Like the inhuman author of *Credences of Summer* who meditates with the gold bugs, and like the serpent who meditates in the ferns, the spectre meditates a whole as he lives all lives, and the whole that he envisages is to be, in some season, relentlessly in possession of happiness by being relentless in knowledge. Someday, Stevens hopes, we may find

> The possible nest in the invisible tree,
> Which in a composite season, now unknown,
> Denied, dismissed, may hold a serpent, loud
> In our captious hymns, erect and sinuous,
> Whose venom and whose wisdom will be one.   (437)

But that new composite androgynous stability of serpent and nest, described in "St. John and the Backache," is not attained in *The Auroras of Autumn*, which remains bound in its glittering motion, a brilliant reproduction of Stevens' apprehensive compulsion in change.

To the extent that *The Auroras of Autumn* remains a poem of the sky and motion, it is a dazzling performance. Indoors, it weakens, and it falters in its regressive motion toward childhood, before the serpent entered Eden. The first canto summons up three manifestations of the Fate-serpent, which are rapidly reduced to two, as the visionary image of the serpent transcendent, relentless in happiness, belonging purely to an airy nest, is dismissed. The other two levels of being remain. One is the simple animal nature of the serpent as he lives in the ferns, on the rock, in the grass, like an Indian in a glade, native and hidden; in this nature his head is wholly zoological — flecked, black-beaded, visible. The serpent's pure bestiality makes us disbelieve in his possible transcendence; we are sure of his naturalness as he moves to make sure of sun. But in contrast, there is the changeable serpent, whose head has become air, whose tip is higher than the stars, whose nest is not the low grass but yet is still the earth, this time the earth in total panorama:

> This is his nest,
> These fields, these hills, these tinted distances,
> And the pines above and along and beside the sea.

This changeable serpent lives in present participles, gulping, wriggling, flashing, and emerging, and he is the true genius of the poem. The wholly natural beast, at ease in the glade, is the presiding spirit of Stevens' willful wish, even here, to be entirely at home in the world, to be an Indian in America, an aborigine indigenous to the place. The children who appear in the poem are the regressive human embodiment of the Indian-serpent, which in its pristine innocence is a biological serpent native to Eden, not an interloping malice. This serpent is dismissed in favor of the grimmer changing one, and the epigraph to *The Auroras of Autumn* could well be Donne's harsh couplet from "Twicknam Garden":

> And that this place may thoroughly be thought
> True paradise, I have the serpent brought.

Like Donne, "blasted with sighs" in spite of the garden, Stevens here bids farewell to the idea which engendered *Credences of Summer* — the idea that one could give credence to summer, that the mind could lay by its trouble, that honey could be hived and a festival held. "As the Eye altering, alters all," the luxuriant haymows bleach to an expanse of desolate sand.

The four cantos that follow the appearance of the serpent are like the scenes following an overture. The overture is the warning — hard-surfaced, intellectual, abstract — but the scenes are elegiac, subtle, personal, "toned" as the overture was not. In the last canto of the four (canto v), the elegiac tone is routed in disorder, and the cause of the rout seems to be a surge of violent disgust for the mythologized father of the poem, who is a mixture of Prospero and Caliban. In his Prospero-role, the father "fetches tellers of tales/ And musicians;" he "fetches pageants out of air,/ Scenes of the theatre, vistas and blocks of woods/ And curtains like a naive pretence of sleep." But as Caliban, the father grossly fetches negresses and "unherded herds,/ Of barbarous tongue, slavered and panting halves of breath." The second perspective wins, finally, as the speaker brutalizes the pageant:

> We stand in the tumult of a festival.
>
> What festival? This loud, disordered mooch?
> These hospitaliers? These brute-like guests?
> These musicians dubbing at a tragedy
>
> A-dub, a-dub, which is made up of this:
> That there are no lines to speak? There is no play.
> Or, the persons act one merely by being here.   (v)

With this dismissal of the characters of the inhuman author Stevens turns the puppet theater into a happening with no script. The central figure of the father is rendered barbarous by the iterative sentence pattern into which he is confined. Whereas the mother "invites humanity to her house/ And table" the father "fetches" things and people, and the phrase "the father fetches" is four times repeated in identical form, three times repeated in identical line position, till the father is made an automatic robot. Under this manipulation, the natural ripeness of *Credences of Summer* becomes the decadent and self-involved ripeness of the negresses who "dance/ Among the children, like

curious ripenesses/ Of pattern in the dance's ripening." The
marriage hymns of Oley are replaced by the "insidious tones"
of the musicians who are "clawing the sing-song of their instruments" at the father's behest. The source of the disgust for the
father-impresario seems to be Stevens' revulsion against that
deliberate primitivism of his own which wants summer, not winter, and which sets itself to conjure up negresses, guitarists, and
the "unherded herds" of oxlike freed men, all in a vain attempt
to reproduce on an ignorant and one-stringed instrument the
sophisticated chaos of the self.

But before he arrives at this recoil against his harmonium's
cruder subterfuges, Stevens gives us the beautiful triad of poems
each beginning "Farewell to an idea," where his elegy reaches
a perfection of naturalness and subdued restraint hardly possible
in earlier long poems. These three cantos are an elegy written
before the fact, an anticipatory mourning in which "a darkness gathers though it does not fall." The first (canto ii) is a
brilliant exercise in more and less — a little more in one place,
a little less somewhere else — but in this season even more is
less, since the positive comparatives are mostly pejorative: the
white of the flowers grows duller, and the lines of the beach
grow longer and emptier. Some equivocation remains in the
comparisons, but the direction of atrophy is clear.

Stevens' tendency in the first elegiac canto is to match unequivocal notations of skeletal whiteness against extremely con-
jectural modifiers of that whiteness: his mind, in other words,
must admit the phenomenon, but will not for a long time admit
its significance. Instead, it casts around for ways of explaining
this whiteness, or ways of softening its harshness. The scene
develops brilliantly by slow increments, beginning with a
sketched line:

> Farewell to an idea . . . A cabin stands,
> Deserted, on a beach. It is white.

The mind immediately skitters off into harmless explanations of that whiteness:

> It is white,
> As by a custom or according to
> An ancestral theme or as a consequence
> Of an infinite course.

As soon as Stevens begins on a multiplicity of "or's" we sense his uneasiness. The deadly observant eye returns, and notes that

> The flowers against the wall
> Are white.

But again the qualifiers multiply in haste and confuse the issue beyond any possible clarity: the flowers

> Are white, a little dried, a kind of mark
>
> Reminding, trying to remind, of a white
> That was different, something else, last year
> Or before, not the white of an aging afternoon.
>
> Whether fresher or duller, whether of winter cloud
> Or of winter sky, from horizon to horizon.

Every means is used to distract the attention from the adamant dry whiteness of the flowers, including the rephrasing of "reminding," the evasiveness about time, the unwillingness to decide between fresher and duller, and the uncertainty about cloud or sky. But the relentless eye is not to be put off, and now it is joined in its infallible perception by the whole body, which senses, in the same flat sentence-form used for the eye's notations, that

The wind is blowing the sand across the floor.

With that union of the white sand to the white cabin and the white flowers, the joining is made between the total atmosphere, dominated by the wind, and the deserted cabin, its floors tenanted only by sand. The totality of whiteness is at last admitted wholly:

Here, being visible is being white.

The scene becomes a white-on-white bas-relief, "the solid of white, the accomplishment/ Of an extremist in an exercise."

With this submission to the truth, the mind has left its deceits, and the declarative statements become dominant and unequivocal:

The season changes. A cold wind chills the beach.
The long lines of it grow longer, emptier,
A darkness gathers though it does not fall

And the whiteness grows less vivid on the wall.

The severity of the language justifies a daring play on words:

The man who is walking turns blankly on the sand.

The man, to use Milton's words, has been presented with a universal blank, and becomes himself blanched and blank, like the scene. But because he has finally granted the desolate whiteness in the landscape, he can give up looking to it for sustenance, and can turn his fixed gaze away from the beach and to the sky. What he sees, inhuman though it is, repays his glance: he sees, but only after he has abjured land-flowerings, the great gusts and colored sweeps of the Northern lights, and they are exhilarating:

> He observes how the north is always enlarging the change
>
> With its frigid brilliances, its blue-red sweeps
> And gusts of great enkindlings, its polar green,
> The color of ice and fire and solitude.

The verbal parallels between the celestial aurora and the chilling earthly wind make us realize that the one does not exist without the other, that they are two manifestations of the same force. The identification is made first syntactically: "the wind is blowing" and "the north is . . . enlarging the change" are the canto's only independent clauses in the continuous present. Later, the parallel is made metaphorically, as Stevens borrows the vocabulary of wind in composing his auroras of "sweeps" and "gusts." For the moment, the enkindling fire of the auroras is not metaphorically reinforced, but the fiery color later gives rise to other burnings in the poem, ending in the wonderful invention of "the blaze of summer straw," when Oley goes up in flames.

The splendor of desolation in the sight of Crispin's deserted cabin is not matched again in the poem until the final cantos regather their energies after the repudiation of the father. But there are gentler moments, in which Stevens surmounts the dangers of pathos by having his "observant" eye, not his rhapsodic one, note his fading tableaux. As he watches the dissolving mother (iii), he phrases the scene in short empty sentences, the fatal notation of necessity: [6]

> Farewell to an idea . . .
> The mother's face, the purpose of the poem, fills the room.

They are together, here, and it is warm, with none of the
    prescience of oncoming dreams.
It is evening.
The house is evening, half-dissolved.
Only the half they can never possess remains, still-starred.
It is the mother they possess, who gives transparence to
    their present peace.
She makes that gentler that can gentle be.
And yet she too is dissolved, she is destroyed.
She gives transparence.
But she has grown old.
The necklace is a carving not a kiss.
The soft hands are a motion not a touch.
The house will crumble and the books will burn.

This canto depends on the continuing antithesis of the beauty
and the dissolution of the mother, an antithesis which reaches its
strictest point in the two rigid sentences at the center of the
poem: "She gives transparence. But she has grown old." The
images of this canto and of the next are quarried from the early
ode "To the One of Fictive Music," but the imposition of the
stern syntactic form on the yielding lyric material makes for
a new sort of nostalgia. The modulation from statement to
prophecy is made so unobtrusively that we scarcely notice it
until it has happened:

> She gives transparence. But she has grown old.
> The necklace is a carving not a kiss.
>
> The soft hands are a motion not a touch.
> The house will crumble and the books will burn.

These four symmetrical lines are so tonelessly uttered that the
fourth seems as unarguable, as much a natural fact, as the pre-

ceding three. But the effect of the intensification into prophecy is to send the mind rapidly back to the lulling present of the unsuspecting family:

> They are at ease in a shelter of the mind
>
> And the house is of the mind and they and time,
> Together, all together.

The prophecy reappears, but in a softened rephrasing, first in the deceptive appearance of the approaching consuming fire:

> Boreal night
> Will look like frost as it approaches them
>
> And to the mother as she falls asleep
> And as they say good-night, good-night.

And the inevitable extinction of the family is announced in a sinister but understated mention of the extinguished lights in the bedchambers, lit now only by the flaring auroras outside:

> Upstairs
> The windows will be lighted, not the rooms.

Finally, though, these mitigations and evasions give way to the peremptory doom:

> The wind will spread its windy grandeurs round
> And knock like a rifle-butt against the door.
> The wind will command them with invincible sound.

Stevens' simplicity of response to the mythological mother is replaced in the next canto (iv) by his ambivalent attentions to the father. On the one hand, the father is descended from the outmoded Jehovah figures, giants, mythy Joves, and so on, of earlier poems, but on the other hand, he has agreeable qualities in common with both Canon Aspirin and the angel of *Notes toward a Supreme Fiction*, those acrobatic seraphic figures who leap through space. Stevens' language becomes archaic, as the father is said to sit "as one that is strong in the bushes of his eyes," with a pun on bushy eyebrows and the burning bush. He sits in "green-a-day" (another reminiscence of *Credences of Summer*), but is also perpetually in motion, just as "green-a-day" is also "bleak regard"; he stops in summer to imagine winter, and his rapid oscillations from saying no to no and yes to yes and yes to no are imitated in the poem by the oscillations between the moving and the motionless. Like the girl at Key West who "measured to the hour its solitude" he "measures the velocities of change," and by his motion establishes a norm of nature; but unlike the singing girl, the father is sometimes comic, as "he leaps from heaven to heaven more rapidly/ Than bad angels leap from heaven to hell in flames." The tension of attitudes mounts as Stevens constructs an apotheosis of the father, moving fully into the regressive diction of "To the One of Fictive Music":

> Master O master seated by the fire
> And yet in space and motionless and yet
> Of motion the ever-brightening origin,
>
> Profound, and yet the king and yet the crown —

The sentimental effort breaks here, as Stevens brusquely forsakes his celebratory incantation-weaving and says dismissively:

> Look at this present throne. What company,
> In masks, can choir it with the naked wind?

Exit the whole shebang, as Stevens had said earlier about Crispin's fiction, and with this dismissal we leave, not only this scene, but the throne and the motley company of *Credences of Summer*. The autumnal wind has blown pretenses away, and the creator-father becomes, in consequence, the object of contempt, the "fetcher" of negresses and clawing musicians and slavering herds, the hospitalier of a disorderly riot.[7] With this denial of meaning to poetic gesture, the first half of the poem comes to a close, in a cynicism that touches both the events and their poems: "There are no lines to speak. There is no play."

One could hardly have guessed where the poem might go from here. *Credences of Summer*, too, had come to a halt halfway through, and had had to rephrase itself, first in celestial and then in "low" terms, in order to deal with its original tableau of mountain, tower, and man. Here, Stevens saves himself by forsaking for a moment his family myth and looking again at the auroras. Earlier, they had only been sketched for us; we saw them once directly in the view of the man on the sand, in a vivid blur of motion and color; and later we saw them obliquely, in their sinister approach, when "boreal light/ Will look like frost" as it lights the windows. But now, two great cantos (vi and vii) are devoted to a panorama of the auroras, the first giving a physical account, the second a metaphysical one. We have finally arrived at that anatomy of summer that Stevens had so hoped to postpone, since summer, anatomized, turns immediately to winter.

The first canto (vi) is exquisitely undemanding, as Stevens is content to imagine no revelatory function for the auroras, no purpose to their activity, simply change for the sake of change, transformation idly done "to no end." The absolute parity of all forms is established, emergence equals collapse in interest and beauty, and activity exists for the time being without dénouement. The mountain of *Credences of Summer* is no longer half green, half rocklike air — nothing so stolid as that. In the boreal night the mountain is now rock, water, light, and clouds, all at once, as Stevens describes the aurora:

> It is a theatre floating through the clouds,
> Itself a cloud, although of misted rock
> And mountains running like water, wave on wave,
>
> Through waves of light.

These transformations of the sky occur as an enormous relief to Stevens, as he feels momentarily that he can give up the difficult labor of willed imaginative transformation: the sky will do it all for him. In the past, he had usually represented nature as the fixed principle, and the interpreting mind as the chief source of change: even in "Sea Surface full of Clouds" the variable surface is pressed into doctrinal service, and the changes have to be seen as symbolic and ordered. In more violently willed transformations, the mind plants in the sky a converse to the monotony of time and place, rather as it placed the jar in Tennessee:

Human Arrangement

> Place-bound and time-bound in evening rain
> And bound by a sound which does not change,
>
> Except that it begins and ends,
> Begins again and ends again —
>
> Rain without change within or from
> Without. In this place and in this time
>
> And in this sound, which do not change,
> In which the rain is all one thing,

In the sky, an imagined, wooden chair
Is the clear-point of an edifice,

Forced up from nothing, evening's chair,
Blue-strutted curule, true — unreal,

The centre of transformations that
Transform for transformation's self,

In a glitter that is a life, a gold
That is a being, a will, a fate.   (363)

This forced transformation, set up in defiance of the monotonous scene, reminds us of Stevens' apocalyptic transformations, nowhere more baldly put than in *Owl's Clover*, where the porcelain muses are to repeat *To Be Itself*,

Until the sharply colored glass transforms
Itself into the speech of the spirit.

Such transformations are one-directional, lifting the subject up a notch from the real to the unreal. But the beautiful transformations of the aurora are directionless:

. . . It is of cloud transformed
To cloud transformed again, idly, the way
A season changes color to no end.

Except the lavishing of itself in change,
As light changes yellow into gold and gold
To its opal elements and fire's delight,

Splashed wide-wise because it likes magnificence
And the solemn pleasures of magnificent space.
The cloud drifts idly through half-thought-of forms.

In these childlike phrases, we sense the "innocence" Stevens will later claim for the aurora: it is "splashed wide-wise," it "likes magnificence," it likes the "solemn pleasures" of its playground, magnificent space.

This will to change of the aurora is rather like the will to change of the west wind (in *Notes*, It Must Change, x), in which metaphor is seen as something we imitate from nature, from this "volatile world." The will of *Notes* was directed, human, urgent, "A will to change, a necessitous/ And present way"; the aurora's will is idle, purposeless, lavish, purely pleasurable, and inhuman. Against the aurora there suddenly appear terrified birds, surrogates for the poet as he recoils from the aurora's meaningless if gorgeous will-to-change:

> The theatre is filled with flying birds,
> Wild wedges, as of a volcano's smoke, palm-eyed
> And vanishing, a web in a corridor
>
> Or massive portico.

This matches Tennyson's recoil from the perception of a purposeless universe, as Sorrow speaks to him in *In Memoriam*:

> "The stars," she whispered, "blindly run,
> A web is woven about the sky."

The surrealism of the birds, dehumanized into wedges, made fluid in form like the auroras themselves, startling and evanescent as spurting smoke, tenuous as a web, and mysteriously palm-eyed, is the surrealism of the poet's terrified response as he feels himself momentarily caught up into the metamorphoses of the lights, absorbed into a nature constantly shifting shape. With an effort of mind he rejects the temptation to be drawn into the undertow of these waves, and sets his scholar of one candle against "the earth's whole amplitude and Nature's multiform power consign'd for once to colors," as Whitman once said of a prairie sunset. It is up to the scholar to destroy the aurora, this named thing, and render it nameless by seeing it as a new phenomenon. The intellectual formulation here is suspect and should not be scrutinized, but the confrontation that follows, as the single man opens the door of his house on flames, is a worthy climax to the poem:

> The scholar of one candle sees
> An Arctic effulgence flaring on the frame
> Of everything he is. And he feels afraid.

As changeful light, the aurora is innocent; as flame, it is dangerous; as cold fire, Arctic effulgence, it is the intimidating unknown. Stevens, in this version of "the multiform beauty" (*OP*, 12), has found the final correlative for his reflections on middle age and for the fear and fascination of ongoing process.

When Stevens passes from these illustrations of the aurora to an analysis of it, the advance on *Credences of Summer* is most visible. Instead of the rather sterile playing-off of the day against the year, the queen against her kin, and the soldier against the land, those social and communal questions always less than urgent to Stevens, we encounter a question more immediate to him, as it was to Keats: why it is, and how it is, that the dreamer venoms all his days, and cannot know, as other men do, the pain alone, the joy alone, distinct. Stevens advances in fact (in canto vii) to three questions — his last great interrogation of the world, since he will come, in *An Ordinary Evening in New Haven*, to pure declaration. The first question examines the necessary passage from the pastoral to the tragic:

> Is there an imagination that sits enthroned
> As grim as it is benevolent, the just
> And the unjust, which in the midst of summer stops

To imagine winter?

The summer throne of "quiet and green-a-day" has stiffened
itself into the throne of Rhadamanthus, and the father's motion
from heaven to heaven now becomes more like a leap from
heaven to hell. Stevens' second question personifies the leaper,
now robed and composed in the deathly magnificence of the
auroras:

> When the leaves are dead,
> Does it take its place in the north and enfold itself,
> Goat-leaper, crystalled and luminous, sitting
>
> In highest night?

The third question asks, in a cold horror, and with an echo of
the Psalms, what indeed these heavens proclaim: what is the
source of the aurora's splendid contrast of black sky with white
light; is it true that it adorns itself in black by extinguishing
planets in its snowy radiance, and does it leave unextinguished
only those planets it decides to retain for its own starry crown?

> And do these heavens adorn
> And proclaim it, the white creator of black, jetted
> By extinguishings, even of planets as may be,
>
> Even of earth, even of sight, in snow,
> Except as needed by way of majesty,
> In the sky, as crown and diamond cabala?

The absolute accuracy of these suspicions is confirmed as Stevens
answers his own questions in precisely the fated terms of his
previous formulation, repeating the leaps and the extinguishings;
but putting them, this time, not as nouns, but as instant verbs:

It leaps through us, through all our heavens leaps,
Extinguishing our planets, one by one,
Leaving, of where we were and looked, of where

We knew each other and of each other thought,
A shivering residue, chilled and foregone,
Except for that crown and mystical cabala.

We remain finally only as an adjunct to that diadem which has so swallowed up the known. "To see the gods dispelled in mid-air . . . is one of the great human experiences . . . We shared likewise this experience of annihilation. It was their annihilation, not ours, and yet it left us feeling that in a measure, we, too, had been annihilated. It left us feeling dispossessed and alone in a solitude, like children without parents, in a home that seemed deserted." These sentences from "Two or Three Ideas" (*OP*, 206–207) are not the only possible gloss on *The Auroras of Autumn*, but they are a partial one: on the one hand the great experience of extinction, leaving a hard brilliance like the diamond crown in the impersonal universe, and on the other hand, the dispossessed children, a shivering residue. A superb and unyielding glitter surmounts everything else in these lines, as it dwarfs with its energy and regality the pathos of the disinherited spectators.

But Sevens will not rest in the sublime. True to its nature, the tragic imagination must beget its opposite. As we went from untroubled summer to winter fatality, we now reverse direction, and go "from destiny to slight caprice." The only force regulating the leaper is its necessary polarity: "it dare not leap by chance," but it moves to unmake itself in comic flippancy — or so Stevens says. *The Auroras of Autumn* itself does not rediscover summer in winter after having discovered winter in summer. It is hard to imagine what might undo the aurora borealis, as the aurora "undid" summer. Stevens becomes purely referential:

> And thus its jetted tragedy, its stele
>
> And shape and mournful making move to find
> What must unmake it and, at last, what can,
> Say, a flippant communication under the moon.

This seems an imposed order, not a discovered one, and Stevens' uneasiness with it is visible in his inference from "must" to "can." In later poems, Stevens will "unmake" tragedy, not through flippancy but through a withdrawal from the theatrical mode in which the tragic perception voices itself. From questions, dramas, theaters, histrionics, brilliancies, we pass in Stevens' work to a sober declarativeness. Here, and for the moment, in canto viii, all that Stevens can summon up are gestures of willed assertion:

> But [innocence] exists,
> It exists, it is visible, it is, it is.

In this wish, the mother is replaced by a dream-vision of her absent self, no longer old but rejuvenated, and the imaginary quality of the vision is reinforced by the fictive "as if":

> So then, these lights are not a spell of light,
> A saying out of a cloud, but innocence.
> An innocence of the earth and no false sign
>
> Or symbol of malice. That we partake thereof,
> Lie down like children in this holiness,
> As if, awake, we lay in the quiet of sleep,

As if the innocent mother sang in the dark
Of the room and on an accordion, half-heard,
Created the time and place in which we breathed . . .

We have already seen the wintry fear "unmade" by an imagined comedy or flippancy; now we are offered a resolution by a pure ethereality. But this moving ending, attached to a stanza that began in the arid vein of *Description without Place*, in a toying with the philosophical mode, makes a centaurlike poem, half abstract discussion, half wish-fantasy, with no middle term of the real to join these two detached poles of the unreal. The ninth canto makes a lulling effort to assimilate terror and innocence, affirming simply that disaster

May come tomorrow in the simplest word,
Almost as part of innocence, almost,
Almost as the tenderest and the truest part.

But what is remembered of this poem is not that assumed naïveté, but the etched anticipation of a secularized doomsday:

Shall we be found hanging in the trees next spring?
Of what disaster is this the imminence:
Bare limbs, bare trees and a wind as sharp as salt?

As before, Stevens answers his own question, this time pairing the earthly wasteland with its wonderfully burnished cause, a mustering of the heavenly army:

The stars are putting on their glittering belts.
They throw around their shoulders cloaks that flash
Like a great shadow's last embellishment.

Here, as in the last lines of *The Auroras*, Stevens is remembering

267

a passage in *Owl's Clover* on evening, where the old woman spoils the being of the night:

> Without her, evening like a budding yew,
> Would soon be brilliant, as it was, before
> The harridan self and ever-maladive fate
> Went crying their desolate syllables, before
> Their voice and the voice of the tortured wind were one . . .

That uninhabited evening would have a sky "thick with stars/ Of a lunar light, dark belted sorcerers," and Stevens would wish to be free of the old woman so that he could "flourish the great cloak we wear/ At night, to turn away from the abominable/ Farewells" (*OP*, 45, 46, 71), those farewells that begin *The Auroras of Autumn.* Our disaster (and Stevens would have been conscious of the etymology of the word) is in fact the gathering of the stars, and the green-queen-like embellishments of summer yield to a different kind of jewels. To see the stars in this way is to awake from the stolid sensual drowse of the Danes in Denmark, "for whom the outlandish was [only] another day/ Of the week, [just slightly] queerer than Sunday." Exposed to the auroras, Stevens, like Melville's dying soldier, has been "enlightened by the glare," and the final flippancy of the last canto, juggling discrepant phases of man's feelings and the world's landscapes, still yields, at the end, to the total reign of the auroras, "these lights/ Like a blaze of summer straw, in winter's nick." It is these flaring lights, and the apprehensive questions they raise, that are the radiant center of the poem: Stevens' theatrical auroras and his repeated interrogations of them create his most ravishing lines. From this, the most economical and yet the most brilliant of his long poems, he will pass on to the looser and quieter recapitulations of *An Ordinary Evening in New Haven.*

X. The Total Leaflessness

It is a bough in the electric light
And exhalations in the eaves, so little
To indicate the total leaflessness.

In poetry, as Valéry once said, it is the lack and the blank
that create. *An Ordinary Evening in New Haven* (1949) [1] is
the poem of an old man living in the lack and the blank, and
asking himself whether a conjecture such as Valéry's can be
true. In this, the harshest of all his experiments, Stevens deprives
his poetry of all that the flesh, the sun, the earth, and the moon
can offer, and, himself a skeleton, examines the bare possibilities
of a skeletal life. Even the pond and the greenhouse of "The
Plain Sense of Things" are not allowed to populate this resolutely impoverished poem. Stevens is cruelly stringent and sets
a desolate scene; the poem cannot hope, under these conditions,
to overcome entirely the exhaustion and despair that motivate it.
It is, humanly speaking, the saddest of all Stevens' poems. One
wants it to have succeeded totally, to have proved that Stevens
could find, in life's most minimal offering, something which
would suffice. Poetry, as we can tell from *The Rock*, had not
deserted Stevens, nor he it, but in taking the commonplace for
"reality" he was repressing too much, as he comes to realize in
the course of the poem. The title is polemic: Stevens chooses
New Haven, not the country but a city and a city not even his
own; and chooses evening, not only without the sun but without
the moon; and not a significant Sunday evening (like Sunday

morning) but an ordinary weekday one; and not an evening pale and possessed, but a cold autumnal one monotonously affronted by rain. His self-portraits are the dry Professor Eucalyptus, the meager letters of the alphabet, or squirrels huddled in trees against the winter cold. *An Ordinary Evening* is, in short, almost unremittingly minimal, and over and over again threatens to die of its own starvation.

When it does not die, on the other hand, it composes itself, all by itself it seems and without human intervention, into that great and remote poetry of Stevens' old age, so unlike any other poetry in English. We encounter this poem and the other poems of Stevens' last decade as Wordsworth encountered his old man:

> He travels on, and in his face, his step,
> His gait, is one expression: every limb,
> His look and bending figure, all bespeak
> A man who does not move with pain, but moves
> With thought. — He is insensibly subdued
> To settled quiet: he is one by whom
> All effort seems forgotten; one to whom
> Long patience hath such mild composure given,
> That patience now doth seem a thing of which
> He hath no need. He is by nature led
> To peace so perfect that the young behold
> With envy, what the Old Man hardly feels.
> ("Animal Tranquillity and Decay")

Stevens, though subdued to settled quiet, is not led to perfect peace. Nevertheless, these poems should tell us, if any can, of that undiscovered country of the old, and in fact they do, but it is a country rarely susceptible to language. When Stevens expresses the meaninglessness of his deprived days, the nameless weight of custom heavy as frost and deep almost as life, he cannot use the dramatic terms of his great predecessors. His mythology, to be truthful, has to reflect his region, and for the most part it, like the language of his poem, is in search of the ordinary and the unenhanced. When the poem takes on color and life it is because he has found some interest even in his New Haven hotel room and its rainy waterspout, or, more often, because he evades his subject and has turned away from the city to the sun, to the earth, or to the realm of theory. Painfully, Stevens' tiredness sometimes lapses into that "deliberate redundance" and "randomness trying to lose itself in multiplication" which Alvarez has criticized in this poem and in others.[2]

The impossible task the poem sets itself is to account, in terms of consciousness, for a depression which is overwhelmingly physical — the metabolic depletion in age of the body's responses. In that way, the poem is at war with itself, and becomes a long expansion of Coleridge's disjunction before the moon and the stars:

> I see them all, so excellently fair,
> I see, not feel, how beautiful they are!

Stevens, in his vision, tells himself that day and night are eternally young in their recurrence; why, then, should he see this evening as ancient when it does not see itself as old:

> The oldest-newest day is the newest alone.[3]
> The oldest-newest night does not creak by,
> With lanterns, like a celestial ancientness.   (xvi)

Day and night, sea and sky, eternally youthful, meet at the horizon in an eternal adolescence, "their eyes closed, in a young palaver of lips." But though Stevens in this passage affirms the ageless perpetuity of night, he writes with such unease of reference that he becomes literally unintelligible:

Silently it heaves its youthful sleep from the sea —

The Oklahoman — the Italian blue
Beyond the horizon with its masculine,

Their eyes closed, in a young palaver of lips.

These stanzas are the emotional center of the canto, but they describe a seeing without feeling, as we realize when we read the framing stanzas — all more truly felt — that precede and follow them. In their barely enunciated phrases, they are dessication itself, but this poverty is more centrally present than the day's riches.

The lines that introduce the canto give us Stevens behind a hieratic mask, which hides, with its stiff grandeur, the unimaginable ruin which has befallen the lapidary rock, now that its lapis-haunted air has become "the dilapidation of dilapidations," an inverse Holy of Holies:

Among time's images, there is not one
Of this present, the venerable mask above
The dilapidation of dilapidations.

This knowledge — that his old age had given him a rare subject, rarely written about and so not among the images of time — is Stevens' torment in the poem. He could not say, with Yeats, that he had never had a more excited, fantastic imagination; age had exhausted him soul and body. And yet that too was a topic, but he could not find bravura, or so he suggests in this canto, adequate to that great hymn. The night, he says, is eternally *vierge* and *vivace*, like the day, and yet —

And yet the wind whimpers oldly of old age
In the western night.

These whimpers of the wind are Stevens' own human voice turned beaten beast, the voice of the inner and ultimate dilapidation, an incoherence as the Rock crumbles to dust. When the poet, on the other hand, speaks, it is through the mask, and that mask is, of course, this entire long poem on New Haven.

Stevens' own judgment on *An Ordinary Evening* is offered in the last two triads:

> The venerable mask,
>
> In this perfection, occasionally speaks,
> And something of death's poverty is heard.
> This should be tragedy's most moving face.

But though this eroded decline of the body should be tragic, the more common tragic subject is maturity cut down, when there is everything to regret. Old age in its poetry is an altogether drier and more brittle thing than tragedy:

> It is a bough in the electric light
> And exhalations in the eaves, so little
> To indicate the total leaflessness.

We are, then, to take these cantos as bare tokens, the most meager signs, of what they would convey. Stevens asks that from a stray indication — a bare bough, the rustle of leaves in the gutters — we compose the whole decay of nature, the total leaflessness of his life, the lifelessness of his leaves. In *Esthétique du Mal*, in *Notes*, and in *The Auroras of Autumn*, Stevens had recounted an impotence, it is true, but an impotence composed of vital assertions which then collapse: the tender researches of the sun which continually fail, the doomed leaps of Canon Aspirin, the vanishing finery of Cinderella, the theatricals of the father which become a disorderly rout. Here, in *An Ordi-*

273

nary Evening in New Haven, impotence is not preceded by human effort. It pre-exists everything else, and prevents any acts except the occasional skull-like speaking of the mask. The yellow grassman's aura is replaced by the nakedness of electric light. Whatever the greatness of the later Stevens may be called, it is present in these lines, and as so often, it is a concealed allusiveness that touches us. As we read about the bough in the electric light, we recall not only Shakespeare's boughs which shake against the cold, but also the bough of summer which Stevens had contrasted with the winter branch; and hearing the exhalations in the eaves, we remember another evening in another town:

> How pale and how possessed a night it is,
> How full of exhalations of the sea . . .

"Bough" and "exhalations" are both celestial words, as "branch" is not, and yet each is undone by its context: the bough by the cold electric light and the exhalations in the eaves by their deathly origin. The perfection of western night, like its boughs and exhalations, is undone by the misery of the wind.

Both wind and leaves, when they are left to themselves and not hopelessly compared to the masculine-feminine oldest-newest physical universe, can play another and more energetic role in the poem. Canto xii, in a variation on the "Ode on a Grecian Urn," ends like the ode, in an immortal equation:

> The self,
> The town, the weather in a casual litter,
> Together, said words of the world are the life of the world.

Sun, moon, auroras, and sea are gone and Stevens is alone with the self, the town, and the weather, that restless resemblance to thought. The poem depends on Shelley as well as on Keats, not only on the "Ode to the West Wind," but perhaps on a poem less well known, "Evening: Ponte al Mare, Pisa":

> There is no dew on the dry grass tonight,
>   Nor damp within the shadow of the trees:
> The wind is intermitting, dry, and light;
>   And in the inconstant motion of the breeze
> The dust and straws are driven up and down,
> And whirled about the pavement of the town.

In Stevens, the dust and straws are "leaves in whirlings in the gutters, whirlings around and away." Shelley had prayed to the wind:

> Drive my dead thoughts over the universe
> Like withered leaves to quicken a new birth;

and Stevens takes up the metaphor as he sees leaves

> . . . Resembling the presence of thought,
> Resembling the presences of thoughts.

The night in canto xii, then, is the same night as in canto xxi, and in fact we have reason to believe that these two cantos were composed together, since they appeared as cantos v and vi in the shorter printed version. In canto xvi, as we saw, poetry was the speech of an immobile mask, oracular. But in canto xii,

> The poem is the cry of its occasion,
> Part of the res itself and not about it.

The distinction between being "part of" something and being "about" something is maintained until the poem realizes a third possibility: that words and res both together make a whole

analogous to body and soul, that words of the world are the life
of the world:

> The poem is the cry of its occasion,
> Part of the res itself and not about it.
> The poet speaks the poem as it is,
>
> Not as it was: part of the reverberation
> Of a windy night as it is, when the marble statues
> Are like newspapers blown by the wind. He speaks
>
> By sight and insight as they are. There is no
> Tomorrow for him. The wind will have passed by,
> The statues will have gone back to be things about.
>
> The mobile and the immobile flickering
> In the area between is and was are leaves,
> Leaves burnished in autumnal burnished trees
>
> And leaves in whirlings in the gutters, whirlings
> Around and away, resembling the presence of thought,
> Resembling the presences of thoughts, as if,
>
> In the end, in the whole psychology, the self,
> The town, the weather, in a casual litter,
> Together, said words of the world are the life of the world.
> (xii)

The problem this canto must solve is to establish the veracity
of its famous close, and it does that by catching up the poet's
thoughts until they become not *post hoc* reflections on the scene,
but actors in it. Stevens' perfect ease in passing from one piece
of litter-in-motion to another removes the strain of allegory:
as he remembers the obsolescence of the Statue in *Owl's Clover*,

he converts sculpture made irrelevant with time into yesterday's newspapers blown in the gutter; the newspapers are yesterday's thoughts, and blow with the leaves; leaves are like thoughts and blow like newspapers, all reverberating, re-wording,[4] the letters and litter of the world. In this canto, very little is said about either the poem or the poet. Most of the energy is expended on the reverberation of the windy night, that "mobile and immobile flickering" which had haunted Stevens ever since "Domination of Black." By slow degrees, nature becomes art, as the flickerings, in turn, are

> leaves
> leaves burnished in autumnal
>   burnished trees and
> leaves   in whirlings in the gutters
>   whirlings around and away
>   resembling the presence of thought
>   resembling the presences of thoughts.

The whirlings are first subordinated to the actual leaves, but then take on an appositional life of their own capable of being described: the whirlings resemble in general the presence of thought, but since they are multiple are said to resemble the presences of thoughts, which, in plurality, return us to the leaves. It is this sequence — from actual leaves to actual whirlings to abstract whirlings to an abstract presence to more actual presences back to actual leaves — which enables Stevens, in the end, to group together in a single speaking voice the whole psychology, the self, the town, the weather, the litter, and to make them utter their famous epigram. The invention of the area between is and was, and its attendant flickering, makes the identification between res and cry a possible one, gives them a no-man's-land in which to meet. If it had not been for Shelley's brilliant finding of a use for fallen leaves, Stevens' canto might have despaired in the total leaflessness of its twin, but as it is, he can salvage, not a Shelleyan prophecy, but a vigorous presence of circulating thought in the wintry scene.

Stevens had hoped for the "paradisal parlance" of the Shelleyan voice stopping in winter to imagine summer. But if that were not possible, he would still avoid calling reality "grim," because life is only grim seen with an indifferent eye. Professor Eucalyptus (xiv) hopes for the commodious adjective for the object:

> The description that makes it divinity, still speech
> As it touches the point of reverberation — not grim
> Reality but reality grimly seen
>
> And spoken in paradisal parlance new
> And in any case never grim, the human grim
> That is part of the indifference of the eye
>
> Indifferent to what it sees.

As Stevens wrote to Bernard Heringman about the poem, "My interest is to try to get as close to the ordinary, the commonplace and the ugly as it is possible for a poet to get. It is not a question of grim reality but of plain reality. The object is of course to purge oneself of anything false . . . This is not in any sense a turning away from the ideas of Credences of Summer: it is a development of those ideas" (L, 636–637). In this purgation, the eye, which must not be indifferent, is the governing presence of the entire poem, and many details of the whole become plain in terms of the many conceits Stevens proposes around the eye. It is both depth and surface, both reflector and window, both trustworthy and deceptive, both a blank and a kaleidoscope, both iris and retina, lens and cornea, island and world, sun and space, sky and horizon, egg and well, burning bush, circle, and sphere. In short, it is Stevens' final symbol of both unity and disparity, and he uses it with a reticent versatility, even unconsciously, to gather together his long poem.

"The eye's plain version" of the world seems to be all there is, but Stevens announces at once that his whole poem will compose one long adversative to this proposal — "an and yet, and yet, and yet." In the first place, the eye's plain version is composed of two halves — the day version and the night version. Stevens sees these two as hemispheres which can become "amassed in a total double-thing" as we half create and half perceive the world, and his language, cooperating in this doubleness, remarks the reciprocity of scene and mind, "the enigmatical beauty of each beautiful enigma" (x). In that chiastic symmetry of adjective and noun lies the perfect congruence which, for Stevens, is generally a daytime embrace. At night, the bodiless half of the world — all the light and color conferred by the sun, and the past and future conferred by sun time — vanishes, and dark shapes alone remain, the shapes of Wordsworth's overhanging crag or Hopkins' beak-leaved boughs dragonish. In attempting a comfort in this darkness, Stevens proposes the response with which Hopkins had begun, that the dark half of the world is a maternal womb. But where Hopkins had flinched at the sight of "self in self steeped and pashed," Stevens welcomes the night "unfretted by day's separate, several selves." However, that harmonious sphere of night, "everything come together as one," cannot retain its integration:

> In this identity, disembodiments
>
> Still keep occurring. What is, uncertainly,
> Desire prolongs its adventure to create
> Forms of farewell, furtive among green ferns.   (xxiii)

So the poem confronts its own hollowness, as the theoretically perfect sphere of night uncurls longing fernlike prongs or prolongations toward the objects of desire. Until the final sleep, human restlessness cannot subside, and the hollow spherical will always quest after the uncertain angular:

> We fling ourselves, constantly longing, on this form.
> We descend to the street and inhale a health of air
> To our sepulchral hollows. Love of the real
>
> Is soft in three-four cornered fragrances,
> From five-six cornered leaves.   (viii)

The prolongations of desire make an empty womb of the eye, and the impotence of an old man's desire is as present in this poem as in "Sailing to Byzantium." The third canto ends, not with a golden nightingale, but with an urn yet to be made, still in the formless clay not yet porcelain. That clay nevertheless comes from the Rock, now "dilapidated" to a hill of stones:

> The point of vision and desire are the same.
> It is to the hero of midnight that we pray
> On a hill of stones to make beau mont thereof.
>
> . . Next to holiness is the will thereto,
> And next to love is the desire for love.
> . . . But this cannot
>
> Possess. It is desire, set deep in the eye
> Behind all actual seeing, in the actual scene,
> In the street, in a room, on a carpet or a wall,
>
> Always in emptiness that would be filled,
> In denial that cannot contain its blood,
> A porcelain, as yet in the bats thereof.   (iii)

This esoteric closure may never come to seem natural, but the empty vacuum of the eye in desire is an image not quickly forgotten.

The counterpart to the appetitive human eye is the stern external "eye" presented explicitly in canto xxv, embodying the relentless exactions of the poet's daemon:

> Life fixed him, wandering on the stair of glass,
> With its attentive eyes. And, as he stood,
> On his balcony, outsensing distances,
>
> There were looks that caught him out of empty air.
> *C'est toujours la vie qui me regarde* . . . This was
> Who watched him, always, for unfaithful thought.
>
> This sat beside his bed, with its guitar,
> To keep him from forgetting, without a word,
> A note or two disclosing who it was.
>
> Nothing about him ever stayed the same.
> Except this hidalgo and his eye and tune,
> The shawl across one shoulder and the hat.
>
> The commonplace became a rumpling of blazons.
> What was real turned into something most unreal,
> Bare beggar-tree, hung low for fruited red
>
> In isolated moments — isolations
> Were false. The hidalgo was permanent, abstract,
> A hatching that stared and demanded an answering look.
>
> (xxv)

In a reversal typical of the late poems, Stevens dismisses the isolated moments of triumph or satisfaction, those final integrations, as false. Neither the suffering of Tantalus nor the momentary miraculous fruit-bearing of the bare tree is the image of life; neither is the coming of "blazoned days" among the commonplace. Instead, Stevens offers us an almost silent and yet demanding presence, an eye like a constantly hatching egg, which "stared and demanded an answering look." Fidelity to this unlikely Muse, day by day and moment by moment, is Stevens' new obligation: the serious exchange of look for look, eye for eye. This hidalgo is "the strength at the centre" of canto xvii, the blank which "underlies the trials of device,/ The dominant blank, the unapproachable." Over and around that blank go all the embroideries of imagination, but that universal blank of the *Auroras* still is the ground beneath the figures.

Stevens has given up the hope of entirely covering that ground with easings and ouncings of damask, but he suggests that this impotence is perhaps not failure, but a severity of self-demand, as the inquisitor of structures rejects the less-than-perfect. He had proposed this equivalence of failure with fastidiousness earlier in *Esthétique du Mal*:

> The sun, in clownish yellow, but not a clown,
> Brings the day to perfection and then *fails* . . .
> > And space is filled with his
> *Rejected* years.

Here, in New Haven, he repeats himself:

> The color is almost the color of comedy,
> Not quite. It comes to the point and at the point,
> It *fails*. The strength at the centre is serious.
>
> Perhaps instead of *failing* it *rejects*
> As a serious strength *rejects* pin-idleness. (italics mine)

To abjure the consolations of both comedy and tragedy, and to write of the high serious, is to write from the snowman's perspective, and therefore to acquire a third eye, neither the hungry eye of the human nor the exacting eye of the Muse but the eye of nature itself. That eye Stevens takes from Keats, and it is the bright steadfast evening star,

> in lone splendor hung aloft the night,
> And watching, with eternal lids apart,
> Like nature's patient, sleepless eremite.

In a perfect oneness with nature, the snowman-poet can put himself within the sphere of the universe and can take a celestial vantage point, standing, with the evening star, at the heart of creation:

> To say of the evening star,
> The most ancient light in the most ancient sky,
>
> That it is wholly an inner light, that it shines
> From the sleepy bosom of the real, recreates,
> Searches a possible for its possibleness.   (xxii)

This evening star is another stable counterpart, like the eye of the hidalgo, to the frailty of the human eye. Only "the real" can be both sleepy and open-eyed at once, can include those two opposing states, which Keats, abiding the question between them, puts sublimely side by side in his sonnet.

The human eye lacks the grandeur of the star, and in fact seems reductive as it pulls all of angular life into its narrow circular compass, its toy gazing-globe in which the whole of New Haven hangs pendent:

> Reality as a thing seen by the mind,

Not that which is but that which is apprehended,
A mirror, a lake of reflections in a room,
A glassy ocean lying at the door,

A great town hanging pendent in a shade,
An enormous nation happy in a style,
Everything as unreal as real can be,

In the inexquisite eye.   (v)

In a peculiarly biological metaphor, Stevens then describes the
whole of the human nervous system as an immense tree, with
roots in the earth and branches in the skull, the whole depending
from the eye, which acts as the searchlight of the self, scan-
ning the night sky:

The self, the chrysalis of all men

Became divided in the leisure of blue day
And more, in branchings after day. One part
Held fast tenaciously in common earth

And one from central earth to central sky
And in moonlit extensions of them in the mind
Searched out such majesty as it could find.   (v)

When the eye finds that nocturnal majesty, it reproduces it as
well as it can, as the iris of the eye joins with the iridescences in
nature. Stevens' parable of this unity is the story of the carpenter who projects his better New Haven: he makes a night
space for astral apprentices to create in sun time, and he bases
his design on the natural eccentric:

The life and death of this carpenter depend

On a fuchsia in a can — and iridescences
Of petals that will never be realized,

Things not yet true which he perceives through truth,
Or thinks he does, as he perceives the present,
Or thinks he does, a carpenter's iridescences,

Wooden, the model for astral apprentices,
A city slapped up like a chest of tools,
The eccentric exterior of which the clocks talk.   (xviii)

This parable of the carpenter depends on the aphorisms preceding it — that the eye is not the present nor part of the present, that life and death are never simply physical, and that therefore temperament and one's sense of the world, not New Haven as it bluntly is, are responsible for one's poems. The iridescences, in passing through the carpenter's eye, become necessarily carpenterlike, wooden, and his model city becomes necessarily like a carpenter's tool chest, even though it will serve disciples of the evening star, who will make it a part of a new exterior reality, like the churches and the schools of canto vii.

In the most inhuman use of the eye's plain version, Stevens imagines himself, in Donne's words, "grown all eye," but an eye turned away from the imaginative and the social alike, evading poems and feelings and even, finally, evading the human, the poet's own will. In that case he becomes, in a more sinister way, Emerson's transparent eyeball, a pure sphere, hypnotized by his own reduction of life to outline, as he had been earlier in "The Common Life"   (221):

The imaginative transcripts were like clouds,
Today; and the transcripts of feeling, impossible
To distinguish. The town was a residuum,

A neuter shedding shapes in an absolute
Yet the transcripts of it when it was blue remain;
And the shapes that it took in feeling, the persons that

It became, the nameless, flitting characters —
These actors still walk in a twilight muttering lines.
It may be that they mingle, clouds and men, in the air

Or street or about the corners of a man,
Who sits thinking in the corners of a room.
In this chamber the pure sphere escapes the impure

Because the thinker himself escapes. And yet
To have evaded clouds and men leaves him
A naked being with a naked will

And everything to make. He may evade
Even his own will and in his nakedness
Inhabit the hypnosis of that sphere.   (xx)

The experience of ultimate ascesis conjured up by this canto is immediately repudiated by the canto that follows: "But he may not. He may not evade his will." Nevertheless, it is Stevens' central experience at this time, not only in his response to New Haven but in his confrontation of the entire world. Though he is surrounded by his past poems, those transcripts of blue phenomena, those shapes the world took on in times of feeling, they are cloudy now, unperceived. And though the impossible possible philosopher's man, like the actors in this canto,

> Still walks in dew,
> Still by the seaside mutters milky lines
> Concerning an immaculate imagery   (250),

nevertheless he has dwindled to one of the cold volume of forgotten ghosts.

The truest description of New Haven as it appears in the entire long poem occurs in this canto:

> The town was a residuum,
> A neuter shedding shapes in an absolute.   (xx)

This hard saying makes the town a bleak descendant of the serpent forever shedding his skin in *The Auroras of Autumn*, but the total colorlessness of the absolute, the neuter, and the residuum masks the hidden serpent form. To escape the impure, as Stevens knows, is itself an evasion: to "see, not feel, how beautiful they are" is, as Coleridge saw, not in any way to have attained to a superior reality. The naked being isolated in a chamber, perceiving the world as debris of life and mind, is a true enough picture of Stevens as the composer of this canto and of large tracts of this poem. But at his most desolate, he is compelled into the life of things, swaying with their motion, breathing with their breath.

Stevens' greatest moments of absorption into the eye of nature do not come in *An Ordinary Evening in New Haven*, but they are a necessary consequence of the nakedness there. Eventually that absorption into nature will incarnate itself in several late poems, "The Region November," "Of Mere Being," "The Course of a Particular," and "A Clear Day and No Memories." All of them are written by "an antipodal, far-fetched creature, worthy of birth,/ The true tone of the metal of winter in what it says" (*OP*, 96). These poems are forecast by the canto in which Stevens repudiates his isolation from objects, as the Ananke of earlier poems reappears in the guise of the black shepherd of death:

> He may not evade his will,

> Nor the wills of other men; and he cannot evade
> The will of necessity, the will of wills —
>
> Romanza out of the black shepherd's isle,
> Like the constant sound of the water of the sea
> In the hearing of the shepherd and his black forms
>
> Out of the isle, but not of any isle.   (xxi)

This distant deathly eternity is the vortex of every man's life, a Hades based on Baudelaire's hellish "île triste et noire" of Cythère:

> Dans ton île, O Vénus! je n'ai trouvé debout
> Qu'un gibet symbolique où pendait mon image . . .

The final necessity of annihilation is matched by a visual necessity near at hand — the severe surfaces of the world upon which the eye must pour its transfiguring creative powers if they are to appear beautiful. The eye must give

> Gold easings and ouncings and fluctuations of thread
> And beetlings of belts and lights of general stones,
> Like blessed beams from out a blessed bush
>
> Or the wasted figurations of the wastes
> Of night, time, and the imagination,
> Saved and beholden, in a robe of rays.   (xvii)

The things of this world are beholden because they are beheld: they are saved, and grateful, because we have looked on them and immortalized them. And so, counterpointing the distant tidal romanza of black necessity heard far away, there is the equally mythical romanza of the poverty of earth's surfaces to which we must give:

Close to the senses there lies another isle
And there the senses give and nothing take,

The opposite of Cythère, an isolation
At the centre, the object of the will, this place,
The things around — the alternate romanza

Out of the surfaces, the windows, the walls,
The bricks grown brittle in time's poverty,
The clear.   (xxi)

The rain and the wind, those pervasive elements of this ordinary evening in New Haven, unite the necessity of poverty with the necessity of death, and in this imperfect we must find our paradise:

A celestial mode is paramount,

If only in the branches sweeping in the rain:
The two romanzas, the distant and the near,
Are a single voice in the boo-ha of the wind.   (xxi)

The two romanzas are at once simple, pastoral, balladlike, elemental, and at the same time exotic, foreign, alien to the human. But together they — our environment and our death — enclose us and make the only superhuman that we know.[5]

Within *An Ordinary Evening in New Haven*, the natural (the rain, the wind, the town), the parabolic (the carpenter, Professor Eucalyptus), and the abstract (aphorisms and theories) struggle for dominance, and the submerging of the first two accounts for the finally theoretical cast of the whole. A look at the various "endings" of the poem shows the struggle clearly. Though Stevens knew the dangers of abstraction, he seems to have determined to try its farthest reaches in this poem; and though his courage faltered at an abstract conclusion when he read the poem aloud, he rearranged the stanzas when it was issued in book form so as to give the abstract the beautifully yielding last word:

> It is not in the premise that reality
> Is a solid. It may be a shade that traverses
> A dust, a force that traverses a shade.   (xxxi)

For all the summoning of earthly mortality implicit in this final dust of the Rock, for all the quasi-metaphorical spiritual energy of the shade and the traversing force, still these lines, with their speculative form, their frame of logical terms, and especially their strict forgoing of the decorative "amorist" adjective, give us Stevens as the noble disembodied preceptor-shade, rebuking us for our grosser theories and our inattentive premises. In *Le Monocle de Mon Oncle* he had concluded,

> Until now I never knew
> That fluttering things have so distinct a shade.

We are offered this conclusion again by the seventy-year-old Stevens, but without the lyric "I" or the personal anecdotes of the rose and blue rabbis, or the attendant pigeons. Imagery, though subterraneanly present, is in the late conclusion attendant upon statement, and not the reverse; it exists as a concession. This concluding canto of the final version chooses as its metaphor for apotheosis not the grandiloquent swellings of the Muses in *Owl's Clover* but the diminishing approximations of the calculus, ever approaching closer and closer to the ideal asymptote. Less, once again, is more, and the celestial becomes the little, the less, the lighter, the inner, the fugitive music in sheets of rain among thunderstrokes, and the candle dimmer than day, as Stevens invokes, in canto xxxi, the poetics of the small:

The less legible meanings of sounds, the little reds
Not often realized, the lighter words
In the heavy drum of speech, the inner men

Behind the outer shields, the sheets of music
In the strokes of thunder, dead candles at the window
When day comes, fire-foams in the motions of the sea.

The preciousness of this exquisite aesthetic nevertheless evokes ridicule from Stevens, as the irrationality of preferring a candle to the sun makes him qualify the candle as dead. Accuracy becomes the affectation of preciousness; art becomes

Flickings from finikin to fine finikin
And the general fidget from busts of Constantine
To photographs of the late president, Mr. Blank.

The next effort Stevens makes to define his aesthetic is not comparative at all, as the attempt in these first six lines had been, but absolute. No longer are we given the false dividing of the primitive — the heavy drum, the outer shields, the strokes of thunder, day, and the sea — from the subtle counterpoint of civilized sounds and more evanescent lights; instead, the terms of definition change from means to ends. In considering "the end and the way to the end," all preliminary minutiae of modeling are seen as steps toward the grand scene, just as scales tend toward a symphony, as hues stretch to a spectrum, as an *essai* leads, even destructively, to a truer formulation. The whole canto turns on the phrase "getting at," in which intermittent flickerings are given direction and purpose:

These are the edgings and inchings of final form,
The swarming activities of the formulae
Of statement, directly and indirectly getting at,

Like an evening evoking the spectrum of violet,
A philosopher practicing scales on his piano,
A woman writing a note and tearing it up.   (xxxi)

The delicate and unforeseen ending ("it is not in the premise that reality is a solid") rebukes the canto for its originally static and stolid instances, whether of inner men or dead candles, and darts itself forward on the rapidity of the double traversing. Repudiating reductive earlier words like "flicking" and "finikin" and "fidget," the poem has passed through the neutral phrases "form" and "formulae" into the earned strength and nobility of "force." In such self-realizations, Stevens' abstractions blood themselves, and the poem, intended as theory, rightly ends with theory.

But Stevens had debated at least one, and probably two, alternate endings. The original order (viii, ix, x, xi) becomes, in reordering, viii, xi, ix, x — or, in the later numbering, xxviii–xxxi. Though canto ix (xxx) never formally ended any version of the poem, its creeping toward a penultimate place suggests that Stevens probably toyed with the idea of concluding with it; it clearly "belonged to" the ending. The last four cantos, in short, remain the last four in both versions, but the order of the last three — all of them "satisfactory" endings — troubled Stevens. His first choice of ending was a plotted parable, an earthy Odyssean anecdote, a light evocation of the Goethean land "wo die Citronen blühn." That land, as we know, is one version of paradise, but Stevens' heavy-hanging fruits of *Sunday Morning* have become considerably more tart, and the land presents itself in the frolic of dactyls instead of in grave iambs:

In the land of the lemon trees, yellow and yellow were
Yellow-blue, yellow-green, pungent with citron-sap,
Dangling and spangling, the mic-mac of mocking birds.

The parable tells us, briefly, that there are two lands. Certain big mariners (like Stevens) have come from a maternal autumnal land of elm trees where ripeness is ruddy, not yellow — presumably Stevens' North of apple trees — and their native language is dark-colored, clodlike, inexpressive. In the brisk tropical land of the lemon trees, where ripeness is yellow, there is forever a blond atmosphere of summer, and language is tasted on the tongue: "they rolled their r's, there, in the land of the citrons." The parable proposes an "alteration of words that was a change of nature" and insists that the mariners' "dark-colored words had redescribed the citrons," but it also contains within itself its own subverting recognition. We are given a long induction, and a long preparation, and then, at the end of the voyage, we are prepared for a climactic recognition and change:

> *When* the mariners came to the land of the lemon trees,
> *At last*, in that *blond* atmosphere, *bronzed* hard,
> They said —   (italics mine)

And what did they say, so absorbed in the new, at this moment of bronzed participation in the yellow tropics, but that it was the same as the last stop on their journey:

> They said, "We are back once more in the land of the elm trees,
> But folded over, turned round."

This possibly depressing recognition is certainly anticlimactic, but Stevens expresses it without tone, as though he wished the moment to be neutral. The repetitiveness of experience is no new theme in Stevens, but here he refuses to speak of it either as pleasurable or as diminishing. Instead, it is factual; and he has it both ways:

> It *was* the same,
> *Except for* the adjectives.   (italics mine)

From this point on, the canto asserts the power of language to redescribe nature, and we realize that we are being given here a parable, from Stevens' own point of view, of what Yvor Winters called his "hedonist's progress." It is true that Stevens had gone to the yellow land, but he discovered there that he did not speak the yellow language, the mic-mac of mocking birds; he still spoke his dank native language, his "brown clods, mere catching weeds of talk." Till his visit, the citrons had presumably been described only in yellow language, by natives of the land; now, from this odd conjunction of hedonist object with autumnal language, a new hybrid reality — yellow shaded by brown — is born; Stevens casts ground obliquities on the lemon, and those brown obliquities make "more/ Than the difference that clouds make over a town." His "dark-colored words had redescribed the citrons." In *The Man with the Blue Guitar*, Stevens had made a false boast:

> I am a native in this world
> And think in it as a native thinks.   (180)

But Stevens had withdrawn, in *Notes*, from that bravado, and had admitted,

> We live in a place
> That is not our own and much more, not ourselves.   (383)

We are, in short, wandering mariners taking our "language" (our sense of the world) with us wherever we go. To visit an alien hedonistic land, even to describe it, is not to become a hedonist — it is rather to redescribe hedonism in terms of one's own permanently dark-colored self.

In the end, Stevens placed the canto about the mariners, originally the conclusion, as the antepenultimate canto, and inserted between it and the conclusion a remarkable poem which, it seems likely, represents another version of the last word. With the mariners, he had ended in parable; with the traversing force, he ends with abstraction; but in canto xxx (originally canto ix), he rests in visible nature, ending with the high severity of an autumn scene at the earliest beginning of winter. Stevens had always instinctively sought out any natural interregnum: though humanly he preferred summer to any other season, imaginatively he was caught up by the moment

> Between farewell and the absence of farewell,
> The final mercy and the final loss,
> The wind and the sudden falling of the wind. (152)

In "Not Ideas about the Thing But the Thing Itself" he will speak of "the earliest ending of winter," the period which he had called "the pre-history of February" in "Long and Sluggish Lines"; and in "The News and the Weather" he remarks that for the spirit left helpless, at the winter's end, by the intelligence, there is a moment when "the deep breath fetches another year of life." That deep breath is visibly and audibly present in this thirtieth canto, though here it is being taken in the hiatus between the end of autumn and the beginning of winter.

Stevens opens the poem with a painful exactness of description, saying not that the last leaf has fallen but, with a reminiscence of Shakespeare, that the last leaf that is going to fall has fallen. "That other fall we call the fall" is over, but leaves remain tenacious on the oaks. Later, there will be the crusted glittering of ice on the junipers, an unearthly foliage, but for the moment, the mind is full of nostalgia for the contours and serenities of summer:

> The last leaf that is going to fall has fallen.
> The robins are là-bas, the squirrels, in tree-caves,
> Huddle together in the knowledge of squirrels.

Like Keats's bees, Stevens' squirrels act as the human substitute, and huddle together in their instinctual response to the cold. The wind begins its sound of misery and its spoiling of calm reflections in ponds. On the other hand, winter does not vanquish summer as, in *Notes*, spring was said to "vanish the scraps of winter." Summer is always behind the scenes, waiting, as the robins wait là-bas, as the squirrels wait in their tree caves: the silence of summer, its susurrus of crickets and bees,

> Buzzes beyond the horizon or in the ground:
> In mud under ponds, where the sky used to be reflected.

The poem becomes like a Cézanne landscape, as the obscuring foliage drops away like a shroud or a veil, and resurrected verticals appear like Lazarus coming forth from the tomb:

> The barrenness that appears is an exposing.
>
> . . .
>
> It is a coming on and a coming forth.
> The pines that were fans and fragrances emerge,
> Staked solidly in a gusty grappling with rocks.

The poem becomes not only resurrection but beatific vision, as Stevens continues with a variation on Saint Paul: no longer are we making rubbings on a glass through which we peer; the whole glass is suddenly transparent, and thought, that skeleton in our flesh, is suddenly as clear as the skeletal tree trunks. It is a moment of pure reason, but there is a graceful glance back at the clusters of squirrels in the closing lines:

It is a visibility of thought,
In which hundreds of eyes, in one mind, see at once.

Argus may be subliminally present, but Stevens' peculiar economy would not leave unused the squirrels looking out of tree holes. The sight so insisted on in the numerical hyperbole is an absolutely equable one, undisturbed by the lost fans and fragrances of summer. They are remembered, just as the robins are, just as the summer silence is, but without recrimination. It is true, Stevens implies, that there was song, silence, sensuality; but there is, equally now, the armature of intelligence, the new clarity of outline, and the new unison of sight and thought.

The kind of balance seen in all three possible "endings" of the poem is both the strength and the weakness of *An Ordinary Evening in New Haven.* What in *Notes* had come together as a whole — as a couple, a plural, a balance, a choice not between but of, a compound of Latin and the lingua franca — here has definitively separated out into elements again. The elegiac anticipation of *The Auroras of Autumn* has been fulfilled, and many of Stevens' planets have been extinguished by the grim imagination. In this post-elegiac phase, hope and fear alike disappear and all seasons are given their due — there is a time to be born and a time to die, and the Necessary Angel of the poem is the figure like Ecclesiast, chanting, in the nineteenth canto, that "text that is an answer, although obscure." The best-known canto of the poem, canto vi, is a personification of that text, which mixes, in an inspired analogy, the high quasi-religious and "imaginative" Alpha and Omega with the wholly secular, "real," and in fact comic, A and Z. This canto, like the one just quoted, attempts to deal out honors impartially, and ends, with distributive justice,

> Alpha continues to begin.
> Omega is refreshed at every end.   (vi)

We may be reminded, in the presence of this antiphonal structure, of the duet with the undertaker in *The Man with the Blue Guitar*, but there Stevens had tried to assimilate the two singers into a closer and closer vortex, a more rapid oscillation back and forth, a confluence of characteristics, until the two became inseparable, "all confusion solved." Even in "the lion in the lute/ Before the lion locked in stone" there is an identification in outline. But here, in Stevens' finest example of his latest mode, Alpha and Omega, A and Z, are separate in every respect and particularly in shape. The poem turns on a surprising variation of the spectrum and the scales we have already seen in the canto which concludes the poem; here we see the alphabet first as spectrum, with two fixed points, a beginning and an end, equally separate in Greek and in English. But by the conclusion of the poem, the alphabet becomes a scale which concludes and rebegins on the same note, a note acting as Omega to one scale and as Alpha to the next, forever regenerating itself:

> Reality is the beginning not the end,
> Naked Alpha, not the hierophant Omega,
> Of dense investiture, with luminous vassals.
>
> It is the infant A standing on infant legs,
> Not twisted, stooping, polymathic Z,
> He that kneels always on the edge of space
>
> In the pallid perceptions of its distances.
> Alpha fears men or else Omega's men
> Or else his prolongations of the human.
>
> These characters are around us in the scene.
> For one it is enough; for one it is not;
> For neither is it profound absentia,

Since both alike appoint themselves the choice
Custodians of the glory of the scene,
The immaculate interpreters of life.

But that's the difference: in the end and the way
To the end. Alpha continues to begin.
Omega is refreshed at every end.   (vi)

The change in Stevens' view of the letters is marked exactly halfway through the poem when he begins to group the initial and final characters together instead of separating them, to subsume them under one bracket — "these characters" — and under dual verbs used with "neither" and "both." The larger perspective making possible the use of the dual number in respect to these opposite ends of the alphabet comes about, of course, with the introduction of the human in the pivotal sentence, "These characters are around *us* in the scence." The mind, in short, is larger than its categories, and can contain beginning and end, group them into a continuum, while recognizing their absolute difference in outline.

Not all of *An Ordinary Evening* keeps to its new equilibrium. There are reversions to old manners, notably in the second canto, where Stevens repeats the old motif of inseparability between mind and object, here by giving identical modifiers to opposite principles, so that all becomes shimmering, uncertain, indefinite, hazy:

Suppose these houses are composed of ourselves,
So that they become an *impalpable* town, full of
Impalpable bells, *transparencies* of sound

Sounding in *transparent* dwellings of the self,
Impalpable habitations that seem to *move*
In the *movement* of the colors of the mind,

On Extended Wings

The far-fire-flowing and the dim-coned bells
Coming together in a sense in which we are poised,
Without regard to time or where we are,

In the *perpetual* reference, object
Of the *perpetual* meditation, point
Of the enduring, visionary love,

Obscure, in colors whether of the sun
Or mind, uncertain in the clearest bells,
The spirit's speeches, the indefinite,

Confused illuminations and sonorities,
So much ourselves, we cannot tell apart
The idea and the bearer-being of the idea.   (ii; italics mine)

Stevens, as I have said earlier, represents *An Ordinary Evening in New Haven* as, in its entirety, one long qualification of the proposition that "The eye's plain version is a thing apart,/ The vulgate of experience." This second canto, with its obscure confusions, is the most total "and yet" in the poem, the grand Greek to counter the vulgate, but it can exist only on the supposition of a radical idealism about New Haven — that the houses are composed of ourselves — and on a corresponding supposition of style — that a succession of dependent prepositional phrases and transferred epithets succeed eventually in becoming wholly detached from earth-bound syntax.

Another form of reversion occurs in the fourth canto, with an echo of both *Notes* and *The Auroras*, as we once again meet the cold copulars, winter and spring, but meet them as fairy tale:

So lewd spring comes from winter's chastity.

So, after summer, in the autumn air,
Comes the cold volume of forgotten ghosts,

But soothingly, with pleasant instruments,
So that this cold, a children's tale of ice,
Seems like a sheen of heat romanticized.

With winter comes the recurrence of voluminous memory, and as the past rises in a spectral vapor, we mistake the season of mists for the sheen of summer. The past returns with the familiarity of a twice-told tale; it is legendary, comfortable, disembodied, an etherealizing by two removes of the coarse heat of summer. Heat, in its moisture, gives off a sheen; the sheen is retrospectively in winter acted on once again, romanticized, and yields the antique masque of icy breath. The indulgent, soothing manner of the telling is its own witness to the process which is really taking place, once described, by Emily Dickinson, as "first chill, then stupor, then the letting-go." With increasing age, even the auroras seem less threatening, more romantic, as all capacities gradually numb.

In another reversion, this time to the manner of *The Comedian as the Letter C*, obdurate reality becomes human, not by being absorbed into the mind, as it was in the second canto when houses became impalpable transparencies, but by being seen as projections of other selves. Architecture is the one art of which it may be said most easily that it has become a part of reality: it is visible, as poetry and music are not, and it is primarily useful, while statues and paintings are primarily decorative. In his architecture, the architect is made visible and rocklike: against his will, even, he is truthful. In turning into things, men lose the power to be self-deprecatory and down-to-earth, "practical," given only to "the plain sense of things"; in spite of themselves, their fantasy breaks out everywhere, and the pure architectural products of fancy are as fantastic as confectionery, while the pure products of rigid realism are, as the saying goes, as plain as day:

> In the presence of such chapels and such schools,
> The impoverished architects appear to be
> Much richer, more fecund, sportive and alive.
>
> The objects tingle and the spectator moves
> With the objects. But the spectator also moves
> With lesser things, with things exteriorized
>
> Out of rigid realists. It is as if
> Men turning into things, as comedy,
> Stood, dressed in antic symbols, to display
>
> The truth about themselves, having lost, as things,
> That power to conceal they had as men,
> Not merely as to depth but as to height
>
> As well, not merely as to the commonplace
> But, also, as to their miraculous.

The patisserie of dawn gives way inevitably to daily bread, but both are equally in the baker's mind; men in architecture reassuringly display their miraculous

> Conceptions of new mornings of new worlds,
>
> The tips of cock-cry pinked out pastily,
> As that which was incredible becomes,
> In misted contours, credible day again.   (vii)

Stevens reasserts, this time by way of churches and schools, that man is the intelligence of his soil, and equally truthfully, that his soil is man's intelligence. To see man as a comedian, men as comedy, is nevertheless a backward look for Stevens, since the concern of *An Ordinary Evening* is, as he announced in the seventeenth canto, "serious reflection," which "is composed/ Neither of comic nor tragic but of commonplace."

The theory of the commonplace, of the ordinary, is Stevens' recurrent subject in this long poem, and three cantos of the shorter version belong together as theoretical lyrics — i, ix, and xxviii. Canto xxviii, as I have said, is one of the solid terminal group of four, and remains the first of that group of four in both versions. It is the most ambitious of the three theoretical lyrics, it is even the most ambitious claim in the entire poem, and in fact is a fourth "possible ending" to the whole. "The theory of poetry," Stevens wishes to claim in this canto, "is the theory of life." Toward this equation of the visible with the invisible, all three theoretical cantos tend, but each embodies it differently. The weakest (xxviii) resorts at its close to language not individually Stevens' own, but rather words of somewhat empty celestial-demonic pointings:

> The theory
> Of poetry is the theory of life,
>
> As it is, in the intricate evasions of as,
> In things seen and unseen, created from nothingness,
> The heavens, the hells, the worlds, the longed-for-lands.

Fortunately for the poem, Stevens leaves us not with these borrowed gestures of transcendence, but with his exquisite force that traverses a shade. His earliest closure had imagined, after a gigantomachia, the emergence of a new Jove,

> As if the crude collops came together as one,
> A mythological form, a festival sphere,
> A great bosom, beard and being, alive with age.   (i)

This reminiscence of the father of the Auroras, one of the pure perfections of parental space, is a wistful projection. Both of these cantos have better and more successful passages than their endings, in each case passages describing the eye's plain version rather than the geography or mythology of desire. In the first, Stevens gives us

> These houses, these difficult objects, dilapidate
> Appearances of what appearances,
> Words, lines, not meanings, not communications;

and in the other, he sketches his tableau of poverty:

>   The tin plate, the loaf of bread on it,
> The long-bladed knife, the little to drink and her
> Misericordia.

But the one canto of the three theoretical ones in which, by common consent, Stevens finds his true theoretical conclusion is not the early or the late one, but the middle conclusion:

> We keep coming back and coming back
> To the real: to the hotel instead of the hymns
> That fall upon it out of the wind. We seek
>
> The poem of pure reality, untouched
> By trope or deviation, straight to the word,
> Straight to the transfixing object, to the object
>
> At the exactest point at which it is itself,
> Transfixing by being purely what it is,
> A view of New Haven, say, through the certain eye,
>
> The eye made clear of uncertainty, with the sight

Of simple seeing without reflection. We seek
Nothing beyond reality. Within it,

Everything, the spirit's alchemicana
Included, the spirit that goes roundabout
And through included, not merely the visible,

The solid, but the movable, the moment,
The coming on of feasts and the habits of saints,
The pattern of the heavens and high, night air.   (ix)

Stevens will not resort here to the salvation of metaphor — the
lion of Juda, the whirling leaves. This is a forbiddingly theoretical poem, in spite of its figurative overtones. We are given no
anecdote, no parable, no color, no persona, no natural scene,
no allegory, no instances. Stevens' late style, here at its most
pure and most successful, gives an impression of massive hon-
esty, as it inches backward unwillingly to the real, from the
temptations of the visionary. The verse seems to do a continual
backstitching:

We keep coming back
        and coming back   to the real
                              to the hotel
We seek the poem untouched
                  straight to the word
                  straight to the object
                      to the object
                 [when] it is itself
                 [being] what it is
           a view of New Haven through the eye
                              the eye made clear
                                  with sight
                                  without reflection.

We seek nothing beyond reality
        within it
    everything,
       the spirit's alchemicana included
       the spirit that goes roundabout and through included
    not merely the visible
         the solid
  but   the movable
         the moment
         the coming on of feasts and
         the habits of saints
         the pattern of the heavens and
            high night air.

This is the style so well described by Frank Doggett: "The special quality of the late style is so permeated with the effects of apposition that some criticism has felt that it resembled improvisation. That effect is given because in apposition the poet seems to deliberate about his original concept. He appears to reconsider it by seeking an equivalent in another and another version, continuously altered yet presented as though it were the same." [6] Though it may resemble improvisation, the snail-like slowness by which this style gains ground has nothing of the spontaneous gaiety of improvisation. On the contrary, it shows us Stevens looking harder and harder at the object, trying to see it for what it is and yet to see beyond it into a more satisfactory whole.

The pivotal change of conception in this canto is, of course, the abandoning of the linear and directed gaze of the eye ("straight to the word, straight to the object") for the inner global eyeball, the eye made clear of uncertainty. We move from the arrow pointing beyond, to the volume existing within, from an outgoing eye threaded on a string to a receptive eye as hemisphere. Everything in the canto suddenly becomes round and three-dimensional as the attention shifts from the object to the eye that sees the object. The directed motion outward, earlier in the poem, turns into the reassuring cyclical motion of habitual feasts, recurrent ritual, and familiar constellations expressed in Stevens' equally reassuring tetrameters of lullaby. But in spite of the increasing density of nouns in the conclusion, the fulcrum of the poem is adverbial, as it turns on the single words "beyond" and "within." They, rather than the change of scene, incarnate the change of perspective. The scene *has* changed — from the hotel to the night sky — but the effect of the poem, in its grudging advance, has not been a change in visual perspective (of the sort we find, for instance in Keats's "To Autumn"), but a slow passage through the looking glass, as the outward-directed gaze recedes, touches the surface of the eye, and fades inward. Though this inching style is not peculiar to Stevens' abstract poems, it is most at home there, and must be distinguished from the earlier style it resembles, the piling up of appositional noun phrases to suggest expansiveness and surfeit, as in *The Comedian* and *Owl's Clover*.

The emphasis in this theoretical canto, as elsewhere in *An Ordinary Evening in New Haven*, falls steadfastly on "the real" — in this case the city, the autumn evening, the rain, the hotel. But as Stevens intermittently knows, even in this poem, there are other realities, and they are here allowed a subsidiary place. These more cheerful realities are multiple — the natural rather than the civilized, birdsong rather than piano music, the morning star rather than the evening star, the youthful day rather than the ancient night, Alpha rather than Omega — but in this poem they are kept strictly subordinated to age and death. And yet Stevens denies the too-simple historical myth of a primitive childhood Eden filled with wonder, to be followed by an increasing and cumulative tedium. Milton's Adam and Eve are a false construct: "Creation is not renewed by images of lone wanderers." Eden comes every day: "The sense of cold and earliness is a daily sense,/ Not the predicate of bright ori-

gin." [7] The mandate to the poet is that he must re-create the
world, turning Hesper into Phosphor by turning himself from
a mirror to a lamp:

> To re-create, to use
>
> The cold and earliness and bright origin
> Is to search. Likewise to say of the evening star,
> The most ancient light in the most ancient sky,
>
> That it is wholly an inner light, that it shines
> From the sleepy bosom of the real, re-creates,
> Searches a possible for its possibleness.   (xxii)

In one of the most unexpected turns of his development, Stevens will find, even in the midst of Omega's decrepitude, surprising budding Alphas; and will discover with some awe, in
the dwarf of himself, a newborn child speaking newborn syllables, a chorister whose c precedes, though in winter, the full
choirs of summer.

XI. Naked Alpha: Epilogue

One is a child again.

After *Notes toward a Supreme Fiction*, Stevens discovers no new forms for long poems, and *An Ordinary Evening in New Haven* may seem only an extension implicit in the earlier poems, though with its episodic looseness, its lack of forward motion, and its ruminativeness, it enacts old age contemplating itself in sporadic proliferations, in "long and sluggish lines," as Stevens heavily described them. Sometimes this November voice in Stevens cannot even articulate itself into verse, and must content itself with those feelings, deep but inchoate, which the pine trees intimate in "The Region November," or which the leaves express in "The Course of a Particular." As Stevens speaks in the voice of extreme old age, he and the interior paramour are finally stripped to the total lifelessness foretold by the total leaflessness:

> It is an illusion that we were ever alive . . .
> $\qquad\qquad$ The sounds of the guitar
>
> Were not and are not. Absurd. The words spoken
> Were not and are not. It is not to be believed.
> The meeting at noon at the edge of the field seems like
>
> An invention, an embrace between one desperate clod
> And another in a fantastic consciousness. $\quad$ (525)

This is a version, conceived in wretchedness, of the plain sense of things, "a theorem proposed" about life in this brutally geometric end of reductive memory. If Stevens had ended only with this naked style, we would see it as the fitting gasp of the final poverty, the victory of Madame La Fleurie.

But if, as Stevens said, a change of style is a change of subject, so perhaps a change of subject may be regarded as a change of style. Though there are no more "long" poems after *An Ordinary Evening in New Haven*, certain late poems, taken together, make up what we may call Stevens' poem of infancy, as his west touches his east. He had begun his poetic life as a "marvellous sophomore," already armored with well-traveled sophistication, knowing all the languages and poetries of the world. Now after his summer credences and his autumnal littering leaves, he has come to the "inhalations of original cold, and of original earliness" (481) which, though they lie in midwinter, are yet intimations of the pristine. On the threshold of heaven, Stevens rediscovers earth, and writes a sublime poetry of inception.

The work which best shows the progress from the bitter geometry of age into an unbidden perception of the new is a poem which has gone, in the calendar of Stevens' year, beyond the deaths of October, November, December, and January, into the tenuous midwinter spring of February, with its hint of budding in magnolia and forsythia, its "wakefulness inside a sleep." Stevens begins in the toneless naked language of tedium:

Long and Sluggish Lines

It makes so little difference, at so much more
Than seventy, where one looks, one has been there before.

Wood-smoke rises through trees, is caught in an upper flow
Of air and whirled away. But it has been often so.

The trees have a look as if they bore sad names
And kept saying over and over one same, same thing,

In a kind of uproar.

But that uproar, Stevens suddenly realizes, is a defensive one; the
sad trees reiterate their uproar

Because an opposite, a contradiction,
Has enraged them and made them want to talk it down.

Conjuring up this psychic struggle in nature fills Stevens with
liveliness, and a euphoric fantasy of language dances into play:

What opposite? Could it be that yellow patch, the side
Of a house, that makes one think the house is laughing;

Or these — escent — issant pre-personae: first fly,
A comic infanta among the tragic drapings,

Babyishness of forsythia, a snatch of belief,
The spook and makings of the nude magnolia?

A myth of pre-existence gives the metaphor for the moral to be
drawn:

. . . Wanderer, this is the pre-history of February.
The life of the poem in the mind has not yet begun.

You were not born yet when the trees were crystal
Nor are you now, in this wakefulness inside a sleep.   (522)

Old age, seemingly prehistoric in its survival, is in fact inhabiting a pre-history, as the soul, not yet born, waits to be reincarnated. One morning in March it will wake to find not ideas about the thing, that intellectuality of old age, but the youthful thing itself. At that moment, in the first scrawny cry of the first returning bird, the poet's tentative infancy of perception will sense a signal of the approach of the colossal sun.[1] Though this "bubbling before the sun" is as yet "too far/ For daylight and too near for sleep" (*OP*, 98), Stevens is not daunted from imagining a possible for its possibleness, even in the leaden misery of winter.

In the great late poem "A Discovery of Thought" the perfect ideal is realized — the self is reincarnated as a child who, though newborn, remembers his previous existence and can speak his infant language, not in the rowdy summer syllables of ohoyo, but with "the true tone of the metal of winter in what it says." This extraordinary creature, Stevens' last mythical invention, is the child one becomes in second childhood,[2] in that sickness where the eyes dim, where the body is a chill weight, and the old winning fairy tales of bearded deities become irrelevant. The wintry habitat of the man in second childhood is superbly real:

> At the antipodes of poetry, dark winter,
> When the trees glitter with that which despoils them,
> Daylight evaporates, like a sound one hears in sickness.
>
> One is a child again. The gold beards of waterfalls
> Are dissolved as in an infancy of blue snow.

But in the midst of February's deathly wind and mist, there is a tinkling of hard ice and a trickling of melting ice which coexist, as a continual metamorphosis thwarts finality: there is, in portmanteau language,

A trinkling in the parentage of the north,
The cricket of summer forming itself out of ice.

And though the scene is populated with "blue men that are
lead within" holding leaden loaves in their hands, nevertheless
"when the houses of New England catch the first sun" we think
that "the sprawling of winter" (like the wilderness commanded
by the jar) "might suddenly stand erect":

> Pronouncing its new life and ours, not autumn's prodigal
> returned,
> But an antipodal, far-fetched creature, worthy of birth,
> The true tone of the metal of winter in what it says.

In the strict ending of the poem, which gathers itself together
after the great freedom of the sprawling lines of description,
Stevens defines in three ways, with verse of metaphysical density, that speech of the antipodal creature:

> The accent of deviation of the living thing
> That is its life preserved, the effort to be born
> Surviving being born, the event of life.   (*OP*, 95–96)

The remembered continuity between past life and present life
accounts for the deviation in the accent of this miraculous creature who remembers his previous incarnation; he remembers
the trauma of being born and has no infantile amnesia; his life,
like the life of the pines in *An Ordinary Evening in New Haven*,
is "a coming on and a coming-forth," an e-vent, and he does not
forget its prehistoric origins. Knowing everything, this infant
creature is everything, and he represents Stevens' final image of
perfection, one step beyond the naked majesty of poverty in
which he had left the old philosopher in Rome. If the high stoic

elegies of Stevens' plain sense of things make a fitting close to his withering into the truth, these short late poems, equally truthful, are those liquid lingerings into which the angel of reality transforms, for a moment, the bleak continuo of life's tragic drone.

Notes

Notes

INTRODUCTION

1. The following conventions will be observed. Numbers in parentheses refer to pages in the *Collected Poems* (New York, 1955), except in the case of *Owl's Clover*, where they refer to pages in *Opus Posthumous*. Other parenthetical numbers are preceded by one of the following:

> OP: *Opus Posthumous*, ed. Samuel French Morse (New York, 1957);
> NA: *The Necessary Angel* (New York, 1951);
> L: *Letters*, ed. Holly Stevens (New York, 1966).

Names of long poems, separately treated, have been italicized. Numbers of cantos or sections of long poems are in lowercase Roman numerals. Dates given in parentheses after first mention of long poems are dates of first publication or of first reading.

2. The only shortcoming in Randall Jarrell's otherwise brilliant appreciation of Stevens is his wariness in respect to the long poems. He lists only *Sunday Morning* among his favorites, and includes one canto of *Credences of Summer*. See his review, "The *Collected Poems* of Wallace Stevens," reprinted in *The Achievement of Wallace Stevens*, ed. Ashley Brown and Robert S. Haller (Philadelphia, 1962), pp. 179–192.

3. I adopt in the penultimate line the reading "ear" for "air" from the original printing of the poem in the *Hudson Review*.

4. Harold Bloom, "The Central Man," *Massachusetts Review*, 7 (Winter 1966): 31.

5. Marianne Moore, "Unanimity and Fortitude," a review of *Owl's Clover* and *Ideas of Order*, in *Poetry*, 29 (February 1937): 268.

6. The best remarks on Stevens' style have been made by Frank Doggett, in his extremely interesting article "Wallace Stevens' Later Poetry" *ELH*, 25 (June 1958): 137–154. See especially his pages (145–147) on the use in Stevens of predicate nominative, aphorism, and apposition. Will C. Jumper, in "The Language of Wallace Stevens," *Iowa English Yearbook*, 6 (Fall 1961): 23–24, isolates seven hallmarks of Stevens' style: Gallic diction, long sentences, archaisms of diction and syntax, polysyllabic adjectives, the juxtaposition of apparently unrelated

317

nouns, contrapuntal progressions, and heavy alliteration. The superiority of Doggett's article is that he makes conjectures on the reason for the traits he isolates, always interesting ones ("In its simple forms conventional metaphor has the shape of the predicate nominative . . . The statement of equivalence gives to poetry some of the effect of the axiom, its accepted verity and essential rightness . . . In apposition the poet seems to deliberate about his original concept," and so forth).

7. See the otherwise interesting article by Louis Martz, "Wallace Stevens: The World as Meditation," reprinted from *Literature and Belief*, ed. M. H. Abrams (New York, 1958), pp. 139–165, in *Wallace Stevens: A Collection of Critical Essays*, ed. Marie Borroff (New Jersey, 1963), pp. 133–160, especially pp. 140–141. See also Frank Kermode, *Wallace Stevens* (New York, 1961), p. 67.

8. A. Alvarez, *Stewards of Excellence* (New York, 1958), pp. 133–134, 136–137.

9. See Stevens' own very apt remarks on "La Vie Antérieure" in "Two or Three Ideas," *OP*, 202–204.

10. John Malcolm Brinnin, "Plato, Phoebus and the Man from Hartford," *Voices*, 121 (Spring 1945): 31.

11. R. P. Blackmur, *Language as Gesture* (New York, 1935), p. 437.

CHAPTER I

1. On Stevens' use of "the" truth, cf. Frank Doggett's remarks on William James in *Stevens' Poetry of Thought* (Baltimore, 1966), p. 210. Doggett's own interpretation of the "the" at the end of "The Man on the Dump" differs from mine: to me, Stevens seems contemptuous of the "the," while to Doggett he seems to be praising it.

2. Although "evasion" is a pejorative word, I use it because Stevens himself regarded it as the nature of poetry to evade, and "evasion" and "metaphor" become synonomous in the *Collected Poems*. See for instance pages 199, 272, 373, 388, 486.

3. See, for instance, the end of "Our Stars Come from Ireland, II" (455), and, for the same construction with "if" alone, "Connoisseur of Chaos, II" (215).

CHAPTER II

1. *The Comedian as the Letter C* was composed at the end of 1921, submitted in an early form for the Blindman prize under the title "From the Journal of Crispin" (*L*, 224 and 224n), and first published in *Harmonium*, 1923.

2. Cf. Daniel Fuchs, *The Comic Spirit of Wallace Stevens* (Durham, N.C., 1963), p. 32 and chapter 2 *passim*.

3. R. P. Blackmur, "Examples of Wallace Stevens," reprinted in *The Achievement of Wallace Stevens*, pp. 52–80. See especially p. 80: "What he deals with is not comic; the comedy, in that sense, is restricted to his perception and does not touch the things perceived or himself." Stevens himself (*L*, 778) wrote that his translator should "try to reproduce the every-day plainness of the central figure and the plush, so to speak, of his stage," recognizing, implicitly at least, the limitations of his comedy noted by Blackmur. The disproportion between Crispin and his much elaborated environment may be attributed to a passivity like that which Roman Jakobson noted in Pasternak, "a tendency," as Victor Erlich says in paraphrase of Jakobson, "to substitute the 'action' for the 'actor' and the 'setting' for the 'action,' to resolve the image of the hero into . . . a series of objectified states of mind or of surrounding objects." Erlich, *Russian Formalism* (The Hague, 1955), p. 177, quoting Roman Jakobson, "Randbemerkungen zur Prosa des Dichters Pasternak," *Slavische Rundschau*, 7 (1935): 357–374. Erlich also remarks (p. 211) that in some poems, action is the pretext for what Shklovskii called the "unfolding of the verbal material," and this seems particularly true of a pseudo-narrative like the *Comedian*.

4. I have been reminded by Marie Borroff of the similarity of this description of Crispin to Berowne's description of Cupid in *Love's Labour's Lost* (III, i, 176ff).

5. Reappearing, for instance, in the "ecce" of *The Man with the Blue Guitar* (182).

6. See *Owl's Clover*, the beginning of canto ii and the conclusion of canto vii, for similar invocations of the Muse.

7. The attempts to match the daughters with the seasons, the points of the compass, or any other quaternary group seem vitiated by the lack of specific detail in Stevens' description. He had no children of his own when he wrote the poem, though he had been married since 1909.

8. Herbert J. Stern, in *Wallace Stevens* (Ann Arbor, 1966), says, after quoting the quite horrible lines describing tropical blossoms, that "Stevens shared with Freud the conviction that temporal happiness is attainable only through a release from sensual and sexual repression." But the tropical plants represent no joyous enfranchising of the sexual: they are

> Fibrous and dangling down,
> Oozing cantankerous gum
> Out of their purple maws,
> Darting out of their purple craws
> Their musky and tingling tongues.

Stevens may share, intellectually, Freud's conviction, but he is not, in Arnold's terms, at ease in Zion.

9. "The Collected Poems of Wallace Stevens," reprinted in *The Achievement of Wallace Stevens*, p. 185.

10. This is the formulation of a former student at Swarthmore, Geoffrey Joseph.

11. The poem says that the men will chant, but this is a signal case in which the rhetoric of the stanza, which is prophetic, is belied by the tone, which is nostalgic.

12. *Sunday Morning* was first published, in a five-stanza version, in *Poetry*, 7 (November 1915): 81–83, with the stanzas chosen by Harriet Monroe but arranged by Stevens in the order i, viii, iv, v, vii. *Le Monocle de Mon Oncle* was first published in *Others*, 5 (December 1918): 9–12. Both were republished in *Harmonium* (1923), *Sunday Morning* of course in its full eight stanzas.

13. The movement in the close of the ode *To Autumn* is entirely different. Stevens begins with mountains and ends with a motion downward to darkness, while Keats begins with the barred clouds and ends also in the panorama of the sky. Stevens' broadest clause is his last, while Keats's is the first, on the gnats. Stevens' passage consists of three equal items and a fourth, syntactically parallel but much enlarged; Keats's five items are given 3, 1, ½, 1½, and 1 lines respectively, a subtler distribution entirely than Stevens'.

14. The fact that *Sunday Morning* precedes *Le Monocle de Mon Oncle* does not change the psychological relation between them, since the states involved are bound to alternate with each other.

15. While it is quite true that the Eve to Stevens' Adam has resemblances to the interior paramour (she has "imagery" in stanza v, for example), the persistent reference seems to be to a woman, once Eve, now turned, like the poet, into a grotesque autumnal fruit: "We hang like warty squashes, streaked and rayed." For the pool of stanza xi, see *L*, 144.

16. Joseph N. Riddel, *The Clairvoyant Eye* (Baton Rouge, 1965), p. 96. He adds that Crispin's voyage "is never seen in true focus," but he founds the difficulty in Stevens' "devotion to the physical world" (93), which I think was largely nonexistent. Stevens' *wish* to be devoted to the physical world was of course real.

17. *Ibid.*, pp. 91, 90.

CHAPTER III

1. The poem was first published in *Poetry*, 45 (February 1935): 239–249. Republished in *Ideas of Order* (Alcestis Press, 1935; Knopf, 1936).

For the title, see *L*, 272: "The title refers to the litter that one usually finds in a nigger cemetery and is a phrase used by Judge Powell last winter in Key West."

2. The desire to call *Harmonium* "The Grand Poem: Preliminary Minutiae," is noted in *Wallace Stevens Checklist*, ed. S. F. Morse (Denver, 1963), p. 10.

3. The poem was apparently written in November 1934. See letters to Zabel (*L*, 271, 272). Autumn, as Stevens wrote to Latimer (*L*, 349), is a metaphor.

4. Stevens seems too modest in saying that this section "consists of the statement of two unrelated ideas: the first is that we do not die simply; we are attended by a figure. It might be easier for us to turn away from that figure. The second is that we should not die like a poor parishioner; a man should meet death for what it is" (*L*, 349). The ideas may be unrelated, but the imagery is not; the ecclesiastical "parish" calls up the sacerdotal Death.

5. Stanzas vii, viii, xv, xxii, xxv, xxix, xxx, xxxii, xxxiii, xxxvi, xlvii, xlviii, in my reading.

6. Stevens' own explanation of this section is generalized, as usual: "An anthropomorphic god is simply a projection of itself by a race of egoists, which it is natural for them to treat as sacred" (*L*, 349). He leaves unexplained the image of egoists as sausage makers, but as I say above, it seems an ironic self-reference, given this linked poem.

7. Cf. *Notes*, I, vi, constructed on this principle.

8. The stanzas, Stevens said, were composed on the way to and from the office, discontinuously (*L*, 272).

9. Stanzas xiii, xiv, xxv, xxx, xxxiii, xlvi.

10. First published in *Others*, ed. Alfred Kreymborg (Knopf, 1917); republished in *Harmonium* (Knopf, 1923).

11. Herbert J. Stern remarks on the debt to Keats in his *Wallace Stevens* (Ann Arbor, 1966), p. 131.

CHAPTER IV

1. *Owl's Clover* was first published in New York by The Alcestis Press in 1936 in a version of 861 lines. When it was reprinted in *The Man with the Blue Guitar and Other Poems* (New York, 1937), it was in a shortened version of 667 lines. The first and longer version is the one reprinted in *Opus Posthumous* and used here. Page references in this chapter are to *Opus Posthumous*. References to poems in the *Collected Poems* are in this chapter preceded by *CP*.

2. Stevens' notes on *Owl's Clover* in letters to Hi Simons (*L*, 366–375, *passim*), are more than useful. I assume familiarity with them, since

they are far too long to quote, except here and there. I am not conscious of having violated any of Stevens' own statements, which are as usual general rather than particular, though more particular here than in any other of his commentaries.

3. See, for instance, "A Duck for Dinner," I, in which Stevens paused to elaborate on the word "rise" in lines 7–14. He cut it all, as well as four lines beyond the expansion.

4. The title shows Stevens' social concern: "The point of this group . . . is to try to make poetry out of commonplace: the day's news; and that surely is owl's clover" (*L*, 311). Stevens himself is of course the owl who browses in this false clover.

5. The line between Stevens' pentameters and tetrameters is often blurred, and at certain points in *The Man with the Blue Guitar* the tetrameter becomes a crypto-pentameter, the reverse of his effect here. Of the two, the pentameter line is more apt for meditation of Stevens' ruminative sort, and in fact his tetrameters are always inserted for special effects, whether of lulling harmony, as they are here, or of primitive balladlike vigor, as they are in the *Blue Guitar*.

6. For a classic modern use of the mythical or paradisal "there" see Yeats's poem of that name in his *Collected Poems*, New York, 1956, p. 284:

> There all the barrel-hoops are knit,
> There all the serpent-tails are bit,
> There all the gyres converge in one,
> There all the planets drop in the Sun.

Wordsworth invokes the same insistent "there" in his account of the visionary power of nature in verse in *The Prelude*, V, 598–602:

> There, darkness makes abode, and all the host
> Of shadowy things work endless changes, — there,
> As in a mansion like their proper home,
> Even forms and substances are circumfused.
> By that transparent veil with light divine.

And here are two instances at random from Shakespeare: the first is clearly mythical, and comes from *A Midsummer Night's Dream* (II, i, 250–251, 253–256):

> I know a bank where the wild thyme blows,
> Where oxlips and the nodding violet grows . . .
> There sleeps Titania sometime of the night,
> Lull'd in these flowers with dances and delight;
> And there the snake throws her enamell'd skin,
> Weed wide enough to wrap a fairy in.

The second, though not betraying its "paradisal" reference directly, does so by its elegiac tone and the repetition of the adverb (*Hamlet*, IV, vii, 168–170, 174–177):

Queen.   Your sister's drown'd, Laertes.

Laertes.   Drown'd! O, where?

Queen.   There is a willow grows aslant a brook,
             That shows his hoar leaves in the glassy stream.
             There with fantastic garlands did she come . . .
             There on the pendent boughs her coronet weeds
             Clamb'ring to hang, an envious sliver broke,
             When down her weedy trophies and herself
             Fell in the weeping brook.

Marie Borroff adds the paradisal "there" in Spenser's Garden of Adonis, *FQ*, III, vi, 42.

7. The natural images in the passage are in delicate and gentle opposition to each other (in contrast to the whirling separations of colorless light). The "natural" placing of the stronger sun and summer light before the "weaker" moon and winter light is played off against a chiasmus of temporal succession:

     (later)   (earlier)   (earlier)   (later)
       Sun and moon at dawn . . . Summer-light and winter-light
                                                   in autumn.

8. Stevens identifies the lights as the waste of the past and the waste to come (*L*, 367), and in their spectral light (a foretaste of the Auroras), the Solitary Urn is seen.

9. The "forcing" of Stevens' apotheosis here has been noticed by Louis Martz, who rightly calls it "a rhetoric of empty assertion," but weakens his case by preferring to the Subman "the daylight figure who shears away this outworn pomp," the man with the blue guitar. ("Wallace Stevens: The World as Meditation," reprinted in *Wallace Stevens: A Collection of Critical Essays*, p. 141.) The guitarist, with his primitive instrument, is at least as "evasive" a persona for Stevens as the ampler Subman.

10. "Credences of Summer" and other poems like it may seem counterinstances, and I deal with them later.

11. Henry Wells, *Introduction to Wallace Stevens* (Bloomington, 1964), p. 204.

12. Ananke reappears abortively in the "Stanzas for 'Examination of the Hero in a Time of War'" (*OP*, 83) but nowhere else by name.

Stevens writes (*L*, 370) that Ananke was, at the time *Owl's Clover* was written, the only thing in which he believed.

13. Stevens serves as "the volcano Apostrophe, the sea Behold," as he urges us to see the statue in many ways. The poem is generically related to other poems of *Bildgedicht*, specifically to "the variant in which the poet (who points at the work of art: 'behold . . . behold . . .') describes it for an ideal spectator or re-enacts, as if personally moved, the scene represented in the work of art as dramatic action." Hellmuth Rosenfeld, *Das Deutsche Bildgedicht* (Leipzig, 1935), quoted by Leo Spitzer, *Essays on English and American Literature* (Princeton, 1962), p. 92.

14. The odd line "Like a word in the mind that sticks at artichoke/ And remains inarticulate" is explained rather feebly by Stevens: "The failure of an era is as if a man was trying to find a word in his mind and could not formulate it: as if the word was *artichoke* and he could get no nearer to it than *inarticulate*, rather an heroic pun." (*L*, 366)

15. For the "return to surfaces," see Wordsworth's sonnet "Composed by the Side of Grasmere Lake," and the rewarding discussion of the poem by Paul DeMan, "Symbolic Landscape in Wordsworth and Yeats," in *In Defense of Reading*, ed. Reuben Brower and Richard Poirier (New York, 1962), pp. 22–37.

16. Whether the impression of spontaneity is consistent with Stevens' rather lugubrious pentameters in these poems is open to question, especially when we see the same device in the brisk tetrameters of *The Man with the Blue Guitar*, III (166). A signal Romantic instance of a similar procession of infinitives to assert copiousness, spontaneity, and continuation without time limit occurs in the ode "To Autumn," as the goddess of the season conspires with the sun to load, to bless, to bend, to fill, to swell, to plump, and to set budding.

CHAPTER V

1. *The Man with the Blue Guitar* was first published entire in the volume of that title (New York, 1937). Earlier that year, twelve cantos (ii, ix, xv, xvii, xviii, xxiv, xxvii, xxviii, xxix, xxx, xxxi, and xxxiii of the complete version) were published in *Poetry*, 1 (May 1937): 61–69. A few rejected stanzas are printed in *Opus Posthumous*, pp. 72–73.

2. "The Balloon of the Mind," *Collected Poems*, p. 153.

3. The image of a mirror as a possible solution is disavowed in "Americana" (*OP*, 93–94) and in "Madame La Fleurie" (507).

4. Another instance of this lulling by grammatical resemblance occurs in canto viii, where there are strong similarities between two quatrains that are in theory opposed to each other. One represents the morning

sky, seemingly propitious to poetry, the other the frustrated feelings of the guitarist (*L*, 362):

> The vivid, florid, turgid sky,
> The drenching thunder rolling by,
>
> The morning deluged still by night,
> The clouds tumultuously bright,
>
> And the feeling heavy in cold chords
> Struggling toward impassioned choirs,
>
> Crying among the clouds, enraged
> By gold antagonists in air.

Both quatrains depend on similar sounds as well as on the present and past participles in each to emphasize the reciprocity of the two antagonists, and to prepare us for the final statement that although the guitar seems as puny as reason in respect to a storm, it nevertheless, as Stevens says (*L*, 362), states the milieu.

5. Stevens' reference here, conscious or unconscious, seems to be to Wordsworth, from whom he takes the favorite word "intercourse." See especially the 1850 *Prelude*, XII, ll. 10–15:

> Ye motions of delight, that haunt the sides
> Of the green hills; ye breezes and soft airs,
> Whose subtle intercourse with breathing flowers,
> Feelingly watched, might teach Man's haughty race
> How without injury to take, to give
> Without offence.

And see also the 1805 *Prelude*, XII, ll. 1–14:

> From nature doth emotion come, and moods
> Of calmness equally are nature's gift,
> This is her glory; these two attributes
> Are sister horns that constitute her strength;
> This twofold influence is the sun and shower
> Of all her bounties, both in origin
> And end alike benignant. Hence it is,
> That Genius which exists by interchange
> Of peace and excitation, finds in her
> His best and purest Friend, from her receives
> That energy by which he seeks the truth,
> Is rouz'd, aspires, grasps, struggles, wishes, craves,

From her that happy stillness of the mind
Which fits him to receive it, when unsought.

6. See *L*, 364, for Stevens' remarks on this canto.

7. Cf. the Snowdon vision, *Prelude*, 1850, XIV, for Stevens' great archetype. The relations of mist, cloud, vapor, water, rain, frost, and ice are part of Stevens' allegiance to Romantic metaphor.

CHAPTER VI

1. *Examination of the Hero in a Time of War* was published in book form (after a preliminary publication in the *Harvard Advocate*, April 1942) in *Parts of a World* (New York, 1942). "Study of Two Pears" and "Oak Leaves are Hands" also appeared in that volume, but were both separately published before, in 1938 and 1942, respectively.

2. Cf. Elder Olson, "The Poetry of Wallace Stevens," *College English*, 16 (April 1955): 396.

3. Michel Benamou, "Wallace Stevens: Some Relations between Poetry and Painting," reprinted in *The Achievement of Wallace Stevens*, p. 241.

4. Marie Borroff, in describing this poem, suggests that the speaker is a Johannisberger named Hans, but the first-person form of the ending presses strongly toward identification of Hans as a person addressed, and to Johannisberger as a wine, which it is. For her reading, see her essay "Wallace Stevens: The World and the Poet," in her collection *Wallace Stevens: A Collection of Critical Essays*, p. 20.

5. For these remarks of Doggett, see his *Stevens' Poetry of Thought*, pp. 88–90, a discriminating reading of the poem, as all his readings of Stevens are.

6. Hydaspia, the place where Lady Lowzen lives, is probably named from the ancient Hydaspes River in the Punjab. Kali, according to the *Encyclopedia Brittanica*, "is usually regarded as a goddess of death and destruction, is depicted as black, four armed . . . wears a necklace of skulls, corpses as earrings, and a girdle of snakes."

7. Marie Borroff has suggested in a very helpful letter that this last appellation, "the chromatic Lowzen," is an honorific like "the divine Tosca," or "the incomparable Lind." Though Stevens may have intended that effect, he "spoils" it by using a descriptive adjective ("chromatic") of neutral value, rather than an honorific adjective. However, Lady Lowzen is certainly, as Miss Borroff points out, "another manifestation of 'the ever-never-changing same,/ An appearance of Again, the diva-dame' (353). There is a play on ideas in the poem similar to that in *diva*: at once mythological goddess and prima donna." Sister M. Bernetta Quinn has shown that Lady Lowzen's exalted state makes us read "an-

cestral hells" as a parody of "ancestral halls" ("Metamorphosis in Wallace Stevens," in *Wallace Stevens: A Collection of Critical Essays*, p. 69).

8. Northrop Frye, "The Realistic Oriole: A Study of Wallace Stevens," in *Wallace Stevens: A Collection of Critical Essays*, p. 168.

9. I am grateful to Margaret Shook of Smith College for the suggestion that the otherwise baffling twelve legs of Flora MacMort may arise from Gray's Ode, "The Fatal Sisters" in which the Fates are "weaving many a Soldier's doom" on "the loom of Hell." In the "Preface" to his *Poems of 1768*, Gray writes: 'On Christmas Day (the day of the battle) a native of Caithness in Scotland saw at a distance a number of persons on horseback riding at full speed towards a hill, and seeming to enter into it. Curiosity led him to follow them, till looking through an opening in the rocks, he saw twelve gigantic figures resembling women: they were all employed about a loom: and as they wove, they sung the following dreadful song; which when they had finished, they tore the web into twelve pieces, and (each taking her portion) galloped six to the North, and as many to the South." *Gray's English Poems*, ed. D. C. Tovey (Cambridge, Eng., 1911), p. 238.

Marie Borroff, in a letter, has proposed that "if she is a goddess of perpetual change, with hands that disappear and reappear like the leaves of a deciduous tree, then it doesn't seem strange that she should be "twelve-legged" — a kind of embodiment of the processional twelve months of the year."

10. *Parts of a World* (New York, 1942), p. 183.

11. Unhappily, "more" is not included in the Stevens concordance: it would be a guide to his "celestial" passages, and a help in assessing his use of simile, since so many of the similes are comparative.

12. Jerome, according to Stevens, begat instrumentation; perhaps Stevens says this because in contrast to the anonymous community of the postapostolic Christians, Jerome is the first solitary rhetorical voice to enunciate the poetry of religion.

13. See S. F. Morse's comments in his introduction to *Opus Posthumous*, p. xxiv.

14. Wordsworth, "Written after the Death of Charles Lamb."

CHAPTER VII

1. First published by The Cummington Press (Cummington, Mass.) in a separate edition in 1942, and reissued in 1943. Its place as the closing poem in *Transport to Summer* (1947) is therefore chronologically deceptive.

2. One signal claim relinquished by the poem is any overt social or

human connection. The introduction, as Stevens tells us (*L*, 538), has "nothing to do with Mr. Church" to whom the poem is dedicated — it is addressed to the interior paramour, and signifies Stevens' final acceptance of his remorseless, if involuntary, isolation from the human world: "And for what, if not for you, do I feel love?" The only alternative object of love proposed is "the extremest book of the wisest man," not any human being. In ceasing to attempt the poetry of human relation, Stevens becomes, paradoxically, most human.

3. Doggett, *Stevens' Poetry of Thought*, p. 101.

4. The Man in the Old Coat, or major man, is of course Stevens' "new" version of the hero. In abandoning the hero, Stevens could abandon his strenuous attempts at apotheosis voiced in *Examination of the Hero*, and could return to the "old fantoche" of *The Man with the Blue Guitar* (xxx).

5. In *Stevens' Poetry of Thought* Doggett offers this sexual interpretation of melon, bananas, and pineapples, a reading which seems likely.

6. Frank Kermode, in his " 'Notes toward a Supreme Fiction': A Commentary," *Annali dell'Istituto Universitario Orientale: Sezione Germanica* (Naples, 1961), p. 187, thinks that "unaffected" means "without affectation," but I would agree with Harold Bloom in his " 'Notes toward a Supreme Fiction': A Commentary," in *Wallace Stevens: A Collection of Critical Essays*, p. 86, that it means "one not influenced," "an insensitive man."

7. The triadic form, of which *Notes* is the first major example, had been congenial to Stevens as early as *Harmonium* (where it is most remarkable in "Sea Surface Full of Clouds"). In *The Making of Harmonium* (Princeton, 1967), p. 213, Robert Buttel suggests its origin in terza rima, and offers the unpublished poem "For an Old Woman in a Wig" (ca. 1916), a long effort in terza rima, as undeniable evidence. Stevens' emancipated triads became his major poetic resource, and he toyed with the canto forms into which they could be cast — a group of seven triads for *Notes*, eight for *The Auroras of Autumn*, and six for *An Ordinary Evening in New Haven*, for instance. These experiments indicate a range of from eighteen to twenty-four lines as a comfortable canto-length for Stevens, and in fact in many of his other stanza forms he approximates this number of verses. *Credences of Summer*, for instance, has fifteen-line cantos (each composed of three five-line stanzas), and the range in *Esthétique du Mal* is from twenty to twenty-six lines to a canto. One of the difficulties of the stanza of *Examination of the Hero* is in fact its brevity, which does not allow Stevens the room for expansion that he needs in a discursive poem: its cantos (with one exception) have only fourteen lines, and those lines are short ones. Some earlier poems, like *Le Monocle de Mon Oncle* with its eleven-line stanzas and *Sunday Morning* with its fifteen-line stanza, suggest that Stevens'

basic canto form derives from the sonnet, and a glance at the construction of the stanzas of these poems bears out the intuition. The narrative emphasis and continuous form of *The Comedian as the Letter C* is so alien to Stevens' temperament that one wonders at his actually finishing the poem. The sonnet is naturally suited, in its division into complication and solution, to reflective poetry, but Stevens seems to have preferred the Shakespearean form to the Petrarchan, perhaps because expansions followed by epigram seemed more congenial than the more severe Petrarchan development. *Le Monocle de Mon Oncle*, especially, sometimes seems to follow a 3–3–3–2 variant of the 4–4–4–2 Shakespearean model. In any case, Stevens needed, for any successful long poem, a constant canto form, as he seems to have realized after the comparative shapelessness of *Esthétique du Mal*. It is significant that though Stevens thought of adding a fourth section to *Notes*, to be called "It Must Be Human" (*L*, 863–864), he never did so: his need to transcend his triads and his isolation both could not be enacted.

8. Cf. *L*, 444–445.

9. Cf. *L*, 433, 434. In a manuscript poem of 1909, Stevens had written of "an Arab moon." The poem is quoted by Buttel, *The Making of Harmonium*, p. 61.

10. As Harold Bloom wittily says in "The Central Man": Emerson, Whitman, Wallace Stevens," *Massachusetts Review*, 7 (Winter 1966): 37, "A qualified assertion remains an assertion; it is *not* an asserted qualification."

11. Cf. *The Irrational Element in Poetry* in *OP*, 216–229, especially pp. 220–221, and 229.

12. This is not the same as the desolate "absence of the imagination" in "The Plain Sense of Things," as Frank Kermode seems to imply (*Commentary*, p. 181). On the contrary, it is an energetic and strenuous effort to isolate the Supreme Fiction, for purposes of speculation, in an isolated state (cf. *L*, 434). "The Plain Sense of Things" is a poem about the loss of that strenuous joy in conjecture and fancy.

13. Cf. "Long and Sluggish Lines" (522).

14. Kermode conjectures (*Commentary*, p. 185) that the poem should read, "The seraph is satyr *or* Saturn, according to his thoughts," but Satyr and Saturn are not contraries: the seraph, if he so chooses, can be lustful, a satyr in the sphere of Saturn, a participant in a Saturnalia, with a pun on "Satyrnalia" included.

15. The daring use here of the intransitive verb "to vanish" in a transitive sense springs probably from the wish to pun on "vanquish," but since the vanquished, however defeated, are still present on the battlefield, that image will not do for winter, which vanishes in the presence of spring. Neither will it do to say, as I have just done, that winter vanishes, since that implies a voluntary dwindling and not a

forced putting-to-rout. Compare Whitman's use of "fades" in *Song of Myself*, 24:

> To behold the day-break!
> The little light fades the immense and diaphanous shadows,
> The air tastes good to my palate.

16. "Materia Poetica," in *View*, 1 (September 1940): 3. When the passage was reprinted (*OP*, 158) the second sentence was omitted.

17. Harold Bloom, in "Notes: a Commentary," p. 94, takes this passage more heroically than I am able to do, and sees no self-disgust implied. The poet locates himself within his escapades of death, however: "*these* external regions."

18. Doggett, *Stevens' Poetry of Thought*, p. 119.

CHAPTER VIII

1. *Esthétique du Mal* was issued separately by the Cummington Press (1945), and later included in *Transport to Summer* (1947). Book publication had been preceded by publication in the *Kenyon Review*, 6 (Autumn 1944): 489–503. *Description without Place* was read by Stevens at Harvard as the Phi Beta Kappa poem in June 1945, and was then published in the *Sewanee Review*, 53 (Autumn 1945): 559–565.

2. R. P. Blackmur, in an inexplicable lapse in taste, singled out "How red the rose that is the soldier's wound" for special praise, along with a few other poems from *Transport to Summer*, saying that they "go into that canon against which other poems merely beat; the canon of poems, no matter what their idiosyncrasy, which create sensibility in desperation." "Poetry and Sensibility: Some Rules of Thumb," a review of *Transport to Summer*, in *Poetry*, 71 (February 1948): 274–275. His usual faultless response was at work, on the other hand, in his remarks on two exquisite cantos of *Notes* — the "bethou" canto and the one beginning "A lasting visage in a lasting bush." Some relic of enthusiasm for the metaphysical poets may have prompted the praise of the rose-red wound.

3. Frank Doggett's reading (*Stevens' Poetry of Thought*, p. 173) equates the sun with day and the bird with night, and adds that "the bird feeding on the sun suggests the darkness and the void that feeds on light and reality . . . Sun is a consciousness continually creating experience, and the bird is man's inner darkness of subconsciousness feeding upon the rejected experiences, the blooms falling downward." Stevens' many self-representations as a bird would tend to contradict Doggett's interpretation.

4. See N.E.D. *s.v.* redden.

CHAPTER IX

1. *Credences of Summer* was first published in *Transport to Summer* (Knopf, 1947). *The Auroras of Autumn* followed the next year in *The Kenyon Review*, 10 (Winter 1948): 1–10, and was republished in the volume of which it was the title poem (Knopf, 1950).

2. Frank Kermode's simplistic account of Stevens' "tone of rapture" in his "total satisfaction, the moment of total summer . . . the paradise of living as and where one lives," in this "passionate celebration of this August heat" (*Wallace Stevens*, pp. 106–107) has been somewhat corrected by later readers. Joseph Riddel, for instance, sees a "lingering nostalgia" but concludes that "it is a time for marriages, for balances" (*The Clairvoyant Eye*, pp. 218, 223), a phrase which scants Stevens' own uneasiness that will find full voice in *The Auroras of Autumn*.

3. See "Wallace Stevens" by Michael Lafferty, *Historical Review of Berks County*, 24 (Fall 1959): 108: "The whole series, 'Credences of Summer,' seems written in reminiscence of a hike over Mount Penn, from whose Tower Stevens could see 'Oley, too rich for enigmas.'"

4. It seems possible that Stevens' central construct in *Credences of Summer* — the mountain, the throne, the old man — may owe something to Wordsworth's *Excursion* (IX, 48ff):

> Rightly it is said
> That man descends into the VALE of years
> Yet have I thought that we might also speak,
> And not presumptuously, I trust, of Age,
> As of a final EMINENCE; though bare
> In aspect and forbidding, yet a point
> On which 'tis not impossible to sit
> In awful sovereignty; a place of power,
> A throne, that may be likened unto his,
> Who, in some placid day of summer, looks
> Down from a mountain-top, — say one of those
> High peaks, that bound the vale where now we are.
> Faint, and diminished to the gazing eye,
> Forest and field, and hill and dale appear,
> With all the shapes over their surface spread.

5. Harold Bloom in "The Central Man," *Massachusetts Review*, 7 (Winter 1966): 38, cites Emerson and Dickinson as other users of the image of the auroras.

6. I adopt here the punctuation of the first printing of *The Auroras of Autumn* in the *Kenyon Review*. The sense and cadence of this passage seem to require a period, not a comma, after "dreams," and the

Collected Poems has no absolute authority. There is no punctuation at all, for instance, in the *Collected Poems* following the word "base" (*Auroras* i, l.13) though something is clearly needed. The *KR* version has Stevens' familiar three periods. In vi, the *KR* does not have the hyphens in "half-thought-of," and it has a simple period instead of three periods after l.18. There is also a simple period closing viii. The next edition of Stevens will doubtless be a variorum.

7. I have been told by Harold Bloom that Chatillon is the proper name of a Renaissance translator of the Bible from Hebrew into Latin and French, one Sebastián Castellio (1515–1563), or Castalion, as he is sometimes called (see *Enciclopedia Universal Illustrada*, Madrid, *s.v. Castalion*). The passage remains obscure, and perhaps the choice of name may rather be dictated by Stevens' recurrent châteaux, built by his figures resembling, in their desire for a *mise-en-scène*, the father of *Auroras*. See, for instance, "Architecture," an early poem later dropped from *Harmonium*:

Architecture

> What manner of building shall we build?
> Let us design a chastel de chasteté.
> De pensée . . .
>
> In this house, what manner of utterance shall there be?
> What heavenly dithyramb
> And cantilene?
> What niggling forms of gargoyle patter?
>
> And how shall those come vested that come there?
> In their ugly reminders?
> Or gaudy as tulips? . . .
> As they climb the flights
> To the closes
> Overlooking whole seasons?
>
> Let us build the building of light.
> Push up the towers to the cock-tops.
> These are the pointings of our edifice,
> Which, like a gorgeous palm,
> Shall tuft the commonplace.
>
>   . . .
> How [shall we] carve the violet moon
> To set in nicks? (*OP*, 16–17)

This sketchy poem reads like a first draft of the idea for *Credences of Summer* and *The Auroras of Autumn*, both poems composed in "the closes/ Overlooking whole seasons." The tower, the company of actors, their speech, their garments, even the word nick (though perhaps in a different sense) are all points in common, as is the prescribing of a ritual.

CHAPTER X

1. *An Ordinary Evening in New Haven* was read, in a shortened form, on November 4, 1949, at a meeting of the Connecticut Academy of Arts and Sciences, and was printed in the *Transactions of the Connecticut Academy of Arts and Sciences*, 38 (December 1949): 171–172. This shorter form, reprinted in the Faber *Selected Poems*, consists of eleven cantos. The long version appears in *The Auroras of Autumn* (New York, 1950), where the original sections fall into the following order: i, vi, ix, xi, xii, xvi, xxii, xxviii, xxx, xxxi, xxxix. As in *Sunday Morning*, Stevens shifted endings.

2. A. Alvarez, *Stewards of Excellence* (New York, 1958), pp. 134, 136.

3. Stevens may echo here the Sonnet "Artémis" from *Les Chimères* of Gérard de Nerval:

> La Treizième revient . . . C'est encore la première;
> Et c'est toujours la seule, — ou c'est le seul moment;
> Car es-tu reine, ô toi! la première ou dernière?
> Es-tu roi, toi le seul ou le dernier amant? . . .

4. The punning use of "reverberation" occurs as early as the *Comedian*, iv, and probably derives from *The Excursion*, where Wordsworth says that the soul reverts to childhood because in age she "thence can hear/ Reverberations" (IX, 40–41).

5. Frank Doggett (*Stevens' Poetry of Thought*, pp. 184–186) offers a more heartening view of the black shepherd's isle as "the universal creative source," an interpretation which seems to ignore Stevens' emphasis on death.

6. "Wallace Stevens' Later Poetry," *ELH*, 25 (June 1958): 146.

7. As Stevens said in *Adagia*, "We never arrive intellectually. But emotionally we arrive constantly (as in poetry, happiness, high mountains, vistas)" (*OP*, 173).

CHAPTER XI

1. Stevens wrote, shortly after writing the poem, that "robins and doves are both early risers and are connoisseurs of daylight before the actual presence of the sun coarsens it" (*L*, 879).

James Benziger in *Images of Eternity* (Carbondale, 1962), 241–243, has written very interestingly of this last poem, "Not Ideas about the Thing," as an escape from solipsism: "The 'Supreme Fiction' has now become a revelation." I think the appreciation of "naked Alpha" is the theme common to these late "infancy" poems, and that alpha may be the given, the infant self with which we are born, that temperament and sense of the world which Stevens at first disliked so much in himself, and required such elaboration of.

2. Stevens' earlier criticism of the child one becomes in second childhood is contained in the poem "Questions are Remarks" (462), turning on three questions, asked of nature: "Why are you: What is that: Who are you." The second of these questions, the only proper one, is asked by Stevens' grandson: the first and third are asked by Stevens as a "drowsy, infant, old man" and they are improper anthropomorphic harassments of nature. The ailing sun rises anew, but the old man still vests it in antique appearances, in old rhetoric, and in the pathetic fallacy, wanting a maternal principal in nature. Stevens ends with a comment on the child's question about the sun:

> His question is complete because it contains
> His utmost statement. It is his own array,
> His own pageant and procession and display,
>
> As far as nothingness permits . . . Hear him.
> He does not say, "Mother, my mother, who are you,"
> The way the drowsy, infant, old men do.   (462–463)

Stevens' exhilarating change to the proclamation of value in "second childhood" is an example of his continuing fertility of thought, as is the metamorphosis from the old man as dwarf (208) to the old man as child, a "bad" shrunkenness changed into a (potentially) "good" one.